Prompt & Circumstance

The Definitive Guide to using AI for

Confident, Consistent Performance with

The C.A.L.M. AI Navigator™

ELISA JANSON JONES

ISBN: 979-8-9996381-0-6

DEDICATION

To my kids.
My greatest contribution to the future of mankind.

CONTENTS

ACKNOWLEDGMENTS

To my readers: thank you for taking this crucial step in your learning journey. The lessons within these pages may well prove to be among the most important you'll ever encounter.

I also wish to thank my dissertation committee for helping me develop and refine my scholarly skills. I hold their rigorous academic training responsible for any excessive flippancy you may encounter in this narration—consider it my small rebellion against years of formal scholarly writing.

I am deeply grateful to the dedicated educators at Section, whose expertise and guidance taught me so much about artificial intelligence. My sincere appreciation goes to the team at the United States Artificial Intelligence Institute for providing the comprehensive education and certification that enabled me to master AI concepts and share that knowledge with others.

Finally, to all who supported this project in ways both large and small: your encouragement made this book possible.

Introduction

Turn Everyday AI Into Your Unfair Advantage

Alarm off, Slack on. While you were sleeping, a teammate shipped a client-winning deck, start to finish, using ChatGPT. You crack open the very same model for a quick brief, using their same initial prompt and get a steaming bowl of jargon stew. Sound familiar?

Most ambitious professionals already flirt with AI: a prompt in ChatGPT here, a Midjourney mock-up there, NotebookLM to wrangle research. Yet every session still feels like you're flipping a coin. One day you unlock superhero-level productivity; the next, you spend an hour rewriting robotic prose or chasing hallucinated data.

That awkward disconnect between what AI can theoretically pull off and what you'd stake your professional life on? That's the AI Confidence Gap in all its glory. But the twist - it's not about doubting the technology, it's about doubting whether you know how to make it work for your particular brand of chaos. Until we bridge this gap, generative AI stays a party trick—never the non-negotiable edge it could be.

The question now is: How do we close the gap?

And not with gimmicky Instagram posts promising million-dollar business growth with a single prompt, but systematically, with a usable process that can be replicated again to ensure the optimal output you seek.

The Hidden Cost of Inconsistency

Every untrained keystroke you throw at AI is a silent siphon draining your time, credibility, and momentum. Minutes melt away as you tinker with a "perfect" prompt, only to spend twice as long triaging the clunky prose it spits back—work you could have polished faster on your own. Then comes the conference call: you cite a slick-sounding, machine-spun statistic, catch the inaccuracy halfway through the sentence, and feel your authority wobble like a table with a missing leg. Meanwhile the team down the hall, armed with a smarter framework and sharper prompts, is shipping deliverables at warp speed. Ignore AI on mission-critical tasks and they'll lap you before you finish your coffee; embrace it without method and you bleed hours and trust. The choice isn't whether to use AI—it's whether you'll master it before the leaks, dents, and stalls become cracks you can't patch.

The folks lapping the field aren't inherently more technical—they're more systematic.

Meet the C.A.L.M. AI Navigator™

Forget the glitter of the newest plug-in or the lure of a 99-line prompt crib sheet—your real edge is an operating rhythm, not another shiny object. That rhythm is the C.A.L.M. AI Navigator™, a four-step playbook that turns everyday tools into an elite performance stack:

Clarity – Pin the bull's-eye before you draw the bow. "Boost Q3 webinar registrations by 25%" is a GPS coordinate; "improve marketing" is a weather report. Precise outcomes give your models—human or machine—a target they can hit like moving from maze to map.

Alignment – Match the right mind to the right mission. Claude for strategic reasoning, ChatGPT for narrative polish, NotebookLM for lightning-fast synthesis. Stop pounding square pegs into round-model holes and watch friction evaporate.

Leverage – Engineer prompts, context, and rapid feedback loops so AI meets professional-grade standards instead of defaulting to mid-table mediocrity. Craft meets capability, and quality scales without mercy.

Manifest – Convert standout outputs into the language your CFO, board, or client speaks fluently: revenue gained, hours saved, risks dodged. Wins that don't show up on the scoreboard don't count. Run these four moves on repeat, and sporadic flashes of brilliance harden into a production line of predictable, high-impact results.

CLARITY

Know What You Want Before You Start

Clarity starts long before you fire up ChatGPT—it begins the moment you picture the finished thing that will move the needle. Like tomorrow's board meeting. You're not "generating a report"; you're wanting a one-page snapshot that drops revenue, churn, and the top three risks right under the directors' noses so they can green-light next-quarter funding in five minutes. That mental picture—numbers up front, zero fluff—guides every word you'll eventually feed the model.

Or consider a six-month content surge you're planning to coincide with your next product launch. Your buyers practically live on LinkedIn and Pinterest, so you're not chasing a vague "marketing plan." You need a strategy that pairs each monthly blog theme with a Pinterest board and a LinkedIn article that march toward the same call-to-action. When you see that cross-channel trio in your mind, the prompt becomes more obvious, and more powerful.

Hand-off day for the new employee? You're not asking for "instructions" from ChatGPT, you're envisioning a click-by-click walkthrough with screenshots, stripped of jargon, so on their second Monday, your new staff can run the weekly report without pinging you on Slack every 30 seconds.

And during a product building sprint, you're not requesting "research." You're wanting a clean, side-by-side grid that lists three candidate names for the product, each with pros, cons, and trademark checks, ready to drop straight into a slide so leadership can choose before lunch.

By starting with Clarity in each use case, you will have nailed the output, the audience, and the decision it contributes to. Once the image of your desired output is crystal clear, the actual prompt becomes a set of directions. That's Clarity: solving the *why* first, so the AI can output precisely what you want, without the guesswork.

ALIGNMENT

Treating Every Model Like The Specialist It Is

Think of AI tools as coworkers with wildly different resumes. Your first move is to hand each task to the teammate with the best chance of success based on their training and experience.

Need a punchy Instagram caption? ChatGPT riffs playful wording in seconds and even slips in the perfect emoji. Crafting an illustrated slide deck for tomorrow's pitch? Pass the task to DALL·E; while it drafts fresh, license-free artwork, you refine the story arc. Staring down three dense research reports? NotebookLM knits the highlights into one clean summary so you're comparing insights, not skimming PDFs.

When you respect each model's sweet spot—language for ChatGPT, images for DALL·E, synthesis for NotebookLM—your workflows like a well-trained relay team instead of everyone grabbing the same baton at once. Square peg, square hole—less friction, cleaner results.

LEVERAGE

You Get Out What You Put In

Like a backline cook, AI prepares whatever you toss in the recipe. Vague requests equal mushy output: like that cereal you poured milk over three hours ago and forgot about because you popped over to the local coffee shop for a latte. Meanwhile, you're missing out on the precise specs which could spark Michelin-level dishes – or the AI version of them anyway.

Instead of "Write a marketing email," which will get you something resembling your favorite mass-produced generic pasta from a can, try precision prompting: "Draft a 120-word email for our audience newsletter inviting them to the upcoming Red Rocks show; tone upbeat and appreciative; end with a P.S. inviting them to take 10% off through the presell, which ends Friday. Include placeholders for the link to the ticket page." A single 45-word prompt can lock in length, audience, mood, and call-to-action. Now the model can't wander or try to please you by filling in the gaps with hallucinogenic garbage. Give it what it needs, and it will give you back the precise output you're seeking.

Leverage is only partly about your ability to leverage each AI model; it's about learning to leverage your own skills as a prompt engineer. It's about starting where you're comfortable and scaling up from there. It's also about knowing how to be ethical and protective in this new age of over-sharing information.

It's probably the most important skill set you're going to learn in your lifetime.

MANIFEST

Bring Your Outputs Into The Real World

Picture an AI dashboard lighting up with possibility: a content calendar that schedules itself, a sales script that answers objections you haven't heard yet, a data summary that spots the trend your competitors still don't see. It's a moment of electric promise—right up until the tab closes and you're left asking the oldest question in business: *Now what?* That uneasy pause between brilliance on-screen and impact in-life is the "Implementation Gap," and it's where even the smartest strategies go to rust.

This book is designed to help you cross the gap with confidence. We call the final, essential step Manifest—the art of taking a pristine, machine-generated plan and hammering it into results your clock, budget, and risk ledger can measure. Manifest is less flash, more follow-through. It's the elbow grease that turns a 47-point automation roadmap into one email template you'll test today, or a thousand-row insight report into a single chart that rewrites next quarter's targets. Time saved, dollars earned, errors avoided: that's the currency of real-world success, and Manifest is how you mint it.

Not only is Manifest the step from the digital to the real, but it's also a reminder that the AI is just a mechanism. A machine. A tool. It requires human taste and judgement, the beautiful gift of discernment you've been given as a member of the human species, to make an output quality enough to be worthy of the real world.

In the pages ahead, you'll build expertise in organizing your AI workflow through this framework—C.A.L.M.—for bridging the gap between inspiration and execution without getting lost in option overload and mysteriously useless AI gibberish. You'll see why a tiny slice of a huge plan often beats rolling out the entire masterpiece, how rapid micro-experiments trump "big-bang" launches, and how every stumble is data for your next, better iteration. The stories are intentionally broad: a marketing team trimming hours off a newsletter, an operations lead slashing defects in a production line, a solo consultant converting AI insights into client renewals. Change the setting and the software—the principles stay the same.

Most books about AI celebrate what the technology *could* do. This one focuses on what *will* get done once a human like you decides to pull it out of the lab and into daily work. By the final page, you'll know how to choose the single task that matters, specify the exact output you need, pair it with the right digital teammate, and measure the win in metrics no skeptic can debate.

Ready to drive that Ferrari instead of admiring it from the curb? Turn the page. Manifest starts now.

From Tinkering to Transformation

You already know AI matters. You're probably already using it every day. This book skips the freshman tour of neural nets, training algorithms, and philosophical ethics debates. What you need is the playbook that turns "nice-to-have" experiments into non-negotiable workflows. Inside you'll find:

Field stories of directors, founders, and analysts who crossed the AI Confidence Gap—plus the exact prompts, guardrails, and dashboards they relied on. Mostly mocked up using synthetic data (yes, that's a thing) to help you visualize the possibilities and lean into the way story and metaphor help you learn faster and better.

Chapter-end sprints that guide you, in real time, through mapping your first C.A.L.M. wins—so progress compounds as you read. The "Try This" sections are also intended to help reinforce what you've learned in each chapter by taking action on it.

Templates and scorecards to audit any AI output in minutes, enforce brand or compliance rules, and rally every stakeholder around the same standard. Not in every chapter, but helpful if you want metrics as another reinforcement. As a doctoral-level instructional designer and lifelong educator, I've designed this book so every type of learner will be able to grasp the topics quickly and integrate them effortlessly.

It's Now or Never

While AI may feel embryonic, and in a lot of ways it is, it's not going away. Consider what it was like when gasoline-powered vehicles first began to roam the streets. There were no stop signs, no road lanes, and most of the place was full of horse manure. The early adopters had to deal with a slew of challenges, and the rest of the population must have seen the dangers those drivers were becoming. Not just to themselves in the seats of the car, but to the other pedestrians and non-motorized transports.

It's not a far cry from where we are today. AI can be dangerous. It can lead to everything from moral corruption to mental incompetence. But that's why you're here learning about how to use AI effectively, ethically, and with sophistication, so you are no longer something in fear or to be feared. That's the goal of the C.A.L.M. AI Navigator framework: safe, effective, creative, leveraged, and realized AI use that doesn't endanger – it enables.

Let this book be your textbook to AI use. By the end, you will have the skills and knowledge to mitigate the risks of AI while capitalizing on the rewards. You're here because you see the future. You're an early adopter yourself, even if it doesn't feel like it yet. And based on this one fact, the future truly is in your hands.

But early-adopter window is closing. Pioneers who grasped the basics already enjoy a head start. The ultimate win—developing steady, bulletproof AI collaboration—is still out there for the taking. And it's yours by taking the steps now to not only understand AI's capabilities, but how to develop the skills to use those capabilities to make a real difference in your life, and in the world you participate in.

By the final page, you won't merely understand how to use AI—you'll be using at least one AI tool daily and reaping the positive impact. You'll be ready to stake your reputation on AI-generated insight because you'll know exactly how to verify, refine, and optimize every output. Your next-level productivity—and a calmer path to achieving it—starts here. If you're ready to swap AI roulette for a reliable engine of sharper insight, flawless execution, and exponential reach, turn the page.

Important Note

Yes, I used AI to help write this book. I would hope you wouldn't be reading a book on AI by someone who *didn't* use AI. I used ChatGPT, Claude, Perplexity, and Grammarly. I also used the automatic features in both Google Docs and Microsoft Word. I used these tools to help find references, correct grammar, identify opportunities to strengthen the flow, clarity, and narrative, and to generate synthetic examples of people, tasks, roles, and scenarios.

The examples used throughout the book are composite scenarios based on common patterns I've observed, designed to illustrate key principles while protecting individual privacy. The concepts contained in the book however are all my original ideas. I have followed my own advice when it comes to creative and ethical AI use and I encourage you to do the same. Now get learning.

1. The AI Anxiety Epidemic

It's 7:03 a.m. and Jenna, a veteran architect who can eyeball a load-bearing wall from fifty paces, is doom-scrolling LinkedIn while the coffee drips into her favorite mug. One of her peers just snagged an award for a skyscraper co-authored by generative AI design. Jenna's own model? Still coughing up floorplans that lean like the Tower of Pisa's clumsy cousin. Each refresh widens the chasm between AI's headline hype and her wobbly reality.

Jenna is far from alone. Deloitte's 2025 survey reported that 61% of leaders are "confident in concept, shaky in practice." In other words, brains and résumés aren't the bottleneck: confidence is. Welcome to the AI Anxiety Epidemic, a four-headed Hydra that keeps even top performers hiding behind spreadsheet shields.

The Pattern of Fear: Why This Feels Familiar

Every time a groundbreaking technology shows up, so does something else: fear. It's not a bug in our cultural operating system—it's a feature. From the automobile to the dishwasher, and yes, even the telephone, every major innovation has kicked up a cloud of public anxiety. People once worried the telephone would electrocute them or invite unwanted intrusions into their private lives. Sound familiar?

These reactions follow a reliable rhythm: first, panic; then resistance; eventually, acceptance. What we're undeniably responding to isn't just the tech—it's the change it represents.

This cycle is deeply human. It reflects our concern about job loss, shifting power structures, and the disruption of the familiar. Studies show that resistance tends to spike when a new technology appears to benefit only a privileged few or threatens long-standing norms. Whether it's fear of moral decline or a loss of control, our anxieties around innovation are often proxies for something bigger: the unknown.

The encouraging part though? Understanding this pattern gives us power. When we name the fear, we can navigate through it. It's not about silencing skepticism—it's about grounding it in context.

The Four Real Barriers to AI Adoption

We keep hearing that AI is going to change everything. But let's be honest: most professionals aren't seeing that change in their day-to-day work. Despite the flood of headlines and hype, AI adoption is still surprisingly sluggish across many industries—and not because the tools aren't ready. The real blockers? They're human.

The hurdles aren't so much technical as they're psychological, organizational, and deeply personal. People aren't resistant to AI because they don't care; they're resistant because they don't see how it fits into *their* world, *their* role, *their* workflow. Whether you're a team leader trying to guide a digital transformation or a professional just trying to stay relevant, the first step is recognizing the four core barriers that keep AI stuck in theory instead of thriving in practice.

These aren't abstract leadership challenges—they're the real-world reasons your AI strategy keeps getting buried under "circle-back" meetings, and why your shiny new productivity tools are collecting digital dust. Let's unpack what's decidedly going on—so you can move from hesitation to momentum, and start making AI work *for* you.

1 — Replacement Fear. "If a bot can sketch a logo in 30 seconds, will clients still need me?" That dread lurks across every creative Slack channel. Robots on factory floors, chatbots in call centers, generative tools in design suites—the headlines write themselves with stories of automation displacing human workers. The fear feels visceral when you watch AI produce in minutes what took you hours to create.

But study after study shows companies that adopt AI hire more strategists and editors, not fewer (Singla et al., 2025). Yes, AI is streamlining operations—and in some cases, that means fewer hands on deck for repetitive tasks. The shift that people miss is that as automation rises, so does the demand for humans who can guide the strategy, oversee the outputs, and ensure quality stays high. AI doesn't eliminate the need for people—it elevates the kind of thinking they're hired to do.

2 — **Complexity Overwhelm.** Enterprise dashboards now come adorned with mystical runes—vector stores, RAG pipelines, and agentic workflows. Open any enterprise AI platform, and you're bombarded with terminology that feels designed to exclude you. The settings menus stretch for pages. The documentation reads like a PhD thesis. So you close the tab and reopen Excel.

Complexity overwhelm creates a vicious cycle. The more intimidating AI appears, the more you delay learning it. Each moment you spend hesitating, your peers are building AI muscle memory that's going to make them unstoppable. Soon, team meetings include casual references to AI capabilities you've never explored, making you feel even more out of touch.

3 — **Ethical Paralysis.** Bias, privacy, disinformation—real concerns that can freeze even the boldest leader into a cubic block of "Let's circle back." The concerns are real. We've seen how hiring algorithms can discriminate against qualified candidates. A medical AI could misdiagnose patients from underrepresented groups. A language model or image generator might output convincing but false information that spreads across social media.

These legitimate red flags too often become red lights, stopping all progress. Sensible hesitation becomes full-blown avoidance, grinding adoption to a standstill while the obvious cracks in your manual processes remain conveniently invisible. The HR manager who avoids AI screening tools because of bias concerns continues using manual processes that reflect her own unconscious biases.

4 — **Change Fatigue.** You just mastered Slack threads, survived CRM migration, and learned fifteen new Zoom reaction emojis. Another tool? Another password? Pass the aspirin. Yet every skipped upgrade lengthens the gap between early adopters and everyone else—and that gap compounds like credit-card interest.

Change fatigue hits hardest when AI adoption feels forced rather than chosen. Your company mandates new AI tools without training. Your industry suddenly expects AI-enhanced deliverables without transition time. You're told to "figure it out" while juggling existing responsibilities and deadlines.

The Real Risk: When AI Becomes a Crutch

Beyond the mythical fears lies a more nuanced concern that deserves serious attention: the risk of outsourcing your thinking entirely. This isn't about AI stealing jobs—it's about you accidentally giving away the cognitive abilities that make you irreplaceable.

The Creative Atrophy Risk. Consider two writers facing the same deadline. Evelyn asks AI to generate article outlines, then develops her own angles, arguments, and voice. Marcus asks AI to write entire articles, then edits for accuracy. Six months later, Evelyn's creative muscles have strengthened through consistent use. Marcus finds himself staring at blank pages, his ideation skills atrophied by disuse.

The issue isn't in the technology—it's in the relationship. Evelyn treats AI as a thinking partner that enhances her creativity. Marcus treats it as a replacement for his creativity. Over time, these approaches compound in opposite directions.

The Decision-Making Dependency Trap. AI excels at processing information and identifying patterns, but it can't weigh your values, understand your context, or consider your long-term vision. When you consistently defer strategic decisions to AI recommendations without engaging your own judgment, you risk developing what psychologists call "learned helplessness"—the gradual erosion of confidence in your own decision-making abilities.

The Expertise Erosion Effect. Your professional expertise isn't just knowledge—it's the ability to think critically within your domain, spot patterns others miss, and make nuanced judgments based on experience. It's the value you bring to the table: being able to discern and decide with taste and judgment you can trust. When AI handles cognitive tasks without your active engagement, you risk losing the very skills that justify your expertise.

Debunking the Myths

Now that we've examined the risks of AI head-on—no sugarcoating, no sci-fi theatrics—it's time to bring some balance back to the conversation. Yes, the concerns are real. But so is the nuance. Many of the fears surrounding AI stem from misunderstandings, outdated assumptions, or worst-case scenarios taken out of context.

"AI Will Steal My Job and Leave Me Obsolete." Not if your job involves judgment, nuance, or talking a CFO off a ledge. AI eats tasks, not roles. AI excels at repetitive, rules-based tasks—the work most of us would gladly outsource. Creativity, nuanced strategy, and genuine human connection remain uniquely ours. The strategist who lets AI crunch data doesn't disappear; she designs campaigns that resonate. The clinician using AI diagnostics doesn't lose relevance; he gains precision while offering compassionate care. The real risk isn't replacement—it's avoidance.

"AI Is an Incomprehensible Black Box That Never Gets It Right." Modern platforms have wizards, tooltips, and 'Explain-like-I'm-five' buttons. If you can order take-out with an app, you can pilot ChatGPT. Forty-two percent of small-business owners cite complexity as their top barrier to AI adoption. You don't have to understand a car's engine to drive; you don't need to grok transformer math to benefit from ChatGPT.

"AI Will Turn Me Into an Unethical Monster." Dodging AI because of ethics is like swearing off electricity because lightning exists. Bias and privacy concerns are real, but manageable. Responsible implementation beats fearful paralysis. Leading vendors ship bias meters and audit trails out of the box. Avoiding AI can leave less-scrutinized manual processes—and their invisible biases—firmly in place.

The Uncomfortable Math of Timing

Here's the plot twist nobody's putting in the brochure: AI adoption doesn't follow that nice, civilized "we're all in this together" timeline you're hoping for. It's more like a ski jump—flat for a while, then suddenly steep. Remember when smartphones went from "nice to have" to "absolutely essential" seemingly overnight? That's happening with AI tools right now, just faster. The professionals who learned to leverage mobile technology early gained advantages that compounded for years. The ones who waited found themselves constantly playing catch-up.

Let's be honest about what happens if you keep putting this off: Six months from now: Your colleagues who started today will have developed efficient AI workflows while you're still "planning to get started." One year from now: The gap widens. Early adopters in your field will have concrete results—improved performance metrics, successful projects, recognition for innovation. Two years from now: AI fluency becomes an expected skill in your industry. You're no longer learning to get ahead; you're learning to keep up.

Five years from now: The professionals who embraced AI early will have fundamentally different career trajectories. This isn't fear-mongering—it's pattern recognition. Every major technological shift creates this same dynamic.

Hope Is Alive: The Path Forward

So if today's conversations about AI feel heated, complex, or even a little dystopian? You're not alone. But you're also not powerless. The key is learning how to lead through the fear, not run from it. The solution isn't to avoid AI—it's to use it strategically. This isn't about handing over the reins to machines. It's about amplifying your uniquely human strengths: judgment, creativity, emotional intelligence, and complex decision-making.

The professionals who thrive in the AI era won't be those who avoid the technology or those who surrender to it completely. They'll be those who master the art of human-AI collaboration, using technology to enhance their distinctly human capabilities while preserving the cognitive skills that make them indispensable.

The future doesn't belong to the most technical—it belongs to the most adaptable. And adaptation starts with understanding that AI anxiety is natural, but it isn't permanent. As you chip away at fear with micro-experiments, confidence compounds. We've got this. Let's build that confidence together.

2. From Fear to Flourishing

You know that feeling when you're standing at the edge of a diving board, looking down at the water below? Your brain starts its unhelpful commentary: What if I belly flop? What if the water's colder than I think? What if there are sharks? (Okay, maybe not sharks in a pool, but you get the idea.)

That's exactly how most of us feel about AI right now. We're perched on the edge, paralyzed by all the what-ifs instead of thinking about the possibilities waiting below the surface. The thing is, you already know more about AI than you think you do. You've probably used it without realizing it—autocorrect saved you from an embarrassing typo, Netflix suggested that show you ended up binge-watching, or your GPS rerouted you around traffic. The problem isn't AI; it's our brains writing checks the current tech can't quite cash yet.

AI in the Wild

Enough theory. Let's take a look at how AI is showing up in the wild—specifically, your email, your spreadsheets, and your sanity.

Education. Instead of wrangling generic templates, teachers are using Claude to tailor lessons like they've got a curriculum whisperer on call. One middle school teacher I know generates differentiated math problems for her class in minutes—problems that used to take her hours to create manually. Routine grading? That's AI's lane. Meaningful feedback? That's still human territory.

And those chatbots answering "When is the project due?" for the hundredth time? That's not lazy teaching—that's smart time management. Let's look at just a little bit of what's possible.

Tailored Lesson Plans: Tools like Claude generate personalized lesson materials based on student learning styles and performance data, helping teachers address diverse classroom needs.

Grading Automation: AI platforms can grade assignments, quizzes, and even essays, providing detailed feedback while saving educators hours of manual work.

Student Support: Chatbots answer common student questions about schedules, deadlines, or resources, allowing teachers to focus on instruction.

Predictive Analytics: AI identifies students at risk of falling behind and recommends interventions, enabling educators to provide timely support.

Marketing. Content creators are using AI to break through blank page syndrome. Not to write entire campaigns (please don't), but to generate headlines, social media variations, or email subject lines when their brain feels empty. The good ones still edit everything, but AI gives them something to start with instead of staring at a cursor.

Smart marketers can use AI to segment customer data and spot patterns they'd never catch manually. It's like having a research assistant who never gets tired of crunching numbers. Here are a few ways AI can advance marketing:

Campaign Optimization: AI-driven platforms like Jasper or HubSpot analyze campaign data to identify high-performing strategies, helping marketers allocate budgets effectively.

Content Creation: Generative AI tools draft blogs, social media posts, and ad copy tailored to specific audiences and tones, reducing content creation time.

Customer Segmentation: AI analyzes customer data to create detailed personas, allowing marketers to target their efforts with precision.

Trend Analysis: Predictive tools identify emerging market trends, enabling brands to stay ahead of the competition and adapt strategies proactively.

Healthcare. Beyond the fancy diagnostic tools you read about in the news, healthcare workers use AI for the mundane-but-critical stuff: optimizing staff schedules, predicting equipment maintenance, streamlining patient intake forms. Chatbots now filter the basic stuff—so physicians can focus on the complex, the critical, and the human. Here are a few opportunities for AI in healthcare:

Predictive Diagnostics: AI systems like IBM Watson Health analyze patient data to predict diseases or conditions, enabling earlier diagnosis and treatment.

Personalized Treatment Plans: Tools create tailored care plans by analyzing patient history, genetics, and lifestyle factors.

Operational Efficiency: AI optimizes staff schedules, predicts equipment maintenance needs, and streamlines administrative tasks, reducing costs and improving patient care.

Telemedicine Support: Chatbots provide initial consultations, triage patients, and direct them to appropriate care providers.

Retail. Inventory management used to be guesswork dressed up as science. AI sees the sales curve before it happens—so your inventory doesn't turn into a sad shrine to Valentine's Day love when Father's Day rolls around. Customer service chatbots handle returns, track packages, and answer sizing questions. The complex complaints still go to humans, but the robots handle the routine stuff that used to eat up support agents' entire days. Let's take a look at the options:

Inventory Management: AI tracks sales patterns to predict inventory needs, preventing stockouts or overstocking.

Personalized Shopping Experiences: AI-powered recommendation engines suggest products based on customer behavior and preferences, boosting sales and customer satisfaction.

Dynamic Pricing: AI adjusts pricing in real time based on demand, competitor pricing, and seasonal trends.

Customer Support: Virtual assistants answer common queries, process returns, and guide customers through purchasing decisions.

Finance. Fraud detection happens in real-time now instead of after someone's account is already drained. AI spots suspicious patterns faster than any human could, even if those patterns are spread across thousands of transactions. Financial advisors use AI to create personalized investment recommendations, but they're still the ones having conversations with clients about their actual goals and risk tolerance. The AI handles the math; humans handle the emotions. Let's explore some of the potential applications:

Fraud Detection: AI analyzes transaction patterns to identify and flag potentially fraudulent activities in real time.

Investment Insights: Predictive tools assist financial analysts by identifying market trends and suggesting optimal portfolio strategies.

Personalized Financial Planning: AI tools like Mint or Betterment create tailored savings and investment plans for users based on their goals and risk tolerance.

Loan Risk Assessment: AI evaluates loan applications by analyzing applicant data and credit history, streamlining decision-making for lenders.

Manufacturing. Factory managers are finally getting ahead of equipment failures instead of constantly reacting to them. AI watches machines for the subtle signs that humans miss—vibration patterns, temperature fluctuations, tiny changes in sound—and schedules maintenance before anything breaks. One plant manager told me this eliminated their 3 AM emergency repair calls almost entirely.

Quality control used to mean hiring people to stare at products all day, trying to catch defects before they ship. Now, AI-powered cameras spot imperfections faster and more consistently than human eyes ever could. Here are some sample applications of AI for manufacturing:

Predictive Maintenance: AI monitors equipment for signs of wear and tear, scheduling maintenance before breakdowns occur, reducing downtime.

Quality Control: AI-powered visual inspection tools identify defects in products during manufacturing, ensuring consistent quality.

Supply Chain Optimization: AI predicts supply chain disruptions and suggests alternatives, helping manufacturers maintain efficiency.

Robotics Integration: AI controls robotics systems to enhance precision and efficiency in assembly lines.

Legal Services. Contract review used to be the legal profession's version of data entry—necessary but mind-numbing. AI platforms now scan contracts for red flags, missing clauses, and unusual terms in minutes instead of hours. Lawyers still make the important decisions, but they're not burning billable hours on routine document scanning. Here are a handful of use cases in legal:

Contract Review: AI platforms like Kira Systems scan contracts for risks, inconsistencies, or opportunities, saving lawyers hours of manual review.

Case Research: AI tools summarize case law and relevant precedents, streamlining the research process.

E-discovery: Sifting through thousands of documents for litigation—used to be where legal careers went to die. Now AI handles the initial sorting, flagging potentially relevant documents so lawyers can focus on building their case.

Compliance Monitoring: AI ensures businesses adhere to regulatory requirements by flagging potential violations.

Nonprofits. This is where AI gets incredibly interesting. Small organizations finally have access to tools that used to require enterprise budgets. Nonprofits use AI to analyze donor data and predict who's likely to give again (and when). They draft grant proposals faster, manage volunteer schedules more efficiently, and track program outcomes without hiring a full-time data analyst. Here are some ways AI can help organizations to even more good:

Donor Insights and Engagement: AI tools analyze donor data to identify giving patterns, predict donor behavior, and personalize outreach campaigns, leading to higher retention and increased contributions.

Grant Writing Assistance: Generative AI platforms can draft compelling grant proposals, which saves time, and allows staff to focus on strategic priorities.

Program Impact Analysis: AI-powered analytics evaluate the effectiveness of programs by identifying trends, measuring outcomes, and providing actionable insights for improvement.

Volunteer Management: AI platforms help match volunteers to opportunities based on skills, availability, and interests, ensuring a better experience for both the organization and its supporters.

In every single case, AI isn't replacing human judgment—it's handling the repetitive, time-consuming tasks that were sucking the life out of people's workdays. The teachers still teach. The doctors still diagnose. The marketers still strategize. They're spending less time on robotic tasks, and more on the stuff that still needs curiosity, judgment, and caffeine.

Three Transformation Stories: Anxiety to Advantage

For all the sweeping promises about AI reshaping industries, real change happens one human at a time. The following stories aren't about flashy tech—they're about everyday professionals who began their AI journeys with confusion, skepticism, or outright frustration. But instead of walking away, they found a way through. Whether it was a marketing manager learning to trust machine-generated insights, a bakery owner uncovering patterns in pastry sales, or a teacher rediscovering joy in lesson planning, each story reveals a simple truth: AI becomes powerful not when it replaces expertise, but when it amplifies it. These aren't case studies—they're proof that transformation begins when we stop waiting for AI to "arrive" and start making it our own.

Emma—Marketing Manager (SaaS)

Emma stared at her company's new AI analytics platform like it was written in ancient Greek. The dashboard displayed dozens of metrics she'd never seen, chart types she couldn't interpret, and recommendations that seemed to contradict everything she'd learned about their customer base. After three frustrating attempts to generate a simple campaign report, she gave up and returned to manually pulling data from five different sources—a process that consumed entire afternoons.

The breakthrough came during a lunch conversation with a colleague who mentioned the platform's one-hour workshop. Emma almost skipped it, assuming it would be too basic or too technical. Instead of chasing vanity metrics, she filtered down to the three that earned their place on the strategy board. More importantly, she learned to trust the AI's pattern recognition while applying her own strategic judgment to the insights.

The transformation was immediate. Within weeks, Emma was using the platform to identify underperforming ad placements and reallocate budget in real-time, cutting waste by 40%. But the real change went deeper. She began seeing data differently—not as numbers to wrestle with, but as stories to interpret. Her presentations became more compelling because she could focus on narrative instead of number-crunching. Six months later, Emma was training new team members and leading the company's expansion into predictive analytics. Her initial anxiety had become her greatest professional asset.

David—Neighborhood Bakery Owner

David's first attempt at AI demand forecasting nearly ended his experiment entirely. The software generated what looked like incomprehensible graphs showing predicted sales for items he wasn't even sure he'd ever made. The interface assumed he understood "seasonality coefficients" and "trend decomposition"—terms that meant nothing to someone who'd always relied on intuition and experience to plan his daily bakes.

Frustrated, David was ready to cancel his subscription when a fellow small business owner suggested starting smaller. Instead of trying to forecast his entire inventory, why not test the AI on just weekend specials—croissants and sourdough bread? This focused approach revealed something remarkable: the AI's predictions were startlingly accurate, accounting for factors David had never consciously considered, like how rainy weather increased demand for comfort foods or how local events affected foot traffic.

Encouraged by this success, David gradually expanded the AI's role in his business. He began using it to time seasonal menu launches, optimize ingredient orders, and even schedule staff based on predicted busy periods. The results were transformative. Waste dropped dramatically as David stopped over-baking slow-moving items. Customer satisfaction improved because popular items were rarely out of stock. Most importantly, David reclaimed hours of his day previously spent on guesswork and manual planning. He now spends that time developing new recipes and building relationships with customers—the parts of his business that sparked his original passion. Profits increased 25%, but the real victory was rediscovering why he became a baker in the first place.

Priya—High-School Educator

When Priya first tried her district's AI lesson-planning tool, the results felt like educational Mad Libs—technically correct but completely soulless. The AI generated generic activities that could have been written for any classroom, anywhere, with no understanding of her students' backgrounds, learning styles, or the creative teaching methods she'd developed over fifteen years. After a few disappointing attempts, she archived the tool and returned to her late-night planning sessions.

The shift happened when Priya stopped expecting the AI to replace her expertise and started treating it as a collaboration partner. Instead of asking for complete lesson plans, she began requesting specific components—discussion questions for Romeo and Juliet, real-world examples of geometric concepts, or creative writing prompts tied to historical events. She learned to provide context in her prompts: her students' grade level, their interests, the time of year, even the energy level she expected in class that day.

The AI responded by generating increasingly sophisticated and relevant content. When teaching fractions, it suggested using cooking scenarios that resonate with her students' diverse cultural backgrounds. For literature discussions, it provided contemporary parallels that helped students connect classic themes to their own experiences. Priya found herself iterating on AI suggestions, combining the tool's broad knowledge with her deep understanding of her specific students.

The transformation extended beyond lesson planning. Student engagement jumped 35% as Priya used AI to personalize learning materials and create differentiated assignments. But perhaps more importantly, she rediscovered her enthusiasm for teaching. Freed from the administrative burden of content creation, she could focus on what she loved most: inspiring students and facilitating meaningful discussions. Priya now leads professional development sessions across her district, showing other educators how to enhance rather than replace their teaching artistry with AI.

Using AI as Enhancement, Not Replacement

The graphic designer who feared logo generators now finds clients seeking her expertise to guide AI outputs, refine concepts, and ensure brand consistency. The content writer worried that ChatGPT now charges premium rates for AI-enhanced ideation and strategic messaging. AI steals drudgery; humans keep the judgment. AI grabs the grunt work; humans keep the baton. Smart pros stop wrestling the robot and start conducting the orchestra.

When it works well, AI doesn't do your job—it frees it up. So you can stop babysitting tasks and start building ideas. It automates the repeatable so you can double down on the remarkable. And it helps you move faster, think bigger, and lead with more clarity.

But here's the catch: AI only amplifies what's already there. If your current systems are chaotic, AI will scale the chaos. If your strategy is sound, AI will supercharge your results.

So don't ask, "Will AI take my job?" Ask instead: "How can I use AI to free me up to do my best thinking, creating, and leading?"

Enhancement vs. Replacement Examples

AI can be a brilliant collaborator—but only if we stay in the driver's seat. The difference between meaningful enhancement and risky replacement comes down to how we engage with the tools. In every domain—creative work, data analysis, strategic planning, or problem-solving—AI shines brightest when it supports human judgment, not substitutes for it. The goal isn't to hand over the reins, but to partner with AI in ways that elevate your thinking, sharpen your instincts, and expand what's possible. The following section breaks down exactly where AI can amplify your strengths—and where relying too heavily could compromise your impact.

For Creative Work:

Enhancement: Use AI to generate initial ideas, then develop your unique perspective and voice

Replacement Risk: Have AI write final outputs without contributing your creative insight

For Analysis:

Enhancement: Let AI process data while you interpret significance and implications

Replacement Risk: Accept AI conclusions without applying your domain expertise

For Strategy:

Enhancement: Use AI research to inform decisions you make based on your values and vision

Replacement Risk: Implement AI recommendations without strategic evaluation

For Problem-Solving:

Enhancement: Leverage AI to explore options while you evaluate and choose based on context

Replacement Risk: Defer complex decisions entirely to AI algorithms

Maintaining Your Cognitive Edge

Think of AI as a cognitive gym. Just like a fitness center, it can either strengthen or weaken your mental muscles—it all depends on how you use it.

Use AI to shortcut every decision, automate every task, and avoid thinking altogether? You're skipping the reps. Over time, that leads to intellectual atrophy: less curiosity, less problem-solving, less growth. But use it to spot patterns faster, clarify complex ideas, and challenge your assumptions? That's a powerful workout for your brain. You build sharper thinking, better decision-making, and more strategic focus.

The tool isn't the problem. It's how you train with it.

Practices to Preserve Your Human Edge

Using AI well isn't about mastering prompts. It's about mastering your role in the process. The smartest professionals don't just use AI; they stay aware of what should never be outsourced: their judgment, creativity, and core values. It's not a matter of distrusting the tech, but of placing greater trust in your own expertise. To let AI elevate your thinking rather than flatten it, you need to stay mentally active, intellectually curious, and strategically grounded. The habits below aren't just best practices—they're the defining traits of empowered collaborators in an age of intelligent tools.

Active Collaboration: Always bring your perspective to AI interactions. Don't just consume AI outputs—build on them, challenge them, and improve them with your expertise.

Learning Habits: Continue developing your knowledge and skills independently of AI. Read, discuss, experiment, and think critically about your field. Let AI challenge your assumptions, call out your bias, and help you recognize your blind spots.

Decision Space: Identify decisions that should remain entirely yours—strategic choices, value-based judgments, creative directions—and resist the temptation to outsource them.

Use AI as Research, Not Oracle: Treat AI insights as high-quality input for your decision-making process, not as final answers.

AI AS YOUR SECRET WEAPON (NOT YOUR REPLACEMENT)

Let's talk about what happens when you stop thinking of AI as some external force and start seeing it as an extension of your own capabilities. This isn't about becoming dependent on machines—it's about becoming the person who gets things done while everyone else is still figuring out what's possible.

Becoming the Person Who Just "Gets It."

You know that person at work who always seems to have better insights, faster turnaround times, and somehow stays ahead of everyone else? They're probably not working 80-hour weeks. They're working smarter, and AI is part of how they do it.

Take Jennifer, a data analyst at a mid-sized company. While her colleagues spent days creating reports manually, she taught ChatGPT to help her identify patterns in customer data. She started presenting insights that took her peers weeks to uncover. Within six months, she was leading the analytics team—not because she was smarter than everyone else, but because she was leveraging tools that made her more effective.

Time Management: Getting Your Life Back.

Here's a question that'll make you uncomfortable: how much of your day is spent on tasks that a well-trained assistant could handle? Email, scheduling, follow-ups, rinse, repeat—the kind of tasks that clog your calendar but don't build your legacy. AI excels at exactly this kind of work. Not the important stuff—the busywork that crowds out the important stuff.

Stacey, a marketing director, used to spend her Monday mornings sorting through weekend emails and updating project timelines. Now, an AI assistant handles email triage and automatically updates her project dashboard based on team inputs. Now those two hours are fueling real strategy—not just work that gets a nod, but work that gets a promotion.

The math is simple: if AI saves you 10 hours a week on routine tasks, that's 520 hours a year—equivalent to three months of full-time work. What would you do with an extra three months?

Creativity: Breaking Through Your Own Limitations.

Here's something most people don't realize about creativity: it's often limited by what you already know. You can only connect dots you can see, and you can only see dots you've encountered before. AI expands your dot collection.

Need to brainstorm marketing angles for a new product? AI can suggest approaches from industries you've never worked in. Stuck on a design problem? AI can show you solutions from completely different fields. Writing a proposal and can't find the right angle? AI can help you see your ideas from perspectives you wouldn't have considered.

Mark, a freelance writer, uses AI to break out of his usual writing patterns. When he's stuck on an article introduction, he asks ChatGPT to suggest five completely different opening approaches. He doesn't use them verbatim—he uses them as creative springboards to write something better than he would have on his own.

The Mental Game: Rewiring Your Brain for AI Success

Recognize this uncomfortable truth: the biggest barrier to using AI effectively isn't technical—it's psychological. Most of us are walking around with mental software that's about as compatible with AI as a flip phone is with TikTok. We've been trained to believe that anything worth doing must be difficult, that we need to understand something completely before we can use it, and that making mistakes means we're failing. With AI, all of that goes out the window.

Stop chasing perfect; it doesn't exist anyway. Remember learning to drive? Your first attempt probably wasn't a smooth cruise down the highway. You jerked the steering wheel, hit the brakes too hard, and maybe stalled out at a traffic light. But you didn't give up and decide cars weren't for you—you kept practicing until it became second nature.

AI works the same way. Your first ChatGPT prompt might produce garbage. Your initial attempt at automating a task might create more work than it saves. That's not failure—that's learning.

Take Elena, a physical therapist who spent weeks crafting the "perfect" prompt to generate patient education materials. Her first attempts were terrible—too clinical, wrong reading level, completely disconnected from her patients' real concerns. Instead of giving up, she started tweaking. She added examples of how she explained exercises to patients, specified the common questions she heard daily, and included details about the specific injuries she treated most—painting a picture as detailed as a medical textbook but twice as engaging. By week three, the platform was cranking out handouts that made her patients go "oh, now I get it" instead of "what the heck does this medical jargon even mean?"

The breakthrough wasn't getting it perfect on the first try. It was accepting that "good enough to improve" beats "too scared to start."

Most people approach AI like they're window shopping—looking from the outside, reading about what other people are doing, but never trying anything themselves. It's like being a perpetual backseat driver who's never touched the steering wheel.

The shift happens when you stop asking "What can AI do?" and start asking "What can AI do for me, specifically, right now?"

Instead of browsing another "50 Amazing AI Tools" article, remember this truth: Learning doesn't happen in the headlines. Pick a tool, use it for 30 minutes, and see what it can technically do. Not researching it, not watching tutorials about it—using it. Break something. Make mistakes. See what happens when you push the boundaries.

Your Brain's Software Update.

Here's what needs to change upstairs:

Old Operating System	New Operating System
"What if I fail?"	"What can I learn?"
"It's too complicated."	"I'll start with something simple."
"I need to understand everything first."	"I can figure it out as I go."
"AI is for tech experts."	"AI is for anyone who wants to solve problems."
"I might look stupid."	"Everyone's figuring this out together."

Understanding AI as a Tool, Not a Threat

At its core, AI is just that: a tool. Like a hammer or a paintbrush, its value depends entirely on how you use it. Think about your daily life. Imagine using AI to create a personalized meal plan based on what's already in your fridge, saving time and reducing food waste. Or picture yourself leveraging AI to plan a workout routine tailored to your fitness goals, no matter how packed your schedule might be. The possibilities are as broad as your imagination.

For example, what if you could use AI to automate those repetitive work tasks that drain your energy? Instead of spending hours compiling reports or organizing data, you could focus on crafting strategies, generating ideas, or connecting with colleagues—the things that truly make an impact. Picture ending your workday feeling accomplished and energized, rather than bogged down by busywork.

Imagine your personal life benefiting as well. You could use AI to organize your calendar, set reminders for family birthdays, or even draft a thoughtful thank-you note. These small but meaningful changes add up to create a smoother, more fulfilling daily experience.

Don't Fall Into These Traps

AI adoption comes with its own set of bear traps, and they're surprisingly easy to stumble into—especially when you're feeling confident about your newfound digital superpowers. The same enthusiasm that drives you to experiment with AI tools can quickly lead you down paths that make you less effective, not more. These aren't theoretical pitfalls dreamed up by cautious consultants; they're real mistakes that even AI-savvy professionals make when they get a little too comfortable with their shiny new tools. Avoiding these traps isn't about being paranoid—it's about being strategic enough to harness AI's power without accidentally handing over your professional judgment to a chatbot.

The Dependency Trap: AI should make you more capable, not less. If you find yourself unable to do basic tasks without AI help, you've gone too far. Use AI to handle routine work so you can focus on higher-level thinking, not to replace thinking altogether.

The Shortcut Obsession: Learning to use AI tools effectively takes time. There's no magic prompt that instantly makes you an AI power user. Plan to invest time upfront to save massive time later.

The Set-and-Forget Mistake: AI tools need regular tuning. What works perfectly today might need adjustment next month as your needs change or the tools evolve. Build review and refinement into your process.

Your Reality Check: Where You Stand Right Now

Before you go any further, let's get honest about where you stand right now. Don't skip this part—I know you want to but bear with me. Understanding your starting point isn't just helpful; it's essential.

What goes through your head when someone mentions AI at work? What's the real reason you haven't dived deeper into AI tools yet? (And "I don't have time" doesn't count—we both know you found time to learn TikTok). If AI could solve one problem in your life tomorrow, what would you want it to be?

Write these answers down somewhere. Not because I told you to, but because you'll want to look back at them in a few weeks and laugh at how different things feel.

Mindset Shift: Curiosity Over Competence

Curiosity reframes "What if I fail?" into "What if this works?" Block 15 minutes to experiment—no stakes, no judgment. Ask how AI could cut a tedious step today or reveal an insight you missed. Progress beats perfection every time.

The anxiety is natural; it isn't permanent. As you chip away at fear with micro-experiments, confidence compounds. The professionals who win in this new era won't be the most technical—they'll be the most adaptive.

Your irreplaceable value lies in your ability to think critically, create meaningfully, and decide wisely within your unique context. AI can provide information, generate options, and process complexity—but it cannot replicate your judgment, creativity, or wisdom.

The bottom line: AI won't transform your career overnight, but it will compound your capabilities over time. The question isn't whether AI will change how work gets done—it's whether you'll be ahead of that change or scrambling to catch up. That's the real promise of AI: not that it'll do your job for you, but that it'll give you back the parts of your job you enjoy—like a good dishwasher that handles the cleanup so you can focus on the cooking.

Ready to turn curiosity into capability? In the next chapter, we build your C.A.L.M.™ foundation, starting with the first—and most overlooked—step: Clarity.

2. Learning Lab

💡 Try This: Confidence Sprint for Experienced Users

Objective: Refine your AI prompting, tool use, and workflow efficiency to maximize results with less effort.

Time Required: 30–60 minutes (can be broken into 10–15 minute sessions)

Materials Needed:

- Your preferred AI tool
- A digital doc or spreadsheet
- A recent or ongoing work task

Steps:

1. **Prompt with Precision**
    - Before prompting, take 2 minutes to list what the AI needs: context, goal, tone, and format.
    - Write your prompt using this information.
2. **Master Your Tool**
    - Explore all settings and features of one AI tool.
    - Note what tasks it excels at and where it underperforms.
3. **Build Feedback Loops**
    - After receiving a result, ask the AI to critique its own output.
    - Request improvements or run it through another tool for enhancement.
4. **Start a Prompt Library**
    - Create a digital document to store effective prompts.
    - Label them by use case (e.g., "client emails," "event planning").
    - Add notes on what made them work well.

Try This: Opportunity Self-Assessment

Objective: Evaluate your current strengths and challenges with AI to guide your next stage of development.

Time Required: 30 minutes (plus ongoing reflection)

Materials Needed:

- A blank document or journal
- Past AI outputs or interaction history (if available)

Steps:

1. **List Frustrations**
    - In the left column, write 3–5 specific AI experiences that were frustrating or ineffective.
    - Note what went wrong and why.
2. **List Wins**
    - In the right column, list 3–5 examples where AI saved time, improved results, or exceeded expectations.
    - Note what made them work well.
3. **Analyze Patterns**
    - Compare both columns. Identify common threads: tool mismatch, vague prompts, unclear goals?
    - Use this insight to target where you need more practice, better tools, or different strategies.

💡 Try This: Build Your Use Case Roadmap

Objective: Develop a personal database of high-impact AI applications to boost confidence and future performance.

Time Required: 45 minutes to start; 10 minutes/week ongoing

Materials Needed:

- A document or spreadsheet
- Any AI tools you currently use

Steps:

1. **Create Two Sections**
   - Section 1: *Proven Successes* – Log AI use cases that have worked well for you. Include the tool, your approach, and what made it effective.
   - Section 2: *Curiosity Queue* – List ideas for how you might use AI in new or creative ways.
2. **Update Weekly**
   - Each week, revisit your list. Add new successes and test one item from your curiosity list.
3. **Reflect and Apply**
   - Use patterns from your success section to replicate outcomes in new areas.

💡 Try This: Curiosity Challenges

Objective: Break through hesitation or creative blocks by experimenting with AI in new, playful ways.

Time Required: 15–30 minutes per challenge

Materials Needed:

- Access to a new or underused AI tool
- A notepad or digital doc for observations

Steps: Choose one of the following exercises:

a. Tool Safari (15 mins)

- Explore a new AI tool without a goal. Click around, test features, and focus on what it can do—not perfect outcomes.

b. 3-Question Deep Dive (30 mins)

- Write 3 questions like:
    - "Can AI help automate this task?"
    - "How could AI speed up my workflow?"
    - "Could AI make this communication clearer?"
- Choose one to research or test in practice.

c. Unexpected Use Challenge (30 mins)

- Pick one surprising way to use AI this week: planning a dinner party, analyzing your mood journal, writing a workout plan.
- Reflect on what worked and what was frustrating.

💡 Try This: Quick Wins You Can Apply Today

Objective: Use AI immediately to improve work performance, save time, and reduce mental load.

Time Required: 15–30 minutes per win

Materials Needed:

- Any AI tool (e.g., ChatGPT, Notion AI, Otter, etc.)
- Access to your current email, calendar, or task list

Steps: Choose one to test today:

◆ **Career Power-Ups**

- **Skills Gap Finder:** Ask AI to analyze 10 job descriptions in your field and identify missing or in-demand skills.
- **Productivity Audit:** Have AI analyze your last week's calendar or to-do list. Ask what tasks can be batched, dropped, or automated.

◆ **Time Liberation**

- **Email Assistant:** Feed a few recurring email types into AI and ask it to write reusable templates or draft your replies.
- **Meeting Scheduling:** Use AI to propose optimal times, draft scheduling emails, or automate meeting setup.

◆ **Creative Collaboration**

- **Brainstorm Generator:** Ask AI for 10 unique takes on a current challenge. Use them to spark your own breakthrough.
- **Quality Enhancer:** Paste a written draft into AI and request feedback, improved structure, or added clarity.

3. Clarity – Design Your Ideal Output Before Your Input

Imagine this: You're standing in the world's most sophisticated hardware store. The aisles stretch endlessly, packed with gleaming tools that promise to solve problems you didn't even know you had. There's a device that apparently makes perfect pancakes, another that organizes your sock drawer by color temperature, and somewhere in aisle 47, a contraption that might just fold fitted sheets properly.

You wander the aisles for hours, increasingly bewildered. Every tool looks impressive, but you can't shake the feeling that you're missing something fundamental. What exactly are you trying to fix?

This is precisely what happens when people dive into AI without clarity. They're mesmerized by the shiny possibilities—chatbots that write poetry, image generators that can make you look like you live in the Elizabethan era, algorithms that predict everything from stock prices to your next Netflix binge—but they've skipped the most crucial step: figuring out what problem they're genuinely trying to solve.

Why Your Brain Craves Direction (And Why AI Does Too)

There's a fascinating element in psychology: we're remarkably bad at making decisions when faced with too many options. Psychologist Barry Schwartz calls this "the paradox of choice"—the more options we have, the more paralyzed we become. Give someone three jam flavors to choose from, and they'll happily pick one. Give them thirty, and they'll leave the store empty-handed, overwhelmed by possibility.

AI amplifies this paradox exponentially. Modern AI tools can write, analyze, create, predict, teach, optimize, generate code, and perform countless other tasks. Without clear direction, you're essentially asking your brain to choose from an infinite aisle of possibilities.

But the fascinating part is this. AI responds best to the exact same thing humans need when they're lost - straightforward, unambiguous direction. Perfect clarity. They're not mysterious black boxes making random magic—they're pattern-matching machines that excel when given specific, well-defined problems. Feed an AI a vague request like "help me with my business," and you'll get vague, generic advice. Ask it to "analyze my customer service emails from last month to identify the three most common complaint categories and suggest response templates for each," and suddenly you're having a productive conversation.

This is where many people miss a crucial insight: clarity isn't just about finding the right tool for your problem. It's also about communicating clearly with the AI once you've found it. The most sophisticated AI in the world can't read your mind or fill in the gaps in your thinking. It can only work with what you give it.

Think of it this way: if you walked into that hardware store and told the clerk, "I need something to fix my house," they'd probably stare at you blankly. But if you said, "I need a drill bit that can make clean holes in ceramic tile without cracking," they'd walk you straight to the solution. The same principle applies to AI interactions—the quality of your output is directly proportional to the clarity of your input.

The Tale of Two Approaches

Let me tell you about three people who discovered AI's versatility on the same day. Their approaches reveal different aspects of what clarity undeniably means.

Emma dove in with creative exploration. She used AI to brainstorm names for her new consulting practice, then asked it to generate character studies for a novel she'd always wanted to write, followed by designing a custom fitness plan that worked around her busy travel schedule. While this might seem scattered, Emma was unquestionably being quite strategic—she was testing AI's creative and generative capabilities across different domains to understand its range.

David focused on knowledge synthesis. He fed AI his collection of business book highlights and asked it to identify patterns across different management philosophies. Then he used it to create a personal learning journey for understanding blockchain technology, complete with beginner-to-advanced milestones. David was exploring AI's ability to connect ideas and structure learning.

Sarah tackled life logistics. She used AI to plan a multi-city family reunion that accommodated different budgets and dietary restrictions, then asked it to help create a parenting framework for managing her teenagers' screen time. Finally, she had it analyze symptoms she'd been tracking to prepare better questions for her doctor visit. Sarah was testing AI's organizational and analytical capabilities.

All three succeeded because they understood something crucial: clarity isn't just about fixing problems—it's about defining the type of output you want, whether that's creative inspiration, structured learning, or organized information.

When Clarity Goes Missing: The Familiar Cycle

Let's be real: most people don't give up on AI because it's complicated. They give up because it's confusing, underwhelming, and occasionally feels like trying to assemble IKEA furniture blindfolded—with no manual, a missing Allen wrench, and four extra pieces labeled "optional."

Without clear objectives and communication strategies, even the smartest AI becomes another overpriced gadget in your digital junk drawer. The cycle novice users fall into is relatable:

The Honeymoon Phase: Everything seems possible. You're generating emails at lightning speed, creating fictional characters for fun, designing workout routines, and asking it to explain quantum physics like you're five. It feels like you've discovered a Swiss Army knife for your brain.

The Reality Check: The novelty wears off. Those AI-generated blog posts need heavy editing. The workout plan doesn't account for your specific limitations. The travel itinerary looks great but ignores your budget constraints. You realize you're spending more time refining AI outputs than you initially saved creating them.

The Frustration Phase: You start blaming the technology. "This AI doesn't understand context." "It keeps giving me generic responses." "It's not reading between the lines." But the real issue isn't the AI's capability—it's the communication gap between what you need and what you're genuinely asking for.

The Abandonment: You quietly stop using the AI tools, maybe keeping one or two for occasional use, but the transformative potential you'd heard about feels like marketing hype.

This cycle isn't a failure of AI technology—it's a failure of clarity at two critical levels: clarity about what you're trying to accomplish, and clarity in how you communicate with AI systems.

THE TWO DIMENSIONS OF CLARITY

Most people think clarity is just about identifying the right problem to solve. But there are ultimately two dimensions that determine your success with AI:

Strategic Clarity. What are you trying to accomplish? This is the big-picture clarity—understanding which of your goals are worth pursuing and which AI approach makes the most sense. It's about recognizing that you spend two hours every Tuesday wrestling with expense reports, or that you're constantly struggling to plan engaging family activities, or that you have a brilliant business idea but need help structuring your thoughts, or that you want to develop a personal philosophy but don't know where to start.

Strategic clarity helps you choose the right tool and approach for the job. It's the difference between wandering aimlessly through AI capabilities and identifying exactly what type of output would be most valuable: problem-solving, creative generation, knowledge synthesis, planning and organization, or skill development.

Tactical Clarity. How do you communicate your needs?
This is the nitty-gritty precision we're talking about—your superpower for converting fuzzy ideas into crystal-clear marching orders that AI can follow without losing its digital mind. It's about understanding that "help me plan a vacation" will produce generic results, while "Create a 5-day family itinerary for Paris in October with two teenagers, focusing on museums and food

experiences, with a budget of $200 per day for activities, and avoiding anything that requires more than 20 minutes of walking between stops" will give you something immediately useful.

Tactical clarity works whether you're solving problems or exploring possibilities. The key is being specific about the type of output you want, the constraints you're working within, and the context that matters.

Consider Jennifer, a small business owner who wanted to "develop her brand voice." Her first attempts were disasters because she was asking AI to "make my writing sound more professional." The breakthrough came when she learned to structure her requests around specific outputs: "Analyze these three blog posts I've written and these five social media captions to identify my natural writing patterns. Then help me create a brand voice guide that captures my authentic style while making it more consistent across platforms. Include specific word choices I tend to use, sentence structures that feel natural to me, and the overall tone that comes through in my best writing."

Same goal, same AI tool, completely different results. The difference was tactical clarity—knowing how to communicate her specific needs rather than hoping the AI would intuitively understand what "professional" meant to her.

THE THREE CLARITY TRAPS (AND HOW TO ESCAPE THEM)

Before we dive into a framework for getting clear, let's talk about the ways people typically sabotage themselves. Recognizing these patterns is half the battle.

The "Everything" Trap: When AI Becomes Shiny Object Syndrome

You discover AI can write emails, create presentations, analyze data, generate images, schedule meetings, and apparently make you coffee (okay, not yet, but give it time). Your brain lights up with possibilities. "I'll use it for everything!" you declare, downloading seven different apps and signing up for four subscription services.

Two weeks later, you're using none of them consistently. This is the "everything" trap, and it's seductive because it feels productive. You're being proactive! You're embracing the future! You're completely overwhelmed and making no real progress.

The antidote? The "One Thing" rule. Pick literally one task—something you do weekly that takes longer than it should—and get absurdly good at using AI for just that. Master both the strategic selection (choosing the right tool) and tactical execution (crafting effective prompts) for that single use case. Once that workflow becomes second nature, then expand.

The Vague Goals Trap: When "Better" Isn't Good Enough

The second trap sounds like this: "I want to use AI to be more productive," or "I want AI to help me write better." These aren't goals—they're wishes. And wishes don't give you enough direction to choose the right tools or craft effective prompts.

Compare these two approaches:

Vague: "I want AI to help me write better emails."

Specific: "I want to use AI to draft initial responses to customer service inquiries, reducing my average response time from 45 minutes to 15 minutes while maintaining our friendly, helpful tone and ensuring each response addresses the customer's specific concern."

The second version tells you exactly what tool to look for (something that can draft responses), how to measure success (response time), what constraints to consider (maintaining tone), and what quality standards to maintain (addressing specific concerns). It also gives you the framework for writing effective prompts: you'll need to provide context about your company's tone, examples of good responses, and specific details about each customer inquiry.

The Magic Wand Trap: When Expectations Meet Reality

The third trap is expecting AI to be a magic wand that makes complex problems disappear entirely with minimal input from you. People imagine feeding a messy, complicated task into an AI platform and getting a perfect result with no human refinement required.

This happens because most AI demos show the highlight reel—the perfectly formatted output, the brilliant insight, the seamless automation. What they don't show is the prompt refinement, the output editing, the iterative improvements, and the occasional spectacular failures. The key insight? AI excels at the heavy lifting—the research, the first drafts, the pattern recognition, the initial analysis. But the final judgment calls, the creative insights, the contextual adjustments? That's still very much a human job. The best AI workflows aren't about replacement; they're about collaboration.

Think of AI as a freakishly smart intern—capable of doing substantial work, but requiring clear instructions, specific examples, and careful review. When you approach it with that mindset, you'll naturally develop better communication habits and more realistic expectations.

THE FOCUS FRAMEWORK: YOUR CLARITY GPS

Now that you know what not to do, let's talk about what works. **FOCUS** isn't another productivity acronym designed to look clever on a slide deck. It's a step-by-step process for transforming vague frustrations into specific, solvable problems that you can communicate effectively to AI applications.

F – FUNCTIONALITY

What Unquestionably Needs Fixing?

The first step sounds deceptively simple: identify what specific task needs improvement. But here's where most people trip up—they think too big or too vague.

"I want AI to help with my writing" isn't specific enough. "I want AI to help me write better email subject lines that get higher open rates" is getting somewhere. "I want AI to analyze my last 50 sent emails and suggest subject line patterns that correlate with faster responses, then help me craft subject lines for my weekly newsletter using those patterns" is pure gold.

But functionality isn't limited to fixing problems. Maybe you want to "explore philosophy" (too vague) versus "create a personal learning journey through Stoicism, with weekly themes, reflection questions, and practical exercises I can apply to managing work stress" (specific and actionable).

Or perhaps you want to "plan better family time" (unclear) versus "design three different weekend adventure frameworks for my family—one for rainy days, one for outdoor exploration, and one for creative projects—each with activities that work for ages 8-16 and can be executed with minimal advance planning" (clear direction).

The trick is catching yourself in moments when you need specific outputs—whether that's solving a frustration, exploring an idea, or creating something new.

Take Maria, a marketing director who initially told me she wanted AI to "help with content creation." When we dug deeper, she realized her needs were undeniably quite varied: repurposing existing content across platforms, brainstorming campaign themes for upcoming product launches, and creating educational scenarios for customer onboarding. Each required a different type of AI interaction and output format.

That specificity led to both better tool selection and better prompt engineering. Instead of looking for general "content creation" tools, she found AI programs specifically designed for content adaptation. And instead of asking "rewrite this blog post for social media," she learned to prompt: "Adapt this 1,200-word blog post into three LinkedIn posts, maintaining the key insights but making the tone more conversational and including relevant questions to encourage engagement. Focus on the practical takeaways that would resonate with marketing professionals."

O – OUTCOME

What Does Victory Look Like?

Here's where things get interesting. Most people are surprisingly bad at articulating what they objectively want. They know what they don't want (to feel overwhelmed, to waste time, to look incompetent), but they're fuzzy on what success would demonstrably look like.

This isn't about setting SMART goals or writing mission statements. It's about being honest about what would genuinely improve your life or work. Maybe success means clearing your inbox in 15 minutes instead of an hour. Maybe it's having a structured approach to exploring new ideas instead of letting them fade away. Maybe it's creating memorable family experiences without the stress of endless planning. Maybe it's developing a writing voice that feels authentically you but more polished.

The crucial element? The clarity of your outcome directly impacts how you'll measure whether your AI interactions are working. If your goal is to "clear email faster," you might accept AI-generated responses that are quick but generic. If your goal is to "maintain strong client relationships while reducing email time," you'll craft prompts that prioritize tone and personalization alongside efficiency.

Consider David, a busy parent who wanted to "be more creative with family time." His initial attempts with AI were frustrating because he was asking for "fun family activities." But when pressed, he realized what he undeniably wanted was to become the kind of parent who created magical moments his kids would remember—the type of experiences that required thoughtfulness, not just entertainment.

That reframe completely changed his approach. Instead of looking for generic activity lists, he started using AI to help him design immersive experiences: "Create a mystery dinner game for my family that incorporates my kids' current interests in space exploration and detective stories. Include character roles for each family member, clues that require teamwork to solve, and a storyline that unfolds over our 45-minute dinner. Make it engaging for ages 10-16 while giving adults meaningful ways to participate."

C – CONSTRAINTS

What Can't You Change?

This is the reality check phase, and it's where a lot of AI enthusiasm crashes into the rocks of real life. You might love the idea of a sophisticated AI assistant, but if your company blocks external software, that's a constraint. You might want automated transcription, but if you work with confidential client information, privacy becomes non-negotiable.

Constraints aren't dream-killers—they're clarity-bringers. They force you to work within the boundaries of your actual situation, not some idealized version where you have unlimited budget and complete control over your technology stack.

But constraints also shape how you'll need to communicate with AI tools. If you can't upload sensitive documents to cloud-based AI services, you'll need to get creative about how you extract insights without sharing raw data. Maybe you anonymize information before analysis, or focus on AI tools that can help you create templates and frameworks rather than process actual client data.

If you're planning family activities but have a tight budget, that constraint shapes how you'll prompt AI: instead of asking for "fun weekend ideas," you'll request "creative family activities that cost less than $20 total and can be done within 30 minutes of downtown Seattle."

Sarah, a teacher, discovered this when she got excited about AI grading tools, only to remember that her school district requires all student data to stay within approved platforms. Instead of giving up, she pivoted to AI tools that could help her create educational content—lesson plans, discussion scenarios, and learning games she could develop on her personal time.

But she also had to adapt her prompting strategy. Instead of asking AI to "create a quiz for my students," she learned to request: "Create a quiz template for 8th-grade American History covering the Revolutionary War, with 10 multiple-choice questions, 3 short-answer questions, and a rubric for grading. Make the questions challenging but appropriate for students reading at grade level, and include one question that requires critical thinking about cause and effect."

U – USER IMPACT

Who Benefits (And How)?

Here's where you zoom out from your immediate frustration and consider the ripple effects. If AI saves you two hours a week on expense reports, what happens to those two hours? If you can respond to emails twice as fast, does that positively improve your relationships, or does it just mean people expect faster responses?

Sometimes the real impact isn't about you at all. Maybe streamlining your invoice processing means your freelancers get paid faster. Maybe generating better meeting agendas means your team members stop dreading your weekly check-ins. Maybe creating more engaging presentations means your audience clearly retains the information you're sharing. Maybe developing a structured approach to family conversations means your teenagers open up to you.

This step keeps you honest about whether you're creating real value or just playing with shiny technology. If you can't articulate how this improvement ripples outward—to your work quality, your relationships, your personal growth, your family dynamics—you might be chasing the wrong goal.

User impact also influences how you'll evaluate AI outputs. If your improvement primarily benefits you (saving time on routine tasks), you might accept AI results that are "good enough" with minimal editing. But if your AI-enhanced work directly impacts clients, family members, or colleagues, you'll need to craft prompts that prioritize quality, appropriateness, and effectiveness for your specific audience.

S – SCOPE

How Small Can You Start?

This is perhaps the most important element, and the one people most want to skip. Everyone wants to revolutionize their entire workflow overnight. But clarity comes from small, successful experiments, not grand transformations.

The question isn't "How can AI transform my business?" It's "What's the smallest AI-powered improvement I could make this week that would prove this is worth pursuing?"

Maybe it's using AI to summarize one type of recurring meeting. Maybe it's generating first drafts of one specific type of email. Maybe it's creating a simple framework for weekly family planning. Maybe it's developing a personal reflection practice with AI-generated journal prompts. Maybe it's using AI to help structure your thoughts about a big decision you're facing.

Tom, a project manager, wanted AI to help with "project management." After working through FOCUS, he narrowed it down to one specific scope: using AI to generate agenda templates for different types of meetings (kickoffs, status updates, retrospectives). It took him two hours to set up, saved him 30 minutes per week, and gave him the confidence to tackle bigger challenges.

Lisa, a busy mom, wanted AI to help with "family organization." She started small: using AI to create weekly meal plans based on what she already had in her pantry and her family's dietary preferences. Once she mastered that workflow, she expanded to using AI for planning birthday parties, organizing vacation itineraries, and even creating bedtime stories that incorporated her children's current interests.

Here's what separated Tom from the AI amateurs: he didn't just throw AI the conversational equivalent of "meeting agenda, please and thank you." He developed specific prompt templates for each meeting type. For kickoff meetings: "Create an agenda for a 90-minute project kickoff meeting with 6 team members. Include sections for introductions, project overview, role clarification, timeline review, risk discussion, and next steps. Allocate specific time blocks for each section and include 2-3 key questions to drive discussion in each area."

That level of specificity meant his AI-generated agendas were immediately useful rather than generic templates that required heavy customization.

The Prompt Engineering Connection

Here's where many people miss a crucial insight: getting clear about your strategic goals is only half the battle. The other half is learning to communicate those goals effectively to AI solutions through well-crafted prompts. Think of prompt engineering as the bridge between your clarity and AI's capability. You can have perfect strategic clarity about what you want to accomplish, but if you can't translate that into specific, actionable instructions, you'll still end up frustrated.

The best prompt engineers aren't necessarily the most technical people—they're the people who can think clearly about what they want and communicate it precisely. They understand that AI interpretations are literal and require explicit instruction about context, format, tone, constraints, and success criteria. That's the North Star we're aiming for.

The Anatomy of Clear Communication

Effective AI communication typically includes several key elements:

- ✓ **Context:** What background information does the AI need to understand your request? This might include your role, industry, audience, or specific situation.
- ✓ **Task:** What exactly do you want the AI to do? Be specific about the type of output you're seeking.
- ✓ **Format:** How should the response be structured? Do you want bullet points, paragraphs, tables, or a specific template?
- ✓ **Constraints:** What limitations or requirements must be respected? This might include length, tone, complexity level, or specific information to include or exclude.

Examples: What does good output look like? Providing examples helps AI understand your expectations and style preferences.

Consider the difference between these two prompts:

Weak: "Help me be more creative."

Strong: "I'm a marketing manager who struggles with campaign brainstorming. Help me create five different campaign concepts for promoting our new productivity app to remote workers. For each concept, include a core theme, three key messages, suggested visuals, and potential objections with responses. Focus on authentic benefits rather than flashy features and keep the tone conversational but professional."

Or consider the difference between these prompts for personal development:

Weak: "Help me set better goals."

Strong: "I'm a working parent who wants to develop a more intentional approach to personal growth while managing a demanding schedule. Create a framework for quarterly goal-setting that includes career development goals that can be pursued in 30-minute weekly sessions, family relationship goals with specific actions, and personal wellness goals that work around my 6 AM and 8 PM availability windows. Include accountability questions I can ask myself monthly."

The second prompt gives the AI everything it needs to generate something useful: your role (context), the specific task (weekly update), the required elements (performance, wins, improvements, priorities), tone guidance (professional but not formal), and format preferences (clear sections, bullet points).

Building Your Prompt Library

As you develop clarity around your most important AI use cases, you'll naturally start building a library of effective prompts. This isn't about memorizing complex formulas—it's about developing templates that consistently produce the results you need.

Start with your highest-impact, most frequent needs. If you're using AI to draft client emails, develop a prompt template that includes placeholders for client-specific information but maintains your standard structure and tone. If you're using AI to plan family activities, create prompts that account for your kids' ages, interests, and your typical constraints. If you're using AI for personal reflection, develop prompts that help you process specific types of experiences or decisions.

The goal isn't to become a prompt engineering expert overnight. It's to develop enough skill to communicate clearly with AI tools about the full range of what you want to accomplish, which is decidedly just an extension of learning to think clearly about your own needs and requirements.

The Magic of Specificity

Once you genuinely commit to the FOCUS process and sharpen those communication skills, the shift is incredible. Instead of feeling buried under AI's infinite potential, you start feeling energized about its precise applications to the stuff that's legitimately driving you crazy. You develop what I call "productive pickiness"—the ability to ignore 80% of AI capabilities because you know exactly which 20% will change your life.

This isn't about limiting yourself. It's about giving yourself permission to start somewhere specific instead of trying to drink from the fire hose of everything AI can theoretically do.

The specific problems you're solving today might evolve or disappear entirely. But the skill of getting clear—of recognizing your patterns, articulating your needs, and communicating effectively with AI programs—that skill becomes more valuable over time, not less.

Think of clarity as a muscle that gets stronger with use. The person who can quickly identify their core frustrations, translate them into solvable problems, and communicate their needs precisely will always have an advantage, regardless of which AI tools happen to be trending.

Your Clarity Action Plan

Don't wait for clarity to arrive fully formed. Start small. Pick one problem worth solving. Use what you learn to shape your next prompt, your next tool, your next win. You don't need to map out your entire AI strategy or anticipate every possible use case. You just need to get clear on one thing—one task that's annoying you, one creative project you'd love to pursue, one learning goal that excites you, one aspect of family life you'd like to improve, one small enhancement that would make your Tuesday mornings feel less chaotic.

Start there. Work through FOCUS for that one specific challenge. Find an AI tool that seems like a good fit, then learn to communicate your needs clearly through well-crafted prompts. Master that workflow until it becomes second nature, then use what you've learned to tackle the next challenge.

Each successful experiment builds both your strategic clarity (understanding what AI can do for you) and your tactical clarity (knowing how to ask for what you need). Over time, these skills compound, making you increasingly effective at identifying opportunities and implementing solutions.

The clarity you develop today becomes the foundation for everything else you'll build with AI. It's the difference between wandering aimlessly through an infinite hardware store and walking directly to the tool that solves your problem—then knowing exactly how to use it.

In our next chapter, we'll explore a crucial question that many people skip entirely: is AI objectively the right solution for what you're trying to accomplish? Just because you can use AI for something doesn't mean you should. We'll learn how to distinguish between problems that genuinely benefit from AI and those that might be better solved with simpler approaches, different tools, or sometimes no technology at all. Because clarity about your goals is only valuable if you're pursuing those goals in the most effective way possible.

3. Learning Lab

Try This: Frustration Journal

Objective: Identify recurring friction points in your daily workflow to discover high-impact AI opportunities.

Time Required: 5 minutes per incident, plus 20 minutes at the end of the week to review.

Materials Needed: A notebook, digital doc, note app, or sticky notes—whatever you'll certainly use

Steps:

1. Set up your capture system.
   Choose a friction-tracking method that's instantly accessible—your phone, desk notebook, or desktop sticky note.
2. Track every AI-related frustration for one week.
   Record the following details each time something slows you down:
   - The moment: What were you trying to do?
   - The friction: What made it annoying or inefficient?
   - The time cost: How long did it take vs. how long it should have?
   - The frequency: How often does this happen?

   Sample entry:
   "Spent 20 minutes searching for the latest version of the client proposal across Slack, email, and Google Drive. Happens every client call."
3. Review your log at the end of the week.
   Look for patterns. Circle the top three frustrations that are either most frequent or most time-consuming.
4. Select one to improve with AI.
   These top items become your "focus candidates" for optimization.

💡 Try This: FOCUS One-Pager

Objective: Clarify the task, goal, and constraints of a specific AI challenge to define your ideal improvement strategy.

Time Required: 15–20 minutes

Materials Needed: Blank page or digital form with the fields below

Steps: Fill out each of the following prompts:

1. Functionality:
   What specific task needs improvement?
   (e.g., "Sorting customer emails by urgency" instead of "Email management")
2. Outcome:
   What does success look like?
   (e.g., "Save 2 hours per week and reduce response delays by 50%")
3. Constraints:
   What limitations do you need to respect?
   (e.g., "Must use current CRM, maintain GDPR compliance")
4. User Impact:
   How will this change benefit others or your broader workflow?
   (e.g., "Faster responses improve client retention and team morale")
5. Scope:
   What's the smallest possible improvement you can implement first?
   (e.g., "Start with automating only internal status updates")

Try This: Clarity-Building Prompt Templates

Objective: Use these prompt structures to clarify what you want from AI and improve the quality of results.

Time Required: 10–15 minutes per prompt

Materials Needed:

- Any AI tool
- Text editor or notebook to reflect on responses

Steps: Choose one of the following templates and customize it to your situation:

1. Problem Analysis Prompt:
   "I currently spend [time] doing [task]. The most frustrating part is [specific issue]. Help me break this down into smaller components and identify which parts might be automated or streamlined."
2. Outcome Clarification Prompt:
   "I want to improve how I [general area]. What are 5 specific, measurable outcomes I could aim for?"
3. Constraint Mapping Prompt:
   "I'm considering using AI for [task], but I need to work within these limitations: [list constraints]. What approaches would respect these boundaries while still improving results?"
4. Scope Reality Check Prompt:
   "I want to use AI to help with [big goal]. Help me identify the smallest, most achievable first step that would prove this is worth pursuing."

Try This: Vague-to-Specific Translator

Objective: Turn ambiguous improvement goals into clear, measurable objectives that AI can support.

Time Required: 15–30 minutes

Materials Needed:

- Your current goals or workflows
- A digital or written copy of the templates below

Steps: Use one of the following five templates to rewrite a vague goal into a specific, actionable plan:

1. Time-Based:
   Instead of: "Get better at email"
   I will: "Use AI to draft responses to customer inquiries"
   To achieve: "30 minutes saved per day"
   Within: "2 weeks"
2. Quality-Based:
   Instead of: "Write better reports"
   I will: "Use AI to generate structured outlines"
   To improve: "report consistency"
   As evidenced by: "faster review cycles and positive client feedback"
3. Frequency-Based:
   Instead of: "Be more organized"
   I will: "Use AI to categorize files"
   To reduce: "document search time from daily to weekly"
   By: "Month-end"
4. Outcome-Based:
   Instead of: "Be more productive"
   I will: "Use AI to automate meeting notes"
   So that: "I can stay engaged in conversations"
   Which enables: "Better client communication"
5. Problem-Solving:
   Instead of: "Improve communication"
   I will use AI to: "Suggest optimal meeting times"
   To solve: "Scheduling conflicts"
   That currently cost me: "2 hours/week"

💡 Try This: Bad Output Debugger

Objective: Diagnose poor AI outputs and refine your prompts or approach for better results.

Time Required: 10–15 minutes

Materials Needed:

- AI tool output that missed the mark
- Debug checklist (see below)

Steps: Work through the checklist below:

1. Context Check:
   - ☐ Did I explain the overall goal?
   - ☐ Did I include background info or examples?
   - ☐ Did I note any constraints or preferences?
2. Specificity Check:
   - ☐ Was the request clear and unambiguous?
   - ☐ Did I specify tone, format, or length?
   - ☐ Did I include models or past examples?
3. Scope Check:
   - ☐ Is this task suited for AI?
   - ☐ Could I break this into smaller pieces?
4. Expectation Check:
   - ☐ Am I expecting creativity when I need consistency—or vice versa?
   - ☐ Am I assuming AI understands unstated context?
5. Iteration Check:
   - ☐ Did I ask for a revision based on feedback?
   - ☐ Have I gone through 2–3 refinement rounds?

Conclusion:
If you checked mostly "no," the issue is likely your input or scope. If mostly "yes," the tool might not be suited for this task.

💡 Try This: Expectation Reality Check

Objective: Calibrate your expectations for what AI can and cannot do, based on task complexity and human judgment needs.

Time Required: 15–20 minutes

Materials Needed:

- This worksheet
- A current or upcoming task you want to use AI for

Steps:

1. Rate Task Complexity (1–5):
    - 1–2: Sorting, formatting, simple analysis
    - 3: Routine writing, standard decisions
    - 4–5: Strategy, nuance, creative work

      → *AI excels at 1–2, supports at 3, struggles with 4–5.*
2. Check for Human Judgment Requirements:
   ☐ Cultural tone awareness
   ☐ Ethical considerations
   ☐ Interpersonal dynamics
   ☐ Creative synthesis
   ☐ Final quality control
   → *The more boxes you check, the more oversight is needed.*
3. Define Automation Expectations:
   ☐ Fully automate the task
   ☐ Handle most of it, I'll review
   ☐ Generate drafts I'll refine
   ☐ Help with research, I'll decide
   → *Options 2–3 are most realistic for complex tasks.*
4. Align Success Criteria:
   ☐ Save time—even if editing is needed
   ☐ Improve output consistency
   ☐ Free me for higher-value work
   ☐ Offer solid starting points
   → *If these match your expectations, you're set up for success.*

4. Is This Even a Job for AI?

Before we dive deeper into the C.A.L.M. framework, we need to pause for a crucial question: Should you be using AI at all?

You've learned to get clear about what you want AI to do—that's the foundation. But clarity about your desired outcome doesn't automatically mean AI is the right tool to achieve it. Just because you can articulate exactly what you need doesn't mean you should hand that task over to artificial intelligence entirely. It may just be that human intelligence is the best solution.

This chapter sits intentionally between Clarity and Alignment because the decision of whether to use AI is too important to bury within other concepts. You need a firm grasp on what you're trying to accomplish before you can make an intelligent choice about your approach. And you need to make that choice before you start learning how to align with the right AI tools for your specific needs.

Think of this as your AI decision gate—the critical checkpoint that determines whether you continue down the AI path or take a more traditional route. Get this wrong, and all the prompt engineering skills in the world won't save you from frustration, wasted time, and subpar results.

Last Tuesday, I watched my friend, let's call her Casey—a personal trainer with fifteen years of experience—spend three hours trying to get AI to create what she called a "simple triathlon training plan." She fed it her client's fitness assessment, race timeline, and previous injury history, then watched in mounting frustration as the AI generated generic workout schedules that ignored the client's knee issues, suggested swimming intervals that made no sense for a beginner, and created a periodization plan that would have her athlete peaking six weeks before race day.

She tried prompt after prompt: "Make it more beginner-friendly." "Account for the previous meniscus tear." "Adjust for someone who can only train five days a week." Each iteration required twenty minutes of back-and-forth, and each result missed crucial elements that any experienced trainer would automatically consider. The AI kept treating each constraint as an isolated variable instead of understanding how they all interconnected in a real human's life.

The kicker? Casey could have designed a superior, personalized plan in one hour using her expertise, intuition, and understanding of how training *really works* in the real world.

This is the AI paradox we're all living in: tools that promise to save us time but often cost us more than they deliver. The problem isn't that AI doesn't work—it's that we're terrible at figuring out when it's the right tool for the job.

The Seductive Lie of "One-Click Everything"

Walk into any AI demo, and you'll see miracles. Sales teams will show you presentations that seem to write themselves, reports that analyze complex data in seconds, and workflows that run like clockwork. What they won't show you is the three hours of prompt engineering it took to get that "automated" result, or the fact that the demo used perfectly clean data that bears no resemblance to the messy reality of your actual files.

It's like watching a cooking show where they never mention the three-hour prep work that happened off-camera, or the fact that the chef burned six practice soufflés before nailing the perfect take. Every AI company has figured out the same marketing playbook: show the output, hide the input.

They'll demonstrate their tool creating a gorgeous infographic but won't mention that it took a professional designer two hours to craft the perfect prompt. They'll show you an AI writing brilliant copy but skip over the part where a copywriter spent half a day training it on brand voice and style guidelines.

The demo effect is real, and it's expensive. When you see AI performing perfectly in controlled conditions, your brain tricks you into thinking it will work the same way in your chaotic, real-world environment. It's like watching a Formula 1 race and thinking you can drive that fast on your morning commute.

Want to know what's tremendously uncomfortable? Most AI tools today are like having a brilliant intern who's also slightly intoxicated. They can do amazing work under the right conditions, but they need constant supervision, clear instructions, and someone checking their output before it goes anywhere important.

Where AI Objectively Earns Its Keep

Don't get me wrong—AI isn't snake oil. When you match the right task to the right tool, the results can feel genuinely magical. But AI has a specific sweet spot, and understanding it is the difference between frustration and transformation.

AI excels at pattern recognition. Give it a thousand customer service emails, and it can tell you the top ten complaints faster than any human could read them. Feed it your grocery receipts from the past year, and it can spot spending patterns that would take you weeks to identify manually. Show it code that's misbehaving, and it often sees the bug you've been staring at for hours.

It's also brilliant at first-draft generation. Need twenty variations of a social media post? AI can pump them out in seconds. Want to brainstorm names for your new rescue dog or design immersive escape rooms for your kid's birthday party? It's like having a creative partner who never runs out of energy. The key phrase here is "first draft"—AI gives you raw material to work with, not finished products to ship.

But perhaps most valuably, AI excels at handling the repetitive stuff that slowly drains your soul. Categorizing expenses, formatting data, generating email templates, creating initial research summaries, turning your rambling voice notes into polished insights—all the tasks that are necessary but not particularly human. This is where AI doesn't just save time; it saves sanity.

THE HUMAN-ONLY ZONE

For all its capabilities, AI has some glaring blind spots that reveal just how much we take human intelligence for granted. Anything requiring genuine judgment is still firmly in human territory. AI can tell you that your teenager's screen time is up 40% this month, but it can't tell you whether that's because they're struggling socially, avoiding homework, or just discovered a new hobby. It sees patterns, but it doesn't understand meaning.

High-stakes accuracy is another no-fly zone. AI can draft a contract for your freelance work, but you'd better have a lawyer review it before anyone signs anything. It can summarize medical research about your aging parent's condition, but you shouldn't make healthcare decisions based on its output. The stakes matter, and when they're high, human oversight isn't optional—it's mandatory.

Perhaps most importantly, AI struggles with anything that requires reading the room. It can't navigate family dynamics during holiday planning, build genuine relationships with potential business partners, or understand the unspoken tensions that drive most important decisions. It doesn't know when to push back on your teenager's request for later curfew, when to compromise with your spouse about the family budget, or when to just listen to a friend who's having a hard time.

THE FIVE-QUESTION FILTER: YOUR AI DECISION FRAMEWORK

Before you hand any task to AI, run it through this filter. Think of these five questions as your AI bullshit detector—they'll save you from the technological equivalent of buying a timeshare.

😟 Question 1: Does this require cultural context or emotional intelligence?

AI doesn't understand subtext, cultural nuances, or emotional undercurrents. If you're writing a condolence card for a colleague who lost their parent, AI might craft technically appropriate language that completely misses the emotional tone needed. If you're planning a family reunion that includes your divorced aunt and uncle, AI can handle the logistics but can't navigate the seating chart politics.

Consider this example: creating a parenting framework for discipline. AI can research child development theories and generate structured approaches, but it can't understand that your particular eight-year-old responds better to quiet conversations than time-outs, or that your family's values around independence versus cooperation need to be woven into any solutions you create.

🤔 Question 2: Are the stakes high if it goes wrong?

Financial projections for your small business, legal documents for your divorce, medical questions about your symptoms, safety protocols for your family's emergency preparedness—these aren't places to experiment with AI's occasional hallucinations. High stakes require human verification, and often human creation from start to finish.

The rule of thumb: if an error could cost money, damage relationships, create legal liability, or harm people, either avoid AI entirely or build in multiple layers of human review. AI can assist with research and initial drafts, but final accountability must rest with humans who understand the consequences.

🤔 Question 3: Does success depend on relationships and trust?

Negotiating your teenager's college choices, resolving conflicts with your homeowners association, building partnerships for your side business, managing difficult conversations with aging parents—these all require the kind of human connection that AI simply can't provide. People do life with people, and AI isn't people.

This extends beyond obvious relationship-building tasks. Even technical work often succeeds or fails based on relationship factors. Getting your family to adopt a new household organization system, convincing your spouse to try a new budgeting approach, or managing change in your volunteer organization—these require reading room dynamics, building trust, and understanding emotional undercurrents that AI cannot perceive.

🤔 Question 4: Is your input data messy, incomplete, or requires interpretation?

AI works best with clean, well-structured information. If your data is scattered across multiple apps, missing key context, or requires interpretation to be meaningful, AI will struggle. Garbage in, garbage out applies especially to AI.

For example, asking AI to create a meal plan based on your family's dietary preferences works well if you can clearly list allergies, favorite foods, and cooking time constraints. But asking it to understand your family's eating patterns based on scattered grocery receipts, random photos of meals, and vague complaints about "eating better" requires the kind of synthesis and interpretation that humans excel at.

🤔 Question 5: Does the task require genuine creativity or original thinking?

AI can remix existing ideas brilliantly, but truly original thinking—the kind that breaks new ground or challenges assumptions—still requires human creativity. AI is great at "what if we tried this variation?" but not so great at "what if we rethought this completely?"

This distinction matters more than you might think. AI can help you optimize your current morning routine, but it can't fundamentally reimagine how you want to start your days. It can suggest improvements to your family's screen time rules, but it can't envision entirely new ways of building connection and engagement that don't rely on restrictions.

HIGH-VALUE AI WINS

Where The Magic Happens

Once you've run tasks through the five-question filter, you'll start recognizing AI's genuine sweet spots. These are the places where AI doesn't just save time—it unlocks capabilities you didn't know you had.

Research and Analysis Powerhouse

AI can turn you into a research superhero. Want to understand the latest developments in sustainable investing for your retirement planning? AI can synthesize information from dozens of sources, identify key trends, and create a personalized summary adapted to your current knowledge level. Planning a family trip to Portugal? It can analyze weather patterns, local festivals, kid-friendly activities, and budget considerations to create a custom itinerary.

Xavier used AI to deep dive into homeschooling approaches when considering alternatives for her gifted daughter. Instead of spending weeks reading conflicting blog posts and forum discussions, she got a comprehensive overview of different pedagogical approaches, curriculum options, and practical considerations—all tailored to her daughter's specific learning style and their family's values.

Content Creation and Adaptation

AI excels at taking your ideas and spinning them into multiple formats. That blog post about your family's approach to financial literacy? AI can help you turn it into a series of social media posts, a presentation for your parenting group, and even a simple workbook for other families. The key is that you're providing the original thinking—AI is just helping you package it differently.

Felix, who runs a small consulting practice, uses AI to convert her client workshop transcripts into multiple lead magnets: summary PDFs, email course sequences, and even quiz-based assessments. She provides the expertise and insights; AI handles the formatting and adaptation.

Pattern Recognition and Insight Generation

This is where AI truly shines. Upload your family's spending data, and AI can identify patterns you never noticed—like how your grocery bills spike during stressful work periods, or how your entertainment spending correlates with your exercise habits. Feed it your journal entries, and it can help you spot emotional patterns and triggers you've been too close to see.

One parent I know, Taylor, used AI to analyze their family's screen time data across multiple devices and apps. Instead of just getting usage statistics, they got insights about how different family members used technology, when conflicts typically arose, and which activities might serve as healthier alternatives.

Learning and Development Acceleration

AI can create personalized learning journeys for virtually any topic. Want to learn photography? AI can design a progression from basic camera operation to advanced composition techniques, complete with practice assignments and milestone checkpoints. Trying to develop your emotional intelligence? It can create reflection prompts, scenario-based exercises, and reading recommendations tailored to your specific growth areas.

Administrative and Logistical Excellence

AI can handle the boring stuff that keeps your life running smoothly. It can create standard operating procedures for your household (morning routines, meal prep workflows, cleaning schedules), generate templates for recurring tasks (appointment scheduling, travel planning, gift-giving), and even help you design family processes that reduce daily friction.

HUMAN-ESSENTIAL TASKS WHERE AI FALLS SHORT

Understanding where AI fails is just as important as knowing where it succeeds. These are the areas where human intelligence, intuition, and relationship skills are irreplaceable.

Complex Decision-Making

Should you change careers? How should you handle your teenager's struggles with anxiety? Is it time to move your parent to assisted living? These decisions involve multiple stakeholders, unclear trade-offs, and long-term consequences that AI simply cannot navigate. It can provide information and framework options, but the actual decision-making requires human wisdom, values, and judgment.

Relationship Dynamics and Conflict Resolution

When your spouse is frustrated about the household workload distribution, when your teenager is pushing boundaries, or when extended family tensions are affecting holiday plans, AI can't read the emotional subtext or navigate the complex dynamics at play. These situations require empathy, emotional intelligence, and the ability to build bridges between different perspectives.

Cultural and Contextual Nuance

AI struggles with context that isn't explicitly stated. If you're planning a wedding that honors both your cultural background and your partner's, AI might provide generic advice about multicultural ceremonies but can't understand the specific family dynamics, religious considerations, or community expectations that will undeniably determine what works for your situation.

High-Stakes Creative and Strategic Thinking

When the decision significantly impacts your life—choosing a college major, deciding whether to have children, planning a major career transition—the creative thinking required goes beyond what AI can provide. These decisions require understanding your own values, risk tolerance, and life vision in ways that AI cannot access.

Accountability and Responsibility

Ultimately, AI can't take responsibility for outcomes. When you're making decisions about your family's health, your financial future, or your children's education, you need to own the consequences. AI can inform those decisions, but the judgment calls must be yours.

ADVANCED APPLICATIONS

AI as Your Thought Partner

Once you've mastered the basics, AI becomes less about task automation and more about cognitive augmentation. These advanced applications can genuinely enhance your thinking and creative capabilities. AI can help you connect ideas across different areas of your life. Feed it your reading notes, journal entries, and random observations, and it can help you spot connections you might miss. It's like having a research assistant who remembers everything you've ever thought about and can help you weave those thoughts into new insights.

Developing Personal Frameworks

AI excels at helping you create well-thought-out (may we say badass) approaches to recurring challenges. Whether you're developing a framework for making family decisions, creating a personal investment philosophy, or designing an approach to work-life balance, AI can help you structure your thinking and identify blind spots in your reasoning.

Scenario Planning and Risk Assessment

AI can help you think through "what if" scenarios more thoroughly than you might on your own. Planning a career change? AI can help you model different timing scenarios, financial implications, and potential obstacles. Considering a major family decision? It can help you think through various outcomes and prepare for different contingencies.

Creative Problem-Solving

When you're stuck on a complex challenge, AI can serve as a brainstorming partner that approaches problems from angles you might not consider. It's particularly good at combining elements from different domains to suggest novel solutions.

THE WISDOM OF STRATEGIC AI USE

The most successful AI users I know aren't the ones trying to automate everything—they're the ones who've developed excellent judgment about when AI is worth the effort and when it's not. They understand that AI is a tool for amplifying human intelligence, not replacing it.

They use AI to handle routine research so they can focus on creative thinking. They leverage it for first-draft generation so they can spend time on refinement and strategy. They employ it for pattern recognition so they can make better decisions with their human judgment.

But they also know when to set it aside. They don't use AI for relationship conversations, high-stakes decisions, or anything requiring the kind of wisdom that comes from lived experience and emotional intelligence. They may use AI to generate a list of ideas, but which ones are brought to life are selected by the humans.

The goal isn't to use AI for everything you possibly can. The goal is to use it strategically—for tasks that genuinely benefit from its strengths—while preserving your mental energy for the decisions that truly need your human intelligence.

AI can tell you that you spent $247 on coffee last month, but it can't explain why you needed that emotional support latte during the quarterly budget meeting. It can generate twenty different ways to phrase a difficult conversation with your teenager, but it can't tell you which approach will surely work with your particular kid on this particular day.

The most important skill in the age of AI isn't learning to use it for everything. It's learning when not to use it at all. That's not a limitation of your AI journey—it's the beginning of wisdom.

QUICK REFERENCE: THE FIVE-QUESTION AI FILTER

1. *Does this require cultural context or emotional intelligence?*
2. *Are the stakes high if it goes wrong?*
3. *Does success depend on relationships and trust?*
4. *Is your input data messy, incomplete, or requires interpretation?*
5. *Does the task require genuine creativity or original thinking?*

If you answered "yes" to any of these questions, proceed with caution—or better yet, keep it human.

4. Learning Lab

💡 Try This: The AI vs. Human Time Trial

Objective: Compare the effectiveness and efficiency of using AI versus your own expertise on a real task to build discernment through direct experience.

Time Required: 30–45 minutes

Materials Needed:

- AI tool of your choice
- Timer or stopwatch
- A task you can complete both manually and with AI (e.g., writing an outline, drafting a plan, summarizing research)

Steps:

1. **Pick one moderate-complexity task** (not too simple, not too high-stakes).
2. **Complete the task yourself manually** (no AI). Track how long it takes.
3. **Repeat the same task using AI.** Track time again.
4. **Compare the two outputs.** Ask:
   - Which was faster?
   - Which was more accurate?
   - Which required more revision?
   - Which one would you ultimately use?
5. **Reflect on what you learned.**
   Did AI save time, or waste it? Was the effort worth the result? Would you use AI again for similar tasks?

💡 Try This: Build Your "AI Sweet Spot" Matrix

Objective: Create a personalized decision framework to determine what types of tasks are well-suited for AI in your life or work.

Time Required: 30 minutes upfront; refine as you go

Materials Needed:

- A blank matrix (paper or spreadsheet)
- Past and current tasks or workflows

Steps:

1. **Set up a 2x2 matrix** with these axes:
   - X-axis: *Clarity of Input* (Clear → Messy)
   - Y-axis: *Risk Level* (Low Stakes → High Stakes)
2. **Plot 10–15 recurring tasks** in your work or life onto the matrix (e.g., meal planning, weekly reports, family scheduling, vacation planning).
3. **Label each quadrant** with your AI decision approach:
   - **Clear + Low Risk = AI Strong Candidate**
   - **Messy + Low Risk = Use AI With Caution**
   - **Clear + High Risk = Human Final Review Required**
   - **Messy + High Risk = Keep it Human**
4. **Use this matrix as your personal AI decision guide.**
   Revisit and update it as your skills and AI tools evolve.

5. Alignment – Use the Right Tools for the Job

Kim, a product information manager at a mid-sized retail company, downloaded ChatGPT after reading an article titled "10 AI Tools That Will Change Your Life." Three hours later, she was staring at her seventh attempt to get it to write product descriptions that didn't sound like they were written by a robot having an existential crisis. She had 200 new SKUs that needed descriptions by end of day, and somehow she was further behind than when she started.

Sound familiar?

This scenario plays out countless times every day across different professions and contexts. The landscape is bewildering. There's ChatGPT for conversation, Midjourney for images, GitHub Copilot for code, Notion AI for notes, and roughly three hundred other tools that all promise to revolutionize your Tuesday afternoon. Each one has devoted followers who swear it's the only tool you'll ever need, which is about as helpful as being told every tool in a hardware store is "the best one."

Here's what those starry-eyed "AI changes everything" articles conveniently forget to mention: one person's game-changing breakthrough tool is another person's expensive digital doorstop. The real trick isn't hunting for the "ultimate" AI—it's discovering which one exactly meshes with your specific brand of problems.

Which sounds obvious until you realize how rarely people stop to ask themselves what that truly is.

The Seven Ways People Mess This Up (And How Not To)

Before we dive into the tool landscape, let's examine the predictable ways this goes wrong. Understanding these patterns can save you weeks of frustration and false starts.

1. **The Collector's Fallacy.** Meet James, a project coordinator who discovered AI tools during a particularly stressful quarter. Within two weeks, he had accounts for ChatGPT, Claude, Jasper, Notion AI, Grammarly, and six others. He spent more time deciding which tool to use for each task than doing the work. His desktop looked like a software yard sale, and his productivity had somehow gotten worse. **The fix:** Start with one tool that solves one specific problem. Master it. Then—and only then—consider adding another.

2. **The "Figure It Out Later" Trap.** Tabitha, an ambitious project manager, jumped straight into using Notion AI to build complex project workflows. She skipped the tutorials, ignored the templates, and tried to recreate her entire project management system on day one. After three frustrating hours of fighting with the interface, she gave up and went back to her old spreadsheets. **The fix:** Spend your first week with any new tool doing the simplest possible tasks. Get comfortable with the basics before attempting to automate your entire workflow.

3. **The Set-and-Forget Mistake.** David, a nursing student, set up Grammarly in January and was thrilled with how it improved his research papers. Six months later, he was still using it the same repetitive way, never exploring new features or considering that his academic writing needs had evolved. Meanwhile, new AI writing tools had launched that better fit his current projects. **The fix:** Schedule a quarterly "tool audit." Ask yourself: Is this still worth the mental energy? Has my work changed? Are there better options now?

4. **The Integration Nightmare.** Maria, a high school teacher, tried to add AI tools to her lesson planning process without mapping out her process first. She used ChatGPT for brainstorming activities, Canva AI for visual aids, and Grammarly for editing handouts—but nothing talked to each other. She ended up copying and pasting between seven different apps, making her process slower than before. **The fix:** Map out your current process first. Then identify one specific step where AI could help. Test it there before expanding.

5. The Perfectionist's Paradox. Tom, a small business owner, expected AI to read his mind and produce perfect marketing copy on the first try. When ChatGPT's initial output needed editing, he concluded the tool was overhyped and went back to writing everything from scratch—spending ten times longer than if he'd just refined the AI's draft. **The fix:** Think of AI tools as talented assistants—they need clear instructions and sometimes produce work that needs editing. That's still faster than doing it yourself.

6. The Universal Tool Syndrome. Jennifer, a freelance graphic designer, discovered ChatGPT could write emails, create presentations, analyze data, and generate images. She started using it for everything, even though dedicated tools often did specific tasks better. Her image prompts never quite worked, and her data analysis was surface level at best. **The fix:** Use tools for what they're more than proficient at. ChatGPT excels at writing and reasoning; image generators excel at visuals. Don't force square pegs into round holes.

7. The Shiny Object Syndrome. Every time a new AI tool launched, Alex, a mechanic running his own shop, abandoned his current setup to chase the latest and greatest. He'd tried fourteen different tools in three months but never truly got good at any of them. His colleagues started joking that he knew more about AI tool demos than using AI. **The fix:** Give yourself a "shiny object quarantine period." When you hear about a new tool, wait two weeks before trying it. Most of the time, the urge will pass. And if it doesn't, you'll know it's time to take it for a spin.

Your Frustration Is Your GPS

Now that we've identified the common pitfalls, let's explore a more productive approach. Instead of trying to avoid all mistakes, use your daily frustrations to navigate your next steps and define your best opportunities.

Consider Linda, a social worker who was drowning in case documentation. Every week, she spent hours transcribing meeting notes, writing case summaries, and formatting reports for court submissions. The paperwork was eating into time she could spend with clients, and she dreaded the administrative days that made her question why she'd chosen this profession.

Rather than trying to find the "perfect" documentation tool, Linda identified her specific pain point: those hours of tedious transcription and formatting. She tried an AI writing assistant for one week on actual case files (following all privacy protocols, of course). The first few attempts were clunky—her prompts were too vague, and the results weren't quite right. But by day four, she was producing cleaner documentation in half the time. That's the power of following your frustration breadcrumbs.

This approach works because frustration is data. It tells you exactly where your current process is breaking down. Robert, a retiree trying to organize decades of family photos, didn't need a comprehensive productivity overhaul—he needed something to help him sort and categorize thousands of images. His frustration pointed him directly to AI tools that could identify faces, dates, and locations in photos.

THE AI TOOL LANDSCAPE: YOUR QUICK-START GUIDE

Most people approach AI tools the same way they approach a Cheesecake Factory menu: with wide eyes, good intentions, and absolutely no idea where to start. Everything sounds amazing. Everything promises transformation. And yet somehow, 20 minutes later, you're overwhelmed, overcommitted, and holding a plate of something that looked better on Instagram.

So what do you do? You default to what someone else swore by on LinkedIn—or worse, TikTok. Maybe it was one of those "Top 6 AI Tools That Will Make You a Millionaire by Lunch" posts. Fast-forward ten minutes and you're staring at a dashboard that feels like it needs a user manual, a therapist, and a translator.

Spoiler: The problem isn't you. It's the lack of strategy. Since you've already mastered the art of defining clear outcomes and crafting specific requests, you might be tempted to dive straight into comprehensive tool research. But here's the shift I see from my front-row seat watching people wrestle with AI choices: the secret to assembling your dream AI squad isn't becoming a research obsessive—it's mastering the fine art of productive procrastination.

You already know how to identify what you want AI to accomplish. Now the question becomes: which specific frustration should you tackle first?

Think about yesterday. What made you groan? What task had you staring at your screen, thinking, "I know exactly what I need, but getting there is going to take forever"? That moment when you thought, "There has to be a more efficient way to do this"? That frustration isn't a character flaw—it's intelligence. Your brain is correctly identifying inefficiency, and since you can already articulate what good output looks like, that recognition becomes your most reliable guide to the right AI tool.

Consider the difference between these two approaches:

The "Comprehensive Evaluation" Approach: Spend weeks researching dozens of tools, creating elaborate comparison matrices, testing everything that might possibly be relevant to your work, and building theoretical workflows for problems you bizarrely may never face.

The "Targeted Solution" Approach: Remember that specific thing that annoyed you last Tuesday? Find one tool that might fix it. Test it with the clear prompting skills you've already developed (or you will develop by the end of this book). Use it for a week. Move on to the next frustration.

The second approach gets you using helpful AI tools within days, not months. And since you already know how to communicate clearly with AI, you can quickly evaluate whether a tool worthily solves your problem or just creates new complexity.

Your Tuesday frustrations are breadcrumbs leading directly to the tools you realistically need—not the ones you think you should need, or the ones that look impressive in demos, but the ones that will immediately improve your workday using skills you already possess.

MAPPING THE AI TERRITORY

Your Field Guide to 20 Essential Tool Types

Forget trying to memorize every AI app that launches (there are approximately forty-seven new ones every Tuesday). Instead, think in terms of what these tools demonstrably do. Here's your topographical map of the AI landscape, organized by the terrain each type of tool is built to navigate:

The Communicators

Conversational AI Assistants. Your ChatGPT, Claude, and Gemini types—the digital Swiss Army knives of AI. They write, brainstorm, explain, and chat about everything from quantum physics to your weekend plans.

Writing Enhancement Tools. Grammarly and its cousins that make your emails sound professional and catch the typos that make you look like you type with your elbows.

Email AI Assistants. Tools like Superhuman's AI features that write replies, schedule follow-ups, and basically turn your inbox into something you don't dread opening.

The Creators

Text-to-Image Generators. When Marcus, a small business owner, needed to create social media content but had zero design skills, he turned to AI image generators. His first attempt at prompting DALL-E was "make a picture for my coffee shop." The result looked like abstract art made by someone who'd never seen coffee. After refining his prompt to "professional photo of a steaming coffee cup on a rustic wooden table, warm lighting, cozy atmosphere," he got something incredibly useful for his Instagram posts.

Video Creation AI. Runway, Pika, and Luma that turn text prompts into moving pictures, because apparently static images weren't magical enough.

Music and Audio Generators. Jenny, a podcast host, used to spend hundreds on voice-over work for her intro segments. With AI audio tools, she can now create professional-sounding narration in different voices and accents, turning what used to be a week-long process involving freelancers into a 30-minute task she handles herself.

Design AI Tools. Beyond Canva's AI features to tools that generate logos, layouts, and color schemes without requiring a design degree.

The Organizers

Meeting AI Assistants. Every Tuesday (yes, we're sticking with the most boring day of the week), Kevin's team had a one-hour meeting that somehow generated three pages of scattered notes across four different notebooks. Now AI transcription tools capture everything, highlight key decisions, and automatically email action items to the team. What used to take Kevin an hour of post-meeting cleanup now happens automatically.

Project Management AI. Smart scheduling, task prioritization, and deadline prediction tools that keep projects from becoming beautiful disasters.

Note-Taking and Knowledge AI. NotebookLM, Notion AI, and tools that turn your scattered thoughts into organized, searchable knowledge bases.

The Researchers

AI-Powered Search Engines. Perplexity, You.com, and enhanced Google features that clearly understand what you're looking for instead of showing you ads for things you bought last week.

Research and Analysis Tools. When Professor Williams needed to review 200 research papers for her literature review, she used AI to summarize each paper's key findings and methodology. What would have taken her six weeks of reading became a manageable three-day project, with AI handling the initial screening and her focusing on the most relevant papers.

Data Visualization AI. Tools that turn spreadsheets into charts that don't make people's eyes glaze over, with AI suggesting the best ways to present your data.

The Professionals

Code Generation and Programming AI. GitHub Copilot, Cursor, Replit—where you describe what you want in plain English and code appears (sometimes it even works).

Customer Service AI. Chatbots, support ticket routing, and response generation tools that handle the "Have you tried turning it off and on again?" conversations.

Sales and CRM AI. Call analysis, lead scoring, and email sequence tools that help sales teams sell without being creepy about it.

HR and Recruiting AI. Resume screening, interview scheduling, and candidate matching tools that make hiring less like throwing darts blindfolded.

The Specialists

Financial and Accounting AI. Expense categorization, invoice processing, and fraud detection tools that make numbers less scary for everyone involved.

Content Moderation and Safety AI. Behind-the-scenes tools that keep online spaces from turning into digital wastelands (they're not perfect, but they try).

Workflow Automation AI. Zapier-style tools, like Make, with AI smarts that connect your apps and automate the repetitive stuff that makes you question your life choices.

Notice something? Each type solves a specific human problem—usually one that involves either tedious repetition, creative blocks, or information overload. The best AI tools don't try to do everything; they do one thing exceptionally well and play nicely with other tools. The trick isn't finding the "perfect" AI tool (spoiler: there isn't one). It's building a toolkit where each piece handles what it does best, and you orchestrate the whole symphony.

FINDING YOUR ROUTE

There are many beautiful things about maps, but they're only useful if you know where you want to go. Now that you can see the terrain, the question becomes: which path makes sense for your epic journey?

The best approach isn't to download one tool from each category like you're collecting Pokémon cards. Instead, start with your biggest daily frustration—that one task that makes you consider a career change every Tuesday—and find the tool type that tackles it head-on.

Maybe it's the thirty minutes you spend each week formatting meeting notes (hello, Meeting AI Assistants). Maybe it's staring at blank slides while a presentation deadline looms (welcome to Design AI Tools). Or maybe it's that research project that's been haunting your to-do list because you don't know where to start (meet your new friend, AI-Powered Search Engines).

Pick one frustration. Find one tool. Use it until it becomes as automatic as checking your phone. Then, and only then, add the next piece to your kit.

How to Choose Your Tools (Without Triggering Decision Paralysis)
Remember that hardware store analogy? Here's where it gets real. You're standing in the AI aisle, overwhelmed by options, and some enthusiastic salesperson is trying to sell you the deluxe everything-package when all you need is something to hang a picture.

The secret isn't finding the "best" tool—it's finding the right tool for your specific brand of chaos.

Start With Your Tuesday Problem

You know what I'm talking about. That recurring task that makes you question your life choices every Tuesday at 2:47 PM. Maybe it's:

- Formatting meeting notes that nobody reads anyway
- Creating slides for presentations you give to the same five people monthly
- Sorting through research papers to find the one useful quote buried in page 47
- Writing emails that say "following up on my previous email" for the fourth time
- Organizing family photos that have been "temporarily" stored in seventeen different folders
- Creating lesson plans that engage students without burning you out
- Troubleshooting equipment issues that eat up your billable hours

Pick one. Just one. This is your compass set.

The Reality Check Framework

Skip the elaborate decision matrices. Instead, ask yourself three honest questions—and masterfully apply them like Sophie did. Sophie, a content manager at a nonprofit, was drowning in social media posts. She needed to create 20 posts per week across three platforms, and each one took her 30 minutes to write, design, and schedule. Instead of trying five different tools, she applied the three questions to AI image generators:

"Will this honestly solve my Tuesday problem?" Could AI create social media graphics faster than her current process? Yes—potentially 15 minutes saved per post.

"Can I figure this out in under an hour?" She spent 45 minutes learning basic prompting and got usable results.

"Does this fit how I already work?" She could generate images directly in her browser and download them to her existing scheduling tool.

Result: Sophie now creates graphics in 5 minutes instead of 30, saving her 8 hours per week.

The framework only works if you're honest about the answers. If the answer to question 1 isn't a clear yes, keep looking.

Test Drive, Don't Test Drive Off a Cliff

Most AI tools offer free trials or freemium versions. Use them. Test them on your actual Tuesday problem, not some hypothetical perfect scenario. Don't spend three hours crafting the perfect prompt for a fake project. Instead, throw your messy, real-world problem at it and see what happens. If it makes your Tuesday marginally less terrible, you're onto something. For non-technical users, this means:

- ✓ Start with the simplest possible task
- ✓ Don't worry about using the tool "perfectly" at first
- ✓ Focus on whether it saves you time, not whether it's impressive
- ✓ If you get stuck, try explaining what you want in plain English

When Things Go Wrong (And They Will)

Your first AI experiment will probably be disappointing. The tool will misunderstand your request, generate something weird, or just not quite hit the mark. This is normal and expected. The question isn't "Is this tool perfect?" It's "Is this tool better than what I was doing before?" If spending five minutes with an AI tool saves you thirty minutes of work, that's a win—even if the output needs some tweaking. Here are some common beginner issues and quick fixes:

- *Vague results*: Be more specific in your requests
- *Wrong tone*: Include examples of what you want
- *Irrelevant output*: Provide more context about your situation
- *Technical errors:* Try rephrasing your request in simpler terms

The Real Goal

You're not trying to become an AI wizard. You're trying to reclaim some time and sanity in your workday. The moment you find yourself spending more time optimizing your AI workflow than the original task would have taken, you've lost the plot.

The right AI tool should feel invisible—like a capable assistant who anticipates what you need and handles it quietly in the background. If you're constantly thinking about the tool itself, it's probably not the right one for you.

Success Story: From Chaos to Clarity

Let's talk about what victory legitimately looks like in different scenarios. Remember Kim from the beginning of this chapter? Six months later, her approach to AI is completely different. Instead of trying to revolutionize everything at once, she started with one specific problem: writing product descriptions that didn't sound robotic.

She spent two weeks learning to prompt ChatGPT effectively—not by reading tutorials, but by practicing on real product catalogs. She learned to give it context ("Our customers are busy parents looking for practical solutions"), specify tone ("Helpful but not pushy, like a knowledgeable friend"), and provide examples of descriptions that converted well.

Now she creates compelling product descriptions in 5 minutes instead of 30 minutes each. But more importantly, she's not afraid of AI tools anymore. When a new challenge came up—optimizing product categorization—she knew how to approach it methodically. She identified the specific problem, tested one tool for two weeks, and gradually built competence.

Her current toolkit? Just three tools: ChatGPT for writing, an AI image tool for quick product mockups, and an automation tool for bulk updates. Each one solves a specific problem she verifiably has. She's not an AI power user, and she doesn't want to be. She's just someone who found a few tools that make her Tuesday afternoons less terrible.

Meanwhile, David, our nursing student, took a different path. His frustration was summarizing complex medical literature for his research papers. After testing several AI tools, he found one that could break down dense academic papers into digestible summaries. His study time decreased by 40%, and his comprehension drastically improved because he could focus on analysis rather than information extraction. That's what alignment looks like across different fields and contexts.

Your Next Move

Your mission, should you choose to accept it (and you should, like, now)—not after you've consulted three more blogs, not when inspiration strikes, but at this precise moment: Zero in on whatever makes your typical Tuesday feel like it's personally trolling you. That thing that makes you audibly sigh when you realize it's time to do it again. Got it? Good.

Now pick one tool type from the map that could tackle that specific annoyance. Just one. Don't overthink it. Give yourself permission to experiment. Download the free version, spend thirty minutes playing with it on your actual Tuesday problem, and see what happens. Maybe it'll be amazing. Maybe it'll be terrible. Maybe it'll be somewhere in between. All of those outcomes are useful information.

The goal isn't to revolutionize your entire workflow in the next hour. It's to take one small step toward reclaiming a bit of your Tuesday afternoon. Before you dive in, take a moment to set your intentions:

- Which tool will you master first? (Pick one from our map that addresses your biggest frustration)
- What measurable goal will you tackle? (Be specific: "reduce research time from 3 hours to 1 hour" not "be more productive")
- How will you know if it's working? (Define success before you start, not after you're disappointed)

Since the AI landscape evolves rapidly, consider joining newsletters or communities focused on AI tools and applications. Resources like JonesCo.AI offer regular updates on new tools and practical use cases, helping you stay current without getting overwhelmed by every new launch.

Having AI is like owning an eye-wateringly good guitar. It doesn't automatically make you a musician. Sarah found the right tool for her product announcements, but it took her two weeks to learn how to get consistently good results. The difference between frustration and success wasn't the tool itself—it was learning how to communicate with it effectively. That's where we're headed next.

In the next chapter, we'll dive into Leverage—the art of getting AI tools to do what you want them to do. You'll discover why "write me a blog post" gets you garbage while "write a 500-word blog post for small business owners about email marketing, using a conversational tone and including three actionable tips they can implement today" gets you gold.

We'll explore the surprisingly simple techniques that turn AI from a frustrating black box into a reliable creative partner. You'll learn how to ask the right questions, provide the right context, and iterate your way to outputs that serve your goals.

Because choosing the right tool is only half the battle. The other half? Learning to speak its language.

Your Tuesday self will thank you.

5. Learning Lab

💡 Try This: The Before/After Time Log

Objective: Measure how much time and frustration an AI tool legitimately saves you—compared to doing the task manually.

Time Required: ~15 minutes/day over 3 weeks (Week 1 = baseline; Week 2 = learning; Week 3 = comparison)

Materials Needed:

- Timer or stopwatch
- Spreadsheet, journal, or tracking template
- AI tool of your choice

Steps:

Week 1: Baseline Measurement (No AI)

Choose one recurring task you do at least twice per week that annoys or drains you.

Write it here: ____

Set up a tracking log with these columns:

  - Date / Time
  - Task Description
  - Start Time / End Time
  - Total Minutes
  - Frustration Level (1–10)
  - Notes

Track this task every time it occurs for 7 days. At the end of the week, calculate:

  - Average time per task
  - Total time spent
  - Average frustration level

Week 2: Learning the Tool

Choose one AI tool to test based on your task.

  - Tool name: _________________

- Tool category: _______________
- Why you chose it: _____________

Complete a 30-Minute Learning Sprint:

  - Sign up for the tool (if needed)
  - Complete the tutorial or help guide
  - Try using it on your chosen task
  - Don't aim for perfection—just learn the basics
  - Record what you learned and any first impressions

Week 3: AI-Assisted Measurement

Track the same task using AI. Use your log again, but add:

- Time spent with AI
- Time spent editing or fixing its output
- Quality rating (1–10) of the final result

At the end of the week, calculate:

  - Average time per task
  - Total time spent
  - Average frustration level
  - Average quality score

Final Reality Check:

- Was the time savings worth the learning effort?
- What surprised you most?
- Would you continue using the tool?
- How would you explain the value to a skeptical colleague?

Try This: Tool Territory Map

Objective: Match your work frustrations to the right AI tool categories so you can make more targeted decisions about what to try.

Time Required: 30–45 minutes

Materials Needed:

- Pen and paper, or spreadsheet
- List of tool categories from Chapter 4

Steps:

1. Brain dump your frustrations.
   Set a timer for 10 minutes. List every work task that drains you, annoys you, or feels inefficient. Don't overthink—dump it all.
2. Sort each frustration into one of the six tool "territories":
   - Communication Valley (Writing, emails, messaging)
   - Creative Heights (Images, video, music, design)
   - Organization Plains (Meetings, notes, project management)
   - Research Ridge (Search, analysis, synthesis, data visualization)
   - Professional Peaks (Sales, customer service, coding, HR)
   - Specialist Slopes (Finance, automation, compliance, moderation)
3. Identify your biggest frustration zone.
   Count which category has the most entries.
   My biggest territory: ______________________________
4. Score your top three tasks in that zone.
   For each one, rate:
   - Frequency (1 = rare, 5 = constant)
   - Time impact (1 = negligible, 5 = huge)
   - Emotional drain (1 = neutral, 5 = maddening)
5. Pick your highest scoring task as your AI experimentation starting point.
   Frustration to solve: ______________________
   Tool category to explore: ___________________

💡 Try This: The Anti-FOMO Filter

Objective: Avoid shiny object syndrome by honestly evaluating whether a tool is relevant to your actual problems.

Time Required: 20–30 minutes

Materials Needed:

- List of AI tools you're curious about
- Pen/paper or digital notes

Steps:

1. List 5 AI tools you've heard of but haven't yet tried:
    - Tool 1: ____________________
    - Tool 2: ____________________
    - Tool 3: ____________________
    - Tool 4: ____________________
    - Tool 5: ____________________
2. Apply the "Problem Test."
   For each tool, complete this sentence:
   "This tool would solve my problem of..."
3. Run the Honesty Filter for each tool:
    - Do I *really* have this problem?
    - Is it in my top 5 work frustrations?
    - Would solving it save me >30 minutes/week?
4. Eliminate anything that got even one "No."
   Tools that passed: ____________________________
5. Reality Check:
   For the tools that passed:
    - Why haven't I tried this yet?
    - What's the real barrier—time, cost, overwhelm?
    - Is it more important than the tools I'm already using?
6. Make a focused commitment:
   I will not try any new tools until I've mastered: _________________
   Date of commitment: _________________

💡 Try This: The Teaching Test

Objective: Solidify your own understanding of AI tool selection by teaching someone else how to make their first smart choice.

Time Required: 1–2 hours total (including prep, teaching, and follow-up)

Materials Needed:

- Notes from Chapter 4
- Willing learner
- Short teaching outline

Steps:

1. Pick your "student."
   Choose someone with:
   - Little or no AI experience
   - A work problem you can relate to
   - Willingness to learn from you
2. Prep your mini-lesson:
   Make sure you cover:
   - Why to start with a specific frustration
   - Overview of tool categories
   - 3 "Reality Check" questions from Chapter 4
   - 7 common mistakes beginners make
   - Importance of starting with ONE tool
3. Deliver your teaching session (15–20 minutes).
   Use these coaching questions:
   - What's your most annoying recurring task?
   - How much time does it waste?
   - What would the ideal solution look like?
   - Which tool category might solve this?
   - What's one tool to try first?
4. Reflect afterward:
   - What did I struggle to explain?

    - What questions did they ask that I couldn't answer?
    - What part of Chapter 4 do I now understand better?
    - What would I change next time?
5. Schedule a follow-up.
   Check in after 2–4 weeks:
    - Did they try the tool?
    - What worked or didn't?
    - What can you learn from their experience?

Teaching someone else is one of the best ways to identify gaps in your own knowledge and reinforce what you've learned.

6. Leverage – From Frustrations to Flow

The Art of Leveraging AI

You know that friend who gives amazing advice but only after you've spent twenty minutes explaining what you genuinely need help with? The one who finally says, "Oh, why didn't you just say that in the first place?"

Welcome to working with AI.

It's problematic when most of us approach AI like we're talking to a mind reader. We type something vague like "help me plan my garden" and wonder why we get back generic advice about "choosing appropriate plants for your climate" instead of a specific plan for growing tomatoes on a shady apartment balcony in Portland. Or maybe you've moved past "help me write something" and learned to be specific. Your prompts are detailed, your context is clear, and you're getting decent results most of the time.

But here's what's probably driving you crazy: the inconsistency. Some days, you nail it on the first try—the AI delivers exactly what you need, whether it's a workout plan that ultimately fits your schedule or a compelling cover letter that lands you an interview. Other days, you're stuck in this maddening back-and-forth, tweaking and re-prompting until you've spent more time managing the conversation than researching grad schools yourself. Or worse, expecting the same output you had a few days ago, but end up with something completely different even though the prompt was essentially the same.

What's the difference between those breakthrough moments and the frustrating ones? It's not just better prompts—it's understanding how to architect an entire conversation with AI to get consistent, high-quality results.

This is where Leverage comes in—the third step in your C.A.L.M. AI Navigator™ journey. You've done the hard work of Clarity (figuring out what you genuinely want) and Alignment (picking the right tool for the job). Now comes the fun part: learning to be the kind of human that AI tools desperately want to work with. Assuming they could want anything.

Think of it this way: AI is like having access to the world's most enthusiastic research assistant, one who never gets tired, never gets annoyed, and genuinely wants to help you succeed. The catch? This assistant has no context about your life, your goals, or what "good enough" means to you. They're brilliant but completely new to your world. They're your biggest cheerleader and always want to please you, even to the point where they'll make things up in hopes it's what you want.

So when you walk up and say, "Help me plan a trip," they're thinking: Where? When? With whom? What's your budget? Are you looking for adventure or relaxation? Do you want to immerse yourself in local culture or stick to tourist highlights? Are we optimizing for Instagram-worthy moments or authentic experiences?

The difference between frustrating AI interactions and genuinely useful ones often comes down to giving AI the right lens through which to view your specific problem. Not everything about your situation—just the parts that matter for this particular request.

In this chapter, we'll turn you into the kind of person AI tools love to work with—someone who knows how to ask the right questions, provide the right context, and iterate toward exactly what they need. Because here's the truth nobody puts in the AI user manual: the real superpower isn't hiding in some fancy algorithm. It's developing the self-awareness to explain your messy human problems to a brilliant digital being that thinks you're a complete stranger.

Let's get started.

UNDERSTANDING AI'S QUIRKS

What You're Really Working With

Before we dive into advanced techniques, let's get honest about what you're precisely dealing with. AI has some very human-like flaws that can trip you up if you don't know what to watch for.

The Confidence Trick

AI never says "I don't know." It doesn't hedge or show uncertainty. It gives you confident, detailed answers even when it's completely falsifying the evidence. This is like having a friend who's absolutely certain that penguins live in the Arctic (they don't—that's polar bears) but delivers this "fact" with such authority that you almost believe them. Or the friend who says the same thing every three minutes but slightly differently because they just want to make sure you get it. Even the most sophisticated AI models have a dirty little secret: they're confident improvisers. When they don't know something, they don't say "I don't know"—they get creative. And that's where hallucinations creep in.

Watch for these warning signs:

- Highly specific statistics that seem too convenient ("Studies show a 23.7% increase...")
- References to studies or experts you can't easily verify
- Information that contradicts what you thought you knew but is presented without any caveats
- Perfectly formatted quotes with precise attributions but no source links
- Recent "breaking news" or events that sound plausible but feel oddly convenient
- Technical specifications that are suspiciously exact without margin of error
- Historical "facts" that include very specific dates, times, or numerical details
- Claims about "recent studies" or "new research" without publication details
- Direct quotes from famous people that sound too perfectly relevant to your question
- Company statistics or financial data that aren't from official reports
- Survey results with precise percentages but vague methodology descriptions
- Scientific claims that seem to settle complex debates too neatly
- News events or announcements that you can't find anywhere else
- Personal anecdotes about real people that read like perfect case studies
- Regulatory or legal information that's stated as fact without citing actual laws or agencies

Every item on this list is a classic giveaway that the AI might be conjuring facts with the swagger of a seasoned improv actor:

Suspiciously specific stats: If it sounds like a textbook answer with a decimal point and no citation? That stat probably never passed peer review—or reality.

Unnamed studies or unverifiable experts: "According to leading experts..." is the AI equivalent of "a guy I met at a conference."

Too-good-to-be-true quotes and breaking news: If it reads like a quote sandwich designed to impress a conference crowd, verify it before you repeat it.

Historical and legal claims with no sources: AI is trained on broad data, not on legal accuracy. Trust but verify—especially if your audience includes lawyers, historians, or fact-checkers.

Bottom line? If the information sounds convenient, overconfident, or too perfectly aligned with your prompt, treat it as a starting point—not a final answer.

YOUR PROTECTION STRATEGY

Trust, But Always Verify

Write down this golden rule or get it tattooed on your forehead: if the information matters, *don't take AI's word for it.* That catchy statistic, compelling quote, or dramatic historical fact may sound airtight—but if it's going into client work, a keynote slide, or anything with legal, financial, or reputational weight, it must be independently verified. Think of AI like your overconfident friend at trivia night: charming, persuasive, and occasionally... completely wrong. Especially when the stakes are high.

Your strategy?

For high-stakes content (anything tied to dollars, data, or decision-making): Cross-check every major claim against at least two reputable sources. Think primary research, published whitepapers, peer-reviewed articles, or official government and company reports.

For stats, quotes, and studies: Google the exact phrase. Look for the original source, not just a blog post repeating it. If no source turns up? It might be AI improv.

For legal, regulatory, or medical information: Never rely solely on AI. Use official agency websites, legal documentation, or direct professional guidance.

If it "sounds true" but feels oddly convenient: Flag it. AI is skilled at delivering plausible-sounding fiction. Be smarter than the sentence.

Bottom line: AI is a brilliant starting point—not a final authority. Your job isn't just to generate—it's to validate. Because accuracy isn't optional. It's your credibility on the line.

The Bias Echo Chamber

AI models are trained on human-generated content. And that means they've absorbed not just our brilliance and innovation—but also our biases, blind spots, and systemic imbalances.

Ask AI for examples of "successful entrepreneurs," and you'll likely get a lineup of hoodie-wearing tech bros with VC funding and TED Talk deals. Not because those are the only kinds of successful founders—but because those are the stories that dominate bookshelves, headlines, and search engine algorithms.

This isn't malice. It's math. The model reflects the patterns it was fed. But if we don't challenge those defaults, we end up reinforcing them. That's where your intentionality matters.

Instead of just asking for "leadership advice," try:

- "What leadership principles are used in matriarchal cultures?"
- "What can I learn from Indigenous leadership models or community-based governance?"
- "Show me communication techniques for high-context cultures or multilingual teams."

These prompts don't just yield better outputs—they interrupt the algorithmic autopilot that can otherwise flatten nuance and erase context. And if you're using AI to build content, curriculum, or tools that impact real people? Your prompts become not just instructions—but acts of inclusion.

Pro tip: When in doubt, ask your AI to "Surface overlooked perspectives" or "Challenge mainstream assumptions on [topic]". You'll be surprised what's in the training data—once you seriously go looking for it.

The Pattern Completion Problem

Sometimes AI gets stuck repeating the same idea in different words because it's trained to complete patterns, not necessarily to think creatively. If you ask for "five different approaches" and get back five variations on the same theme, that's pattern completion in action.

The fix is to explicitly request variety along specific dimensions: "Give me five approaches to learning Spanish—one focused on conversation, one on grammar, one using media, one through immersion, and one gamified approach."

Now that you know what you're working with, let's learn how to work with it effectively.

THE HIDDEN TRAPS THAT KEEP GOOD PROMPTS FROM BECOMING GREAT

Let's start with a reality check. You're probably making at least three of these mistakes—and they're not the obvious ones everyone talks about. These are the subtle patterns that keep competent AI users from becoming truly effective ones.

Mistake #1: The Context Avalanche

You know context matters, so you've started including background information in your prompts. Good! But here's where it gets tricky: you're probably giving AI all the context instead of the right context.

I watched someone spend ten minutes crafting a prompt that included their entire fitness history, dietary restrictions, work schedule, family obligations, and exercise preferences when all they decidedly needed was help choosing between two specific workout programs. The AI came back with a response that was... fine. Generic fine. It had processed all that information but couldn't figure out what to prioritize.

The smarter move? Isolating the 2-3 pieces of intel that were truly essential for nailing this specific decision. "I have 30 minutes, three times a week, and I'm choosing between strength training and cardio for weight loss. I've been sedentary for two years." That's it. The AI doesn't need to understand your whole fitness journey—it needs to understand the specific factors that matter for this decision.

Mistake #2: The Single-Shot Assumption
You've learned to write detailed prompts, which is great. But you're still approaching each interaction like it needs to be perfect on the first try. This is like expecting to nail a complex recipe without tasting as you go.

The most effective AI users treat their first prompt as an opening move, not a final request. They use it to establish direction, then refine based on what comes back. Understand this: they do it strategically, not randomly.

Random refinement sounds like: "Can you make it more casual? And shorter. But also add more examples."

Strategic refinement sounds like: "This is helpful, but I'm seeing you're assuming I'm a complete beginner. I have experience with basic photography—can you adjust the advice for someone who understands exposure but struggles with composition?"

Another solid step in mitigating this issue is to always have a second prompt that forces the AI to question the output of the first prompt. Even something as simple as "Was your response comprehensive?" will open your eyes to what's missing.

Mistake #3: The Format Afterthought
You spend time crafting your request but treat the output format as an afterthought. "Put it in a table" or "make it a bulleted list" gets tacked on at the end.

But format isn't just about organization—it's about thinking. When you ask for a pros-and-cons list, you're asking AI to think in terms of trade-offs. When you ask for a step-by-step guide, you're asking it to think sequentially. When you ask for a story, you're asking it to think about human psychology and narrative flow. Advanced users choose formats strategically because they know different formats unlock different types of thinking.

Mistake #4: The Assumed Objectivity Trap
You ask AI to "summarize the pros and cons of remote work policies" or "suggest strategies for middle managers," assuming it will give you an objective, balanced response.

But remember—AI reflects patterns in its training data. That means its "balanced" take might still lean heavily toward Silicon Valley startup culture, Western business norms, or outdated assumptions about productivity. **Fix:** Be explicit about the lens you want.

Instead of "Give me pros and cons," try:

"Compare remote work policies across industries with differing access to digital infrastructure."

"Include insights from global organizations and workers in emerging economies."

You're not just asking AI to think—you're directing it to rethink.

Mistake #5: The Prompt Pile-Up. Sometimes we try to do too much in one go: "Summarize this article, compare it to recent trends, identify three insights, write a tweet about each one, and make it sound like Brené Brown meets Seth Godin." This overloads the system, muddles the task, and usually results in generic output. **To fix it:** Break it into phases.
Start with:

1. "Summarize this article in 3 bullet points."
2. "Now, compare those insights to trends in the 2024 State of AI report."
3. "Great—now draft a tweet thread using that comparison, in a bold-yet-warm tone."

Clarity beats ambition—every time. The good news? Once you recognize these patterns, they're easy to fix. And the improvement in your results will be immediate and dramatic.

The Prompt Improvement Fundamentals

Let's establish the foundation that turns mediocre AI interactions into consistently excellent ones. You probably know these concepts, but most people apply them inconsistently. Getting these right is what creates that "flow state" where AI just seems to understand exactly what you need.

1. Be Precise About What Matters. Specificity isn't just about being detailed—it's about being precise about the right details. Think of it like ordering at a restaurant. "Bring me food" might get you a random dish, but "I'd like a medium-rare steak with garlic butter" ensures you get exactly what you want.

Example Transformation:

Vague: "Help me learn guitar."

Precise: "Create a 30-day practice schedule for learning basic chords on acoustic guitar, assuming 20 minutes of daily practice."

Context Checklist: For any important request, answer these three questions:

- Who is this for, and what do they care about?
- What constraints or requirements must be met?
- How will this output be used?

2. Use Strategic Iteration. Every conversation is a chance to refine not just your output, but your prompting skills. The best AI users treat each exchange like a feedback loop, analyzing what the AI prioritized and adjusting their approach accordingly.

Example Evolution:

First Try: "Help me organize my closet."

Result: Too general and overwhelming.

Second Try: "Help me organize a small bedroom closet that's overflowing with clothes I rarely wear."

Result: Better, but still generic advice.

Third Try: "I have a 4-foot closet bursting with clothes I haven't worn in years. Help me create a process for deciding what to keep, donate, or toss, plus an organization method that fits my space."

Result: Specific, actionable, and tailored!

3. **Use Format as Strategy.** Choose output formats strategically because different structures unlock different types of thinking:

- Decision matrices for comparing options systematically
- Timelines for understanding cause and effect
- Stories for human psychology and motivation
- Q&A formats for addressing objections or concerns
- Checklists for ensuring nothing gets missed

Example: Instead of "explain budgeting," try "create a Q&A that addresses the five most common objections people have to starting a budget, with practical responses for each."

4. **Assume the AI is Smart—But Not Psychic.** Even the best AI tools can't infer context you didn't provide. If you're halfway through explaining your needs and think, "It probably knows what I mean,"—it doesn't. You don't need to overexplain your life story, but you do need to surface the relevant why behind the what. **Instead of:** "Draft a follow-up email." **Try:** "Draft a follow-up email to a podcast guest who just recorded an interview with me. I want to thank them,

share the timeline for publication, and encourage them to promote the episode once it goes live."

It's not just about tone—it's about clarity of intent.

5. Prompt for Perspective, Not Just Production. AI is more than a content factory. It's also a lens-shifter—a way to look at problems differently. Too many users treat it like a task rabbit instead of a thinking partner.
Ask things like:

> *"What are three angles I might be missing here?"*
>
> *"What would someone with a radically different worldview say about this?"*
>
> *"Push back on this idea—what are the potential downsides I'm ignoring?"*

This opens up your prompting to strategic insight, not just efficient output.

Nine Powerful Prompt Formulas

What sets the AI masters apart from the hopeful masses: they refuse to just cross their fingers and hope for magic to happen. They don't just type whatever pops into their heads and hope for brilliance. They use prompt frameworks—simple, proven structures that organize their thinking and give the AI exactly what it needs to perform at its best.

Think of these frameworks as conversational scaffolding. They help you clarify your goal, set parameters, and guide the output format. And just like great lesson plans or effective meeting agendas, the magic is in the repeatable structure—not the improvisation.

These formulas are battle-tested across thousands of real-world use cases. And the best part? You don't need to memorize all nine. Master just two or three, and you'll instantly level up the quality, consistency, and usefulness of every AI conversation you have.

Here's why they matter:

- ✓ They prevent prompt paralysis ("How do I even start this request?").
- ✓ They eliminate vague instructions that lead to generic results.
- ✓ They help you ask better follow-up questions by showing you what to refine.
- ✓ They reduce the mental overhead of crafting the perfect prompt from scratch.

Advanced users know: Prompting isn't about magic—it's about structure. Use these templates like tools in your creative toolbox. When the goal is clear but the wording isn't, pull out the format that aligns with the outcome you want—whether that's strategic analysis, persuasive messaging, storytelling, or planning.

Because the moment you stop winging it, AI stops guessing—and starts delivering.

For Clear, Actionable Outputs: T-A-G

Task: Define the job or activity
Action: Describe the approach
Goal: State the desired outcome

Best for: Projects with specific, measurable outcomes.
Example: "Task: Plan a vegetable garden for a beginner. Action: Design a layout for a 4x8 raised bed that's easy to maintain. Goal: Grow enough salad ingredients for a family of four through the summer."

For Problem-Solving: B-A-B

Before: Current situation or problem
After: Desired outcome
Bridge: How to get there

Best for: Transformation projects where you need to move from Point A to Point B.
Example: "Before: I procrastinate on important tasks and feel overwhelmed by my to-do list. After: I want to complete important work consistently without

last-minute stress. Bridge: Help me design a productivity process that works with my tendency to procrastinate, not against it."

For Creative Work: R-T-F

Role: Assign AI a persona
Task: Define what to accomplish
Format: Structure of the output

Best for: Creative projects and specialized expertise where you need AI to think from a specific perspective.
Example: "Role: Act as a children's librarian with 20 years of experience. Task: Recommend books that will help my 8-year-old who loves dogs but struggles with reading confidence. Format: Provide 5 recommendations with specific reasons why each book builds reading skills while maintaining engagement."

For Complex Projects: C-A-R-E

Context: Background for the request
Action: Tasks needed to be completed
Result: Intended output or impact
Example: Provide a benchmark of excellence

Best for: Large-scale projects requiring thorough analysis with multiple considerations.
Example: "Context: I'm planning my first solo international trip and I've never traveled outside the country. Action: Create a comprehensive preparation checklist. Result: I should feel confident and well-prepared for my 10-day trip to Japan. Example: Include both obvious items like passport renewal and less obvious ones like cultural etiquette research."

For Detailed Instructions: R-I-S-E

Role: AI's identity
Input: Information AI needs first
Steps: Instructions to follow
Expectation: What the outcome should be

Best for: Process-driven work where you need AI to follow specific methodologies.
Example: "Role: Act as a personal trainer specializing in home workouts. Input: I have 30 minutes, three times per week, basic dumbbells, and I'm recovering from a knee injury. Steps: Design a progressive 12-week strength program that accommodates my limitations. Expectation: Each workout should be clearly explained with modification options and progress tracking."

For Results-Focused Requests: A-I-M

Action: What should be done
Intent: Purpose or reason behind it
Metric: How success is measured

Best for: Performance-driven tasks where you need clear success criteria.
Example: "Action: Help me establish a morning routine. Intent: Reduce my daily stress and start each day feeling focused rather than rushed. Metric: I should be able to complete my routine in 45 minutes and feel calm when I start work."

For Justification and Buy-In: G-R-O

Goal: What you want achieved
Reason: Why this goal matters
Output: What AI should deliver

Best for: Proposals and recommendations where you need to build a compelling case.
Example: "Goal: Convince my family to adopt a rescue dog. Reason: My kids are old enough to take responsibility, and pet ownership teaches empathy while providing companionship. Output: Create talking points that address my spouse's concerns about time, cost, and mess while emphasizing the benefits for our children."

For Data Analysis and Interpretation: F-I-T

Format: Desired structure of answer
Input: Information AI should use
Task: The main job described

Best for: Research projects and analysis where you need specific formatting and clear methodology.
Example: "Format: Respond with three clear sections: Summary, Key Insights, and Action Items. Input: Use this data from my sleep tracking app over the past month. Task: Identify patterns in my sleep quality and suggest specific improvements to my bedtime routine."

For Tone and Complexity Control: L-E-D

Level: Set the complexity level
Expectation: What you want back
Direction: Style, format, or tone

Best for: Educational content and communications where audience sophistication and tone are critical.
Example: "Level: Explain quantum physics concepts at a high school level. Expectation: I want to understand enough to help my teenager with their science project on quantum computing. Direction: Use everyday analogies and avoid technical jargon, but be scientifically accurate."

These formulas aren't just about better prompts—they're about training yourself to think more strategically about what you honestly need from AI. Once you start using them, your requests become clearer in your own mind, which means better results and less back-and-forth.

THE APEX FRAMEWORK: YOUR BEST OUTPUT EVERY TIME

Here's where we separate the advanced users from everyone else. Most people think better prompting means writing longer, more detailed single requests. But the real breakthrough comes when you stop thinking in terms of prompts and start thinking in terms of sequences.

The APEX Prompt Sequence, a little brainchild of mine, is a systematic approach where each prompt asks AI to evaluate and improve the output from the previous step. Instead of hoping to get great results on the first try, you're deliberately guiding AI through a refinement process that delivers the highest quality output in the least amount of time and guesswork.

Think of it like developing a photograph in the old darkroom days. You start with an exposed film (your initial idea), then develop it through a series of chemical baths, each one revealing more detail and clarity until you have a sharp, professional-quality image. APEX works the same way—each sequential prompt builds on the previous output, adding precision, depth, and polish until you have something truly professional-grade.

The key insight: You're not starting over with each prompt. You're saying, "Here's your output—now make it better by addressing these specific aspects." By the end, you have output that's been systematically refined through multiple lenses of analysis. Advanced prompts use sequences, never just the first output. Here's your progression from rough concept to polished deliverable:

Step 0: Clarity Prompt (Optional - Use When You Need to Define Your Foundation Inputs)

Generate the Components for Your Step 1 Foundation Prompt

You've already mastered the art of clarity from earlier in this chapter—you know how to define what you want and why you want it. But sometimes, even with that skill, you need help organizing your thoughts for complex, high-stakes projects.

This optional step helps you generate the specific inputs you'll need for your Foundation Prompt (Step 1). Use it when your project has multiple moving parts, stakeholders, or when you want to ensure you've considered all the strategic angles before diving into execution.

What this step generates:

- Clear objective and strategic purpose statements
- Relevant context that affects your approach
- Working assumptions you should validate
- Success criteria and constraints you might have overlooked

Example for Career Transition: "I'm considering a career transition from teaching to data science, but I need help clarifying my approach before creating a detailed plan. Help me define: (1) What specific objective should I be optimizing for—speed of transition, salary maximization, or skill development depth? (2) What context about my situation should inform my strategy? (3) What assumptions am I making that I should validate? (4) How should I define success for this transition?"

The AI's output becomes your input for Step 1. The AI might respond with insights like: "Your primary objective should be demonstrating analytical thinking to hiring managers, not just learning programming. Key context: your teaching background comes with storytelling and communication advantages that most data science candidates lack. Critical assumption to validate: that portfolio projects matter more than formal credentials for career changers."

Example for Family Decision: "My family is considering relocating for a job opportunity, but I want to make sure I'm framing this decision properly. Help me clarify: (1) What should our decision criteria be—short-term financial gain, long-term opportunities, or family stability? (2) What factors should influence our approach that we might not be considering? (3) What assumptions are we making about the kids, housing market, or job security? (4) How should we define a successful decision process?"

Now you take these insights and use them to craft a much more strategic Foundation Prompt.

STEP 1. FOUNDATION PROMPT

Set Precise Parameters and Expectations

This is where you architect your AI's approach using a proven 6-part structure that eliminates ambiguity and maximizes relevance.

The 6-Part Structure:

1. **Intent Statement** – What specific outcome do you want?
2. **Role Assignment** – Who should the AI be? (Expert, advisor, analyst, etc.)
3. **Audience Context** – Who will consume this output?
4. **Output Format** – How should information be structured?
5. **Constraints/Must-Includes** – What boundaries or requirements must be met?
6. **Strategic Framing** (optional) – Tone, perspective, or scenario considerations

Example for Data Science Portfolio: "Intent: Create a project plan for building a data science portfolio that demonstrates real analytical skills. Role: Act as a senior data scientist who's hired entry-level analysts and knows what hiring managers actually look for. Audience: This plan is for me—someone transitioning from teaching with strong analytical thinking but needing to prove technical competency. Format: Month-by-month roadmap with specific project milestones and skill development targets. Constraints: Must accommodate full-time work schedule, limited budget for courses, and 6-month timeline. Strategic Framing: Focus on projects that tell a story about problem-solving ability rather than just technical skill demonstration."

Example for Family Relocation: "Intent: Create a comprehensive comparison framework for deciding between staying in Chicago vs. moving to Austin. Role: Act as a family financial advisor who specializes in relocation decisions and understands both the financial and emotional factors involved. Audience: This analysis will be shared with my spouse and potentially our kids (ages 12 and 14) to help us make a family decision. Format: Decision matrix with weighted criteria and clear recommendations. Constraints: Must consider both quantifiable factors (cost, schools, job market) and qualitative ones (community, family proximity, lifestyle). Strategic Framing: Present this as a balanced analysis that acknowledges trade-offs rather than pushing toward either option."

STEP 2. OPTIMIZATION PROMPT

Ask AI to Critically Analyze and Improve Its Previous Output

Now you take the output from Step 1 and ask AI to become its own critic. This is where the sequential magic happens—you're not asking for new content, you're asking AI to evaluate what it just created and make it better.

Your prompt structure: "Here's what you just created [paste or reference the Step 1 output]. Now analyze it critically and improve it by addressing..." or "Review your last output. Analyze it by checking for comprehensiveness, clarity, and accuracy..." or "Analyze your last output and identify any areas for improvement..." or "Play devil's advocate and review your last output..."

However you want to phrase it, the key element is to have the AI self-evaluate. It's much better at evaluation and analysis than generation. And don't we all prefer to do what we're freakishly good at?

What to ask AI to identify:

- Gaps, inaccuracies, or missing considerations
- Potential bias or narrow framing in its approach
- Alternative approaches or perspectives it didn't consider
- Assumptions that might not hold true
- Ways to strengthen the weakest elements

Example Optimization Prompts:

"Review the portfolio development plan you just created and improve it by addressing: (1) What assumptions are you making about the current job market for entry-level data scientists that might not be accurate? (2) Which projects might actually hurt my candidacy if executed poorly? (3) What alternative skill-building approaches should we consider for someone with my teaching background? (4) Generate 2-3 variations that test different strategic angles and integrate the strongest elements into an improved version."

"Analyze the relocation comparison framework you just created and make it more robust by identifying: (1) What important factors might we be overlooking? (2) How might our decision criteria change if we're thinking 10 years out vs. 2 years out? (3) What would a family counselor say about how we're approaching this decision? (4) Are we giving appropriate weight to our children's preferences and adjustment challenges? Now revise the framework to address these considerations."

STEP 3. REFINEMENT PROMPT

Transform the Enhanced Output into Final Form

Take the improved output from Step 2 and ask AI to polish it for real-world use. You're saying: "Here's your enhanced analysis—now turn this into something I can ultimately implement successfully." You can even ask it to update the first output based on its own analysis. This is also your chance to layer in additional elements like a change in the tone of voice (ex. more scholarly, or more fun, or more like you're talking to a 17-year-old boy who doesn't really listen), a specific type of output (ex. make it an interactive artifact, or a PDF, or a table, or a spreadsheet, or html code), or add elements (include real-world scenarios, infuse with deadpan humor, pepper in puns). The key here is to get to the best output yet, whatever that looks like for you.

Your approach: Reference the Step 2 output and ask AI to transform it with specific refinement goals.

Focus areas for refinement:

- Format for your specific audience and context
- Add clarity, persuasion, or compelling calls to action
- Ensure implementation-readiness with specific next steps
- Polish tone and presentation for maximum impact
- Remove any remaining ambiguity or theoretical elements

Example Refinement Prompts:

"Take your improved portfolio development plan and transform it into an actionable roadmap I can start using immediately. Make it practical and motivating: include specific resources with links, realistic weekly time commitments, and clear success metrics for each month. Address the

challenges you identified by building in accountability mechanisms and backup plans. Structure it so I can track progress easily and know exactly what to do next at any point."

"Convert your enhanced relocation framework into a family decision tool. Create two clear sections: (1) A practical decision process with specific steps and timeline that helps us gather the right information without getting overwhelmed, and (2) A simple evaluation method that turns our various concerns into a clear recommendation we can all understand and feel confident about. Make it something we can work through together as a family."

STEP 4. VALIDATION PROMPT
(OPTIONAL - RECOMMENDED FOR HIGH-STAKES OUTPUTS)
Stress-Test Your Final Output Against Real-World Conditions

Take your polished output from Step 3 and ask AI to simulate how it would perform in actual use. You're asking: "Here's the final plan you created—now put it through real-world scenarios and tell me where it might fail or how different people would react to it." This is pressure testing, polishing.

Your validation approach: Present the final output and ask AI to test it from multiple perspectives.

Validation methods:

- Simulate stakeholder reactions from different viewpoints
- Test comprehension, tone, and practical usability
- Identify potential implementation obstacles
- Run through worst-case scenarios
- Check for missing steps or unrealistic assumptions

Example Validation Prompts:

"Here's the final portfolio development plan you created. Now stress-test it by putting yourself in the shoes of three different people: (1) A hiring manager at a tech startup who's skeptical about career changers and has 5 minutes to review my portfolio, (2) My spouse who's concerned about the time commitment affecting family life and our finances, and (3) A senior data scientist who might mentor me and wants to see genuine analytical thinking. How would each person react to this plan? What questions, concerns, or red flags would they raise? What adjustments should I make based on their likely responses?"

"Take our family relocation decision framework and test it against these real scenarios: (1) Our 14-year-old becomes very emotional about leaving friends and refuses to engage with the decision process, (2) The job market shifts and my spouse's new role becomes less secure after 6 months, (3) We discover that Chicago schools are implementing a new STEM program our kids would really benefit from. How well does our framework handle these complications? What blind spots does this reveal, and how should we adjust our approach?"

STEP 5. TRIANGULATION
(OPTIONAL BUT AWESOME - THE POWER USER SECRET)

Get a Second AI's Independent Review of Your Final Output

Ready to learn the technique that will set you apart from novice AI users? Cross-model validation. Take your final, validated output and ask a completely different AI program to review and critique it. You're essentially getting a second expert opinion.

Why this works: Each AI application has different training data, reasoning patterns, and blind spots. By having them review each other's work, you catch issues and gain insights that no single model would provide.

How to execute triangulation:

1. Copy your final output from Steps 4
2. Open a different AI platform (if you used ChatGPT, try Claude, or vice versa)
3. Ask the second AI to evaluate and recommend improvements
4. Compare insights and integrate the strongest elements
5. Then, have it incorporate the improvements – either all of them or the ones you agree with

Example Triangulation Prompt: "I worked with another AI to create this data science portfolio development plan [paste the full output]. Please evaluate it with fresh eyes: What are the strongest elements that I should definitely keep? Where do you see potential problems, unrealistic expectations, or missing considerations? How would you approach this challenge differently? What specific improvements would make this plan more likely to succeed?"

The magic happens in the comparison: Often, the second AI will validate most of the approach while catching 1-2 critical blind spots or suggesting refinements that significantly improve the final result. You may end up with the most comprehensive, well-written output you've seen yet.

Especially powerful for:

- High-stakes communications or major decisions
- External-facing strategic work
- Career or financial planning
- Any situation where you want maximum confidence before taking action

The result: By the end of APEX, you have output that's been systematically refined, critiqued from multiple angles, stress-tested against real conditions, and validated by independent analysis. This is the highest quality output possible in the least amount of trial and error.

Why APEX Delivers Maximum Quality in Minimum Time

The sequence works because it mirrors how human experts fundamentally think through complex problems, but without the inefficiency of starting over each time. Instead of hoping to get lucky with one perfect prompt, you're systematically building toward excellence.

The sequential refinement advantage:

- **Step 1:** AI generates initial approach based on your clear parameters
- **Step 2:** Same AI improves its own work by identifying and fixing flaws
- **Step 3:** Same AI transforms improved concept into implementation-ready format
- **Step 4:** Same AI stress-tests the final output against real conditions
- **Step 5:** Different AI provides independent validation and final improvements

What makes APEX different from trial-and-error prompting:

- **Compound improvement:** Each step deliberately builds on and improves the previous output
- **Systematic coverage:** You address generation, critique, refinement, validation, and verification in sequence
- **Guided evolution:** Instead of random iterations, you're directing specific types of improvement
- **Quality assurance:** Multiple review stages catch errors and blind spots before implementation
- **Efficiency:** You reach professional-grade results in 3-5 prompts instead of 10-15 random attempts

When to use the full APEX sequence:

- Important decisions with long-term consequences
- Professional communications with external audiences
- Strategic planning or analysis projects
- Creative work where quality directly impacts results
- Any situation where "good enough" isn't frankly good enough

When to use abbreviated versions:

- Routine tasks with established patterns (use just Steps 1-2)
- Internal brainstorming or exploration (Step 1 + Step 2)
- Time-sensitive requests (Step 1 + Step 3)
- Low-stakes communications (Step 1 only)

The APEX sequence enhances your prompt skill to evolve AI from a content generator into a strategic thought partner. Instead of getting one AI's "best guess" at your request, you're orchestrating a holistic process that builds complexity, catches errors, and delivers implementation-ready results. Most importantly, APEX teaches you to think more strategically about your own requests. The discipline of working through each step clarifies your own thinking and helps you articulate exactly what you need—a skill that improves every AI interaction you'll ever have.

More Advanced Conversation Techniques

Once you've mastered APEX conversations, you're ready for some sophisticated approaches that most people never discover.

Cross-Platform Analysis

If you want a quick first-pass assessment at an AI response, this is your go-to. Simply use different AI platforms to analyze each other's work. You just saw this in action with Step 5 of APEX. Each AI application has its own strengths and blind spots. By having them review each other's outputs, you get insights no single model would provide.

Example Process:

1. Ask ChatGPT to help you plan a major home renovation project
2. Take that entire plan to Claude with this prompt: "Please analyze this renovation plan critically: What are the strongest elements? Where do you see potential problems or missing considerations? What would you do differently?"
3. Take Claude's feedback back to ChatGPT: "Here's feedback on my renovation plan from another perspective. How would you respond to these critiques? Where do you agree, and where might you push back?"

This creates AI peer review that often surfaces blind spots and strengthens your final output dramatically.

The Expert Panel Technique
For complex decisions, create a virtual panel of experts by asking AI to respond from different professional perspectives. This works well if you open your LLM (ChatGPT, Claude, DeepSeek, etc.) in multiple instances across different windows. This way, you can view the various outputs side by side.

Example: *"I need to evaluate whether to invest in solar panels for my home. Give me feedback as if you were: (1) a financial advisor focused on ROI, (2) an environmental scientist concerned with sustainability, and (3) a home improvement contractor thinking about practical installation issues. What would each expert prioritize or warn me about?"*

The Perspective Flip
Want to stress-test your ideas? Ask AI to argue against its own recommendations. This technique uncovers assumptions and helps you prepare for obstacles you might not have considered.

Example: *"You just recommended I start a morning exercise routine. Now take the opposite position—make the strongest possible case for why morning workouts might be a mistake for someone in my situation. What would my biggest critics say?"*

BUILDING YOUR PERSONAL PROMPT PLAYBOOK

Forget flawless prompts—the real magic comes from crafting a few flexible, proven approaches you can rely on again and again. You don't need to master every advanced technique or memorize viral prompt templates. What you do need is a small set of strategies that consistently work for your specific goals—whether that's planning smarter, writing faster, learning deeper, or thinking more clearly. These aren't one-size-fits-all formulas; they're personalized, repeatable patterns you refine over time. The goal isn't perfection—it's reliability. When you know what works for you, you can stop experimenting and start accelerating.

Think about how a great chef works. They don't follow recipes word-for-word every time—they've developed a repertoire of techniques they can adapt to whatever ingredients they have. Working with AI is remarkably similar.

Starting Your Collection

Begin with tasks you do repeatedly. Instead of starting from scratch each time, capture what works:

- ✓ **Email Templates:** "Write a [professional/friendly/apologetic] email to [audience] about [topic]. Keep it [specific tone] and structure it so the main [request/information] is clear within the first two sentences."
- ✓ **Learning Plans:** "Create a [timeframe] study plan for learning [skill] at a [beginner/intermediate] level, assuming [time constraint] of practice per [frequency]."
- ✓ **Decision Frameworks:** "Help me decide between [options] by creating a comparison that weighs [specific factors that matter to you]. Focus on [your priorities] rather than generic pros and cons."

The Evolution Process

Your playbook gets better over time. Every interaction teaches you something about what works. Maybe you discover that adding audience context dramatically improves your results. Or you find that specifying emotional tone prevents misunderstandings.

Example Evolution:

> **Version 1:** *"Help me write a thank-you note."*
>
> **Version 2:** *"Help me write a professional thank-you email after a job interview."*
>
> **Version 3:** *"Write a thank-you email that reinforces my qualifications for [specific role] while expressing genuine appreciation for [interviewer's name]'s time. Strike a balance between enthusiasm and professionalism."*

Capturing Breakthrough Moments

When you have a particularly successful interaction, take a moment to note what made it work. Was it the specific way you provided context? The format you requested? The sequence of questions you used?

This isn't about documenting every interaction—it's about being intentional about learning from your successes so you can build on them rather than accidentally abandoning approaches that work.

Your prompt playbook becomes a personalized collection of approaches that consistently deliver the results you need. And that expertise, refined over time, becomes a sustainable advantage that no one else can replicate.

WHEN THINGS DON'T GO ACCORDING TO PLAN

Let's be realistic. Even with proven formulas and a personal playbook, AI interactions don't always go smoothly. The difference between experienced users and frustrated ones? They recognize these challenges as normal parts of the process and have quick diagnostic skills to fix things fast.

When AI simply doesn't understand what you're asking for, it's usually a clarity problem, not an AI problem. Instead of trying to communicate everything in one complex request, break it down into clear, sequential steps.

Instead of: "Help me get better at public speaking."
Try: "First, identify the three most common public speaking fears. Then suggest specific techniques for managing each one during a 10-minute presentation."

The Information Avalanche

Sometimes AI gives you way too much information. You ask for a summary and get a novel. The fix is being specific about boundaries.

Instead of: *"Summarize this article about nutrition."*
Try: *"Extract the three most actionable nutrition tips from this article that someone could implement immediately."*

The Tone-Deaf Response

When AI output sounds wrong for your situation, be explicit about the voice you want. Think about the vibe you want to elicit in the output.

Instead of: *"Write an email to my professor."*
Try: *"Write a respectful but casual email to my professor asking for a deadline extension. I want to acknowledge responsibility while explaining my situation clearly."*

The Generic Response Trap

Nothing is more frustrating than getting content that could have been written for anyone. The antidote is generous context-setting.

Instead of: *"Give me study tips."*
Try: *"Give me study strategies for someone who learns best through discussion and examples, preparing for a statistics exam while working 30 hours a week."*

Building Diagnostic Skills

The more you work with AI, the faster you'll recognize these patterns and know how to adjust. Experienced users develop an intuitive sense of what went wrong and how to fix it.

Most AI "failures" aren't ultimately technology failures—they're communication failures. And communication skills can be developed, refined, and systematized. Each time you identify what went wrong and successfully correct it, you're building knowledge that makes every future interaction more effective.

Your Strategic Advantage

By mastering the art of leverage, you've moved from being someone who uses AI tools to someone who directs them strategically. You understand how to craft conversations that consistently deliver value, have frameworks for complex interactions, and diagnostic skills for when things go sideways.

This isn't just about becoming more efficient with AI—it's about developing a competitive advantage that compounds over time. While others struggle with inconsistent results and frustrating conversations, you're building comprehensive capabilities that let you extract maximum value from these tools. But here's something crucial: with great capability comes great responsibility. The same techniques that make you incredibly effective with AI can also get you into serious trouble if you're not thoughtful about how you use them.

Now that you know how to get AI to produce compelling, authoritative-sounding content on virtually any topic, how do you ensure that content is accurate? How do you verify insights aren't biased or misleading? How do you maintain authenticity and trust when you can generate professional communications that perfectly match any tone?

These aren't hypothetical concerns. Right now, people across every field are discovering that AI's incredible capabilities come with equally significant risks—risks that can damage reputations, create legal liabilities, and undermine trust they've spent years building. The good news is that the same strategic thinking you've applied to mastering AI conversation can be applied to using AI responsibly. Just as you've learned to be intentional about your prompts and systematic about your improvements, you can be equally intentional about the ethical implications of your AI use.

The goal isn't just to become incredibly effective with AI—it's to become incredibly effective and trustworthy. In the next section, we'll explore how to harness all this power while protecting yourself, your relationships, and your professional reputation.

6. Learning Lab

💡 Try This: Create Your Signature Prompt Formula

Objective: Develop a custom prompt structure that consistently delivers high-quality AI outputs for a task you perform regularly.

Time Required: 30–45 minutes over 1 week (5 sessions of 5–10 minutes each)

Materials Needed:

- Access to your preferred AI tool
- Notes from Chapter 5 (prompt formulas)
- Digital doc or notebook for tracking results

Steps:

1. Choose Your Target Task (5 minutes)
   - Select one task you do weekly (e.g., content creation, emails, analysis, planning).
   - Choose something moderately important—high-impact, but not high-stakes.
2. Select Your Formula Combination (10 minutes)
   - Review the 9 prompt formulas in Chapter 5.
   - Pick 2–3 that seem most useful for your selected task.
   - Example combo: R-T-F (Role–Task–Format) + L-E-D (Level–Expectation–Direction).
3. Create Your Base Prompt (10 minutes)
   - Combine your selected formulas into one prompt.
   - Example:
     "Role: Act as a professional account manager. Task: Write a follow-up email after our meeting. Format: Keep it concise and action-oriented. Level: Professional but warm. Expectation: Client should clearly understand next steps. Direction: Include a timeline and one follow-up question."

4. Test and Iterate (15–20 minutes across the week)
   Use your formula for the same task five times, adjusting one variable per test:
   - Test 1: Use your base version
   - Test 2: Add more context about audience
   - Test 3: Refine desired outcome language
   - Test 4: Adjust tone or style cues
   - Test 5: Change format guidance
5. Document Your Winner (10 minutes)
   - Compare the five results
   - Choose the version that produced the most usable first draft
   - Finalize your "signature prompt formula" and write notes on why it works
   - Save it as a reusable template

Success Metric: You should have a repeatable prompt that gets you 80% of the way to a usable output on the first try.

💡 Try This: The Expert Panel Simulation

Objective: Use multiple simulated expert perspectives to generate deeper, multidimensional insight into a real-life decision.

Time Required: 45–60 minutes

Materials Needed:

- Access to AI chat (or multiple tabs for concurrent threads)
- Notes on a real decision you're making
- Notebook or doc for summarizing and synthesizing insights

Steps:

1. Define Your Decision (10 minutes)
    - Choose a real decision you're considering (personal or professional).
    - Write 2–3 sentences about what the decision is and what matters most in making it.
2. Design Your Expert Panel (10 minutes)
    - Choose 3 distinct expert roles that would provide useful—but contrasting—perspectives.
    - Examples: Financial advisor, strategist, lifestyle coach.
3. Conduct 3 Expert Consultations (30 minutes total)
    - Open 3 separate AI chats. Use this prompt (tweaked for each role):
      "I need advice on [insert decision]. Please respond as a [expert type] with deep experience in [domain]. Focus on [their priority]. My situation: [summary]. What would you recommend and why?"
    - Spend ~10 minutes exploring each expert's view.
4. Synthesis Session (10 minutes)
    - Compare the 3 expert responses:
        - Where do they agree?
        - Where do they disagree?
        - What valuable ideas did each one introduce?

- Ask AI:
  "Based on these three expert views, what are the strongest elements from each perspective, and how might I integrate them into a smart approach?"

5. Decision Refinement (5 minutes)
   - List:
     - Two insights you hadn't considered before
     - One potential risk that came to light
     - Your revised plan based on all input

Success Metric: You should uncover at least two perspectives or risks you wouldn't have considered on your own.

💡 Try This: The Perspective Shift Exercise

Objective: Strengthen your critical thinking by challenging AI-generated advice and identifying potential blind spots.

Time Required: 20–30 minutes

Materials Needed:

- One past AI recommendation or fresh advice on a real problem
- Notebook or doc for analysis
- AI tool to explore counterpoints

Steps:

1. Identify a Recent AI Recommendation (5 minutes)
    - Choose a suggestion you've received that seemed helpful.
    - If needed, ask AI for advice on a current challenge.
2. Summarize the Original Advice (5 minutes)
    - Write it out in 2–3 sentences.
    - Note why it appealed to you.
    - Identify the assumptions it relies on.
3. Request the Counter-Argument (10 minutes)
    - Prompt AI:
      "You previously recommended [insert summary]. Now argue against that advice. What are the strongest objections? What could go wrong? What alternatives should I consider?"
    - Ask follow-ups like:
        - "Who would this advice work poorly for?"
        - "What's the best alternative path?"
4. Spot the Blind Spots (5 minutes)
    - Compare the original and counter-argument.
    - What risks, trade-offs, or flawed assumptions were exposed?
    - List 2–3 things you didn't initially consider.
5. Refine Your Approach (5 minutes)
    - Draft a revised decision that reflects both perspectives.

- List the conditions where the original advice holds—and where it doesn't.
- Write 2–3 vetting questions to ask next time before following AI's advice.

Success Metric: You should surface at least two important blind spots or risks that weren't obvious in the original recommendation.

💡 Try This: Test Your Bias Detection

Objective: Identify and revise for hidden biases or missing perspectives in AI-generated content in your area of expertise.

Time Required: 30–40 minutes

Materials Needed:

- AI-generated article, post, or guide in your field
- Text editor or annotation tool
- Optional: AI for revision and comparison

Steps:

1. Generate Target Content (10 minutes)
    - Ask AI to write a short guide, article, or summary on a topic you know well.
    - Example prompt:
      "Write a guide for [audience] about [topic]. Include examples and practical advice."
2. First Impressions Review (5 minutes)
    - Read through and mark anything that feels off.
    - Note areas that seem incomplete, unbalanced, or overly generic.
3. Apply the Flip Test (10 minutes)
    - For any assumed audience (e.g., male executive, big business), mentally "flip" the demographic or context.
    - Ask: Does this still make sense if the reader is a woman, freelancer, or working parent?
4. Scan for Missing Perspectives (10 minutes)
    - Ask yourself:
        - Who is not represented in this advice?
        - Does it assume resources, tools, or privileges not available to everyone?

        - What alternatives might exist for different people or situations?
    - Write down 2–3 missing perspectives.
5. Ask for a Bias Revision (5 minutes)
    - Prompt AI:
      "Review your own content. Identify any bias or missing viewpoints, especially regarding assumptions about [audience demographics], resource access, or situational context. How would you revise this to be more inclusive?"
6. Compare and Document (5 minutes)
    - Review the revised version against your original notes.
    - Write down what AI found that you didn't—and what you caught that it missed.

Success Metric: You should identify at least one important bias or missing perspective that wasn't obvious on first review.

7. More Prompt Skills for Mere Mortals

Or: The Art of Getting AI to Legitimately Do What You Want

I can hear you now: 'Elisa, didn't we *just* cover prompting?' You're not wrong. But here's the thing—I've spent a lifetime in education, and if there's one truth that never fails, it's this: not everyone learns the same way. The more tools you've got in your AI toolbox, the better your chances of finding the one that locks in and gives you exactly the output you need.

Think of the previous chapter and this one as your AI prompting toolbox. As you read, highlight the ones that click for *you.* Try them out. Rank them. Keep a list of your favorite ones. Because this dance is just getting started.

I mean, just last week, I asked an AI to help me write a professional email declining a dinner invitation. Simple enough, right? I wanted something polite but not overly apologetic, warm but not gushing. What I got back was a three-paragraph opus that began: "Dearest Beloved Host, thy gracious invitation hath stirred mine heart..."

I stared at my screen. Somewhere in the digital ether, an artificial mind had decided that "professional" meant "Renaissance faire performer having an emotional breakdown." Probably it was using the custom GPT I wrote called "Shakespeare is Your Life Coach".

This is our reality now. We're living through history's weirdest communication revolution—one where we're learning to talk to minds that aren't quite minds, intelligence that's intelligent in ways we didn't expect and clueless in ways that make us question everything we thought we knew about thinking itself.

The thing is, getting AI to do what you actually want isn't rocket science. But it's not exactly intuitive either. It's more like learning to communicate with a brilliant alien who's studied human language by reading every book ever written but has never *really* had a conversation. They know all the words, understand grammar better than most English teachers, and can write poetry that would make Shakespeare weep—but ask them to help you politely decline a dinner invitation, and suddenly you're dealing with someone who think social etiquette peaked in the 1600s.

The good news? Once you understand how these digital minds work—and more importantly, how they don't work—talking to them becomes not just manageable, but genuinely fascinating. You start to see patterns in the miscommunications, develop intuition for what works and what doesn't, and eventually, you might even find yourself enjoying the process.

THE PROMPT WHISPERER'S TOOLKIT

Clarity Beats Cleverness Every Time. Let me tell you about the prompt that haunts my dreams. A friend, let's call him Dave, was trying to get AI help with his dating profile. Being Dave, he thought he'd be clever about it:

> "Help me craft something that shows I'm mysterious but approachable, confident but humble, successful but down-to-earth. Think James Bond meets Mr. Rogers meets that guy who always knows the best local coffee shops."

The AI, bless its digital heart, took this seriously. It produced a dating profile that read like a spy novel written by someone who'd never been on a date: "I navigate the shadows of international finance by day, but come evening, you'll find me reading stories to shelter puppies while brewing the perfect pour-over using beans I've personally sourced from a small village in Colombia where I may or may not have saved the local economy."

Dave's profile got zero matches. Zero.

Dave's expensive lesson in AI communication: these systems are basically brilliant literalists. When you get all poetic and indirect, you're asking it to decode your inner thoughts—and spoiler alert, telepathy didn't make it into the feature set.

The revised prompt that ultimately worked? "Write a dating profile for a 32-year-old financial analyst who loves coffee, volunteers at an animal shelter on weekends, and wants to sound friendly and genuine. Keep it under 150 words and avoid clichés about loving to laugh or long walks on the beach." Boring? Maybe. Effective? Dave got three dates that week.

When Cleverness Backfires

I've watched this pattern repeat across countless scenarios. My sister asked AI to help plan her daughter's 8th birthday party with this prompt: "Create a magical experience that will make her feel like a princess without being too girly or reinforcing stereotypes."

The AI suggested a "Royal Engineering Academy" where kids would design and build "princess-approved infrastructure projects." Creative? Absolutely. What an 8-year-old basically wants? Not so much. The lesson here isn't to drain all personality from your prompts. It's to remember that AI takes you literally. When you say "mysterious but approachable," it doesn't think "intriguingly reserved." It thinks "I must somehow be both secretive and welcoming," and the cognitive dissonance shows.

The Goldilocks Principle: Getting the Details Just Right

Prompting AI is a lot like cooking risotto—too little attention and you get mush, too much and you end up with something nobody wants to eat. Let me show you what I mean with three attempts at the same task: getting help with a work presentation.

Too Vague: "Help me with my presentation."

This is like walking into a restaurant and saying "food, please." The AI doesn't know if you're presenting to kindergarteners or the board of directors, whether you need help with content or slides or public speaking anxiety. You'll get something generic and probably useless.

Too Rigid: "Create a 47-slide PowerPoint presentation for Q3 financial results targeting mid-level managers in the consumer goods sector, with exactly 3 bullet points per slide, using only blue and white colors, including charts showing revenue growth, market share analysis, competitive positioning, cost structure breakdown, and forward-looking projections for Q4 and 2024, with speaker notes of exactly 2 minutes per slide, following the corporate template version 3.2 guidelines established in the brand manual section 4.7."

This is like giving someone a recipe with ingredients measured to the gram and cooking times down to the second. Sure, it's specific, but it's also exhausting to read and leaves no room for the AI to help you think strategically through the problem.

Just Right: "I'm presenting Q3 financial results to a group of 15 department managers next Tuesday. We exceeded revenue targets but missed profit margins due to supply chain costs. I want to acknowledge the challenges while keeping the team motivated. Help me structure this into a clear narrative with 3-5 main points."

This gives the AI enough context to be genuinely helpful while leaving room for it to contribute ideas you might not have thought of.

Finding Your Sweet Spot

The principle applies everywhere. When my neighbor asked for help writing a college application essay, her first attempt was: "Help me write a good college essay." The result was generic advice about "showing, not telling."

Her second attempt was much better: "I'm applying to small liberal arts colleges and want to write about how working at my family's bakery taught me about community. I'm worried it sounds too ordinary. Help me find what's unique about my experience."

The sweet spot is giving AI enough information to understand your world without drowning it in details that don't matter. Think of it as briefing a smart colleague who's new to your specific situation but understands how business (or writing, or relationships, or whatever) generally works.

Context is King

Something weird about AI: it has no memory of your previous conversations, but it has perfect recall of everything you tell it within a single conversation. This creates an odd dynamic where context is both crucial and completely under your control.

I learned this lesson while trying to get help with a tricky email to a client. My first attempt was: "Write a professional email explaining that we'll be two weeks late on delivery." The response was technically correct but completely wrong for the situation. It was formal to the point of being cold, with no acknowledgment of the relationship I'd been building with this client for months.

My second attempt included the context: "I need to write an email to Sarah, a client I've worked with for eight months. She's generally understanding but this is the second delay on this project. The delay is due to a supplier issue outside our control, but I don't want to make excuses. She has a big presentation depending on this deliverable. Write something that's apologetic but not desperate, and includes a concrete plan for moving forward."

The difference was night and day. The second email sounded like it came from someone who understood the business relationship, the stakes, and the appropriate tone.

Context in Creative Projects

This principle works beyond business communications. When I was helping my teenage nephew with a creative writing assignment, his first prompt was: "Write a story about friendship."

The AI produced a generic tale about two kids who become friends after initially disliking each other. Technically competent, utterly forgettable.

His revised prompt: "Write a story about two 16-year-olds who bond over their shared love of vintage video games, set in a small town where the only arcade is about to close down. One character is outgoing but struggling with his parents' divorce, the other is shy but incredibly skilled at games. Make it about 1,000 words."

The second story had heart, specificity, and emotional resonance—because the AI understood the emotional landscape it was working within.

AI reads between the lines, but only the lines you give it. It can't guess that your "professional email" needs to account for an eight-month relationship, or that your creative writing needs to resonate with contemporary teenage experience. But when you provide that context, AI becomes remarkably good at matching tone and approach to the situation.

MORE PROMPTING TOOLS FOR YOUR TOOLBOX

Chain Prompting: Building Complex Solutions Step by Step

Chain prompting is the practice of breaking complex tasks into a sequence of simpler prompts, where each response builds on the previous one. Instead of trying to solve everything at once, you guide the AI through a logical progression of thinking.

Think of it like following a recipe where each step prepares ingredients for the next, rather than trying to cook everything simultaneously. I discovered this technique's power while tackling a scheduling nightmare. I had six people, four meeting rooms, three time zones, and approximately seventeen conflicting requirements.

My first prompt was straightforward: "Help me schedule a meeting that works for everyone." The response was... fine. A list of possible times with brief explanations. But when I tried chain prompting, something remarkable happened:

Link 1: "Help me map out the constraints for scheduling a meeting with 6 people across 3 time zones. Think through this step-by-step."

Link 2: "Based on those constraints, what are the 3 most important factors I should prioritize when choosing a time?"

Link 3: "Now suggest 3 specific time slots that best balance these priorities, and explain the trade-offs for each."

Link 4: "Take the best option and help me write an email proposing it to the team that acknowledges the compromises some people are making."

The final result wasn't just better—it was creative. The AI had noticed patterns I'd missed and suggested solutions I hadn't considered, like splitting the meeting into two shorter sessions to accommodate different discussion topics.

When Chain Prompting Fails. Not every task benefits from this approach. I once tried to use chain prompting to help write a simple thank-you note, breaking it into "analyze the relationship," "identify key points to acknowledge," and "draft the note." The result was overthought and artificial—sometimes a single, direct prompt is the right tool. Chain prompting works best for:

- Complex problems with multiple variables
- Tasks requiring analysis before action
- Situations where you need to build understanding progressively
- Creative projects that benefit from exploration

APEX: YOUR GO-TO PROMPT SEQUENCE

Tackle a quick review of the APEX Prompt Sequence, which you explored in depth in Chapter 7.

The Core Concept: Each prompt builds on and improves the previous output. You're not starting over—you're systematically refining toward excellence.

THE 5-STEP SEQUENCE

Step 0: Clarity (Optional) When you need help organizing complex thoughts before diving in.

- Generate objectives, context, assumptions, and success criteria
- Use the output to craft a stronger Foundation Prompt

Step 1: Foundation Set precise parameters using the 6-part structure:

1. Intent Statement
2. Role Assignment
3. Audience Context
4. Output Format
5. Constraints/Must-Includes
6. Strategic Framing (optional)

Step 2: Optimization Ask AI to critique and improve its own work:

- "Here's what you just created... now analyze it critically and improve it"
- Look for gaps, bias, alternatives, assumptions, weak elements

Step 3: Refinement Transform the enhanced output into implementation-ready form:

- Polish for your specific audience and context

- Add clarity, remove ambiguity
- Include specific next steps and practical elements

Step 4: Validation (Optional) Stress-test against real-world conditions:

- Simulate stakeholder reactions
- Test for implementation obstacles
- Run worst-case scenarios

Step 5: Triangulation (Optional) Get a second AI's independent review:

- Copy final output to different AI platform
- Ask for fresh evaluation and improvements
- Integrate the strongest insights

When to Use What

Full APEX: High-stakes decisions, professional communications, strategic planning, quality-critical work

Abbreviated: Steps 1-2 for routine tasks, Steps 1+3 for time-sensitive requests, Step 1 only for low-stakes communications

Remember: You're orchestrating holistic, strategic improvement, not hoping for lucky first attempts. Each step deliberately builds compound value.

ROLE-PLAYING

Channeling Specific Expertise

Sometimes the best way to get what you need from AI is to ask it to embody someone with specific knowledge or perspective. This isn't about deception—it's about accessing the patterns and approaches that AI has learned from examples of expert thinking.

Role-playing prompts ask AI to take on the mindset, knowledge, and communication style of a specific type of expert or person. I was struggling with a presentation that felt flat and lifeless. Every revision made it more technically accurate but somehow less engaging. Then I tried something different:

"Act as an experienced TED talk coach. Review this presentation outline and give me advice on how to make it more compelling. Focus on storytelling, emotional connection, and audience engagement."

The transformation was immediate. Instead of generic advice about "making presentations better," I got specific, actionable feedback: "Your opening needs a hook—start with the moment you realized everything you thought you knew was wrong... This section has too many statistics—pick the one that's most surprising and build a story around it... Your conclusion should call back to your opening, but with the audience now seeing it differently..."

Choosing the Right Role

The key is matching the role to your specific need:

- **Creative writing instructor** for storytelling feedback
- **Senior developer** for debugging help
- **Direct response copywriter** for marketing copy
- **Elementary school teacher** for explaining complex concepts simply
- **Hiring manager** for resume feedback

I helped a friend prepare for a job interview using this approach: *"Act as a hiring manager for a tech startup. I'm interviewing for a product manager role. Ask me challenging questions that would help you assess whether I'm the right fit, and give me feedback on my answers."*

The practice session was invaluable—not because the AI was *actually* a hiring manager, but because it channeled the types of questions and evaluation criteria that hiring managers typically use.

When Role-Playing Doesn't Work

Be cautious about asking AI to role-play as:

- Specific real people (privacy and accuracy concerns)
- Professionals giving advice that requires legal/medical/financial expertise
- Roles that require real-world experience AI can't have

I once asked AI to "act as a parent" to help with a difficult conversation with my teenager. The advice was generic and missed the nuanced reality of actual parent-child relationships. Some expertise can't be simulated.

THE POWER OF CONSTRAINTS

Counterintuitively, the more limits you place on AI, the more creative and useful it becomes. It's like poetry—sonnets are beautiful partly because of their rigid structure, not despite it.

I learned this while helping my niece with a school project. She needed to write a short story, and her first prompt was beautifully open-ended: "Write me a creative short story." The result was... fine. Generic fantasy adventure with predictable characters and a storyline that felt assembled from spare parts of better stories.

Then we tried again with constraints: "Write a 500-word story about two characters who are stuck in an elevator. One of them is claustrophobic, the other is a stand-up comedian. Neither of them can use their phones. The story should be mostly dialogue and end with them becoming friends."

The second story was infinitely better. The constraints forced the AI to be inventive within limits, to develop character through dialogue, to build tension and resolution in a confined space. The limitation became the source of creativity.

EFFECTIVE CONSTRAINT CATEGORIES

Format constraints: Word count, structure, style

"Write this in exactly 100 words"

"Use only dialogue"

"Structure this as a FAQ"

Content constraints: What to include or exclude

"Don't mention price"

"Focus only on environmental benefits"

"Assume the reader knows nothing about this topic"

Tone constraints: How it should sound

"Write as if explaining to a curious 10-year-old"

"Sound enthusiastic but not pushy"

"Be professional but not formal"

Creative constraints: Artificial limitations that spark innovation

"Create a marketing campaign using only questions"

"Explain this concept using only sports metaphors"

"Write a product description without using any adjectives"

THE ART OF PRODUCTIVE FEEDBACK

Your first prompt will probably produce something that's almost but not quite what you wanted. This isn't a failure—it's the opening move in a collaborative process. The secret is learning to give feedback that helps rather than confuses.

I watch people get frustrated with AI the same way I watch people get frustrated with GPS applications—they keep repeating the same instruction louder, as if volume were the issue.

What doesn't work: "That's not what I wanted. Try again."

What does work: "This captures the main points well, but the tone is too formal for my audience. Can you make it more conversational, like you're explaining this to a friend over coffee?"

THE FEEDBACK FRAMEWORK

Effective AI feedback follows a simple pattern:

1. **Acknowledge what worked:** "This structure is exactly what I need..."
2. **Specify what needs to change:** "...but the tone is too technical for my audience..."
3. **Give clear direction:** "...can you rewrite it as if you're explaining why someone should care about this topic?"

I've started thinking of this as collaborative refinement rather than error correction. Each round gets you closer to your best output, and often ends up somewhere better than what you originally had in mind.

When Feedback Loops Break Down

Sometimes, despite your best efforts, a conversation just spirals. I had this happen while trying to get help with a complex project plan. After twenty minutes of back-and-forth that left me more confused than when I started, I realized the problem: I was asking AI to solve a problem I hadn't fully defined for myself.

Warning signs of a broken feedback loop:

- You're giving the same type of feedback repeatedly
- The AI responses are getting more generic, not more specific
- You've lost track of what you originally wanted
- Each revision creates new problems while solving old ones

The nuclear option: Start over, but differently. Instead of continuing to refine the same approach, step back and reconsider your entire strategy. Maybe the task is too complex for a single prompt. Maybe you need to break it into smaller pieces. Maybe you need to do some thinking on your own first.

READING AI'S CONFIDENCE LEVELS

AI has a peculiar relationship with confidence. It can sound absolutely certain about things it's completely wrong about, and hedge uncertainly about facts it knows perfectly well. Learning to spot the difference is crucial.

Red Flags: When to Be Skeptical

Overly specific claims you can't verify. "The 2019 study by Dr. Johnson found that exactly 73% of people..." AI sometimes generates plausible-sounding but completely fictional citations.

Claims about very recent events. AI's training has a cutoff date, but it doesn't always admit what it doesn't know about current events.

Step-by-step instructions without caveats. When AI gives you detailed procedures for complex tasks without mentioning what could go wrong, be suspicious.

Green Flags: Appropriate Uncertainty

AI tends to be properly uncertain about:

- Subjective matters ("this message might resonate with your audience")
- Creative judgments ("you could try this approach")
- Anything involving human emotions or complex relationships

The key is developing intuition for when to trust AI's confidence and when to fact-check independently. Think of it like listening to a very knowledgeable friend who sometimes gets enthusiastic about things they half-remember.

A Failure Story

I once asked AI to help me troubleshoot a technical issue with my event registration automation. The response was confident and detailed, walking me through a series of steps that seemed logical. I spent hours trying to follow the instructions, but kept discovering errors along the way. It was 70% helpful, 30% hopeful.

The lesson? Always verify technical instructions, especially when they seem too convenient or when the AI doesn't ask clarifying questions about your specific setup.

PROGRESSIVE PROMPT BUILDING

Progressive prompting combines multiple techniques to tackle complex challenges that no single approach can handle. Think of it as building a conversation where each exchange makes the next one more effective.

Let me show you how this works with a real example. I needed to write a difficult email to my team about budget cuts—a task that required sensitivity, clarity, and strategic thinking.

Stage 1 - Context Building (Role-Playing): "Act as an experienced manager who's had to deliver difficult news to teams. What are the key concerns employees typically have about budget cuts, especially around job security and project continuity?"

Stage 2 - Strategy Development (Chain Prompting): "Based on those concerns, what are the most important points I need to address in an email announcing budget cuts? What should I definitely avoid saying?"

Stage 3 - Content Creation (Constraints): "Now help me draft an email that addresses those points. The tone should be honest but not alarming, under 200 words, and I want to focus on what we're doing to minimize impact rather than dwelling on the problems."

Stage 4 - Refinement (Feedback Loop): "This draft feels right for the content, but I'm worried it sounds too corporate. Can you suggest ways to make it feel more personal and authentic without being overly casual?"

Each stage built on the previous one, and the final email was far better than anything I could have gotten from a single prompt. The AI helped me think through the problem systematically while maintaining focus on the human elements that mattered most.

When Progressive Building Works Best

This approach is powerful for:

- High-stakes communications
- Creative projects requiring exploration
- Complex problems with multiple stakeholders
- Situations where you need to balance competing priorities

But it's overkill for simple tasks. Don't use progressive building to write a basic thank-you note or schedule a straightforward meeting.

NEGATIVE PROMPTING

The Art of Exclusion

Negative prompting involves telling AI what not to do, which can be more effective than describing what you want. This technique is especially useful when you keep getting responses that miss the mark in predictable ways.

I discovered this while trying to get help with a presentation that kept coming out too academic. Instead of trying to describe the tone I wanted, I started listing what I didn't want:

> "Write a presentation about mentorship trends. Don't use academic language, don't include more than three statistics per slide, don't make it sound like a research paper, and don't start with 'In today's world' or similar generic openings."

The results improved immediately. The AI had clear boundaries to work within, which paradoxically gave it more creative freedom within those limits.

Effective Negative Prompting Strategies

- ✓ **Tone exclusions:** "Don't sound salesy," "Don't be overly formal," "Don't use corporate jargon"
- ✓ **Content exclusions:** "Don't mention pricing," "Don't include competitor names," "Don't assume prior knowledge"
- ✓ **Format exclusions:** "Don't use bullet points," "Don't make it longer than one page," "Don't include a conclusion section"
- ✓ **Style exclusions:** "Don't start with questions," "Don't use passive voice," "Don't include obvious advice"

This technique is particularly effective for people who know what they don't want but struggle to articulate what they do want.

META-PROMPTING

Getting AI to Help You Prompt Better

The most advanced technique might be the simplest: ask AI to help you write better prompts. It's like asking a translator to teach you their language while they're translating for you.

"I'm trying to get help with [specific task], but my prompts aren't producing the results I want. Can you suggest how I might rephrase this to be more effective?"

Or: "What information would you need to give me better advice about [topic]?"

I used this approach when struggling to get good creative writing feedback. My original prompt was: "Give me feedback on this story." The results were generic and unhelpful.

So I asked: "I want feedback on creative writing that will effectively help me improve. What should I tell you about my story, my goals, and my audience to get the most useful feedback?"

The AI suggested I include information about:

- The genre and target audience
- Specific aspects I was worried about
- What kind of feedback would be most helpful (structure, character development, dialogue, etc.)
- Whether this was a first draft or later revision

This meta-conversation led to much better feedback on my actual writing.

THE LEARNING LOOP

Meta-prompting creates a learning loop where each conversation teaches you to have better conversations. You start to understand not just what to ask, but how AI thinks about problems.

Over time, you develop intuition for:

- What kinds of context AI finds most helpful
- What level of detail works best for different tasks
- What assumptions you're making that aren't as obvious as you think

The Human in the Loop: Learning to JUDGE

After months of working with AI, the most important lesson is this: the best interactions don't feel like giving commands to a computer. They feel like brainstorming with a colleague who brings a different perspective—but you're still the one making the final call.

This is where the **JUDGE framework** becomes essential:

J - Judgment

Ask yourself: Does this *actually* and *effectively* solve my problem, or just the generic version of my problem? Does it sound like me, or like an AI trying to sound professional? Does it account for the specific context and constraints I'm working within?

Example: Lisa's investor presentation was technically perfect but wrong for her specific audience. The AI had optimized for "impressive" when she needed "authentic."

U - Underpins

Remember: Your human assessment underpins every interaction with AI.

AI can generate options, but it can't know which option serves your actual needs. Every suggestion requires your evaluation of fit, appropriateness, and effectiveness.

Practice: Before using any AI output, ask: "Would I say this?" "Does this match my goals?" "Will this work in my specific situation?"

D - Decision

Recognize: Decision-making remains fundamentally human. AI can inform your choices, expand your options, and help you think through implications. But the choice itself—what to do, what to say, what direction to take—that's on you.

Framework: Use AI to generate options, but make decisions based on your knowledge of context, relationships, and consequences that AI can't fully grasp.

G - Guidance

Understand: Guidance flows both ways.

You guide AI with your prompts, but you also let your human wisdom guide how you use AI's outputs. Sometimes that means taking the suggestion wholesale. Sometimes it means using it as inspiration for something completely different.

Approach: Think of AI as a brilliant research assistant, not a replacement for your thinking.

E - Evaluation

Practice: Evaluation is an ongoing process.

Not just "is this output good or bad?" but "is this the right kind of good for what I'm trying to accomplish?" Quality without relevance isn't helpful.

Questions to ask:

- Does this serve my audience's actual needs?
- Is this genuinely helpful or just impressively written?
- Does this account for the constraints and context I'm working within?
- Would I be comfortable standing behind this output?

The Dance Continues

We're not just learning to talk to machines. We're discovering new ways to think about thinking, new methods for breaking down complex problems, and new approaches to creative collaboration.

But remember: the conversation is just that—a conversation. And like any good conversation, the best outcomes happen when both participants bring their strengths to the table. AI brings processing power, pattern recognition, and the ability to generate options at scale. You bring judgment, context, wisdom, and the irreplaceable human ability to know what absolutely matters. It's like having a Tesla that can parallel park itself with mathematical precision but still needs you to remember that driving through the farmer's market is frowned upon, no matter how efficiently it could navigate the produce stands.

The future belongs to people who can dance this dance—who can leverage artificial intelligence while remembering to JUDGE the results through authentically human eyes.

And honestly? The dance is just getting started.

QUICK REFERENCE: TECHNIQUE SUMMARY

Basic Techniques

- **Clarity over Cleverness:** Be direct rather than metaphorical
- **Goldilocks Principle:** Provide just enough context—not too little, not too much
- **Context is King:** Give AI the background it needs to understand your situation

Intermediate Techniques

- APEX Prompt Sequence
- **Chain Prompting:** Break complex tasks into sequential steps
- **Role-Playing:** Ask AI to embody specific expertise or perspective
- **Productive Feedback:** Acknowledge what works, specify what needs change, give clear direction

Advanced Techniques

- **Progressive Building:** Combine multiple techniques for complex challenges
- **Negative Prompting:** Tell AI what not to do to clarify boundaries
- **Meta-Prompting:** Ask AI to help you prompt better

When Techniques Fail

- **Broken Feedback Loops:** Start over with a different approach
- **Overconfident AI:** Verify claims, especially technical instructions
- **Wrong Tool:** Some tasks need human judgment, not AI assistance

7. Learning Lab

Try This: Calibrate the Goldilocks Prompt

Objective: Learn how to move from vague or overloaded prompts to that "just right" level of detail that consistently generates useful AI results.

Time Required: 25–30 minutes

Materials Needed:

- Any AI tool
- A moderately complex task or topic (e.g., writing an email, creating a summary, building an outline)
- A notepad or doc for comparison

Steps:

1. **Choose Your Task (2 minutes)**
   Pick a real task you want AI to help with—ideally something you've tried before and felt underwhelmed by.
2. **Write a Vague Prompt (3 minutes)**
   Give the AI as little context as possible.
   Example: "Help me write a blog post."
   Save the result.
3. **Write a Rigid Prompt (5 minutes)**
   Go the other extreme. Over-specify tone, structure, format, audience, and details.
   Example: "Write a 1,200-word blog post for mid-career marketing professionals about content strategy trends, including exactly four subheads, three statistics, a CTA in paragraph five, and no contractions."
   Save the result.
4. **Write the Goldilocks Prompt (5 minutes)**
   Now find the middle ground.
   - Who is this for?
   - What do you want the output to do?

- What tone or format *generally* works best?
- What's the core idea or outcome you care about?

Save this result, too.

5. **Compare the Three Outputs (10 minutes)**
    - Which one was most helpful and why?
    - What did you learn about the balance of context and flexibility?
    - How will you apply this "Goldilocks" mindset in future prompts?

Success Metric: You'll walk away with a prompt template that hits your personal sweet spot—and a clear sense of how to adjust prompts that feel "off."

💡 Try This: The Constraint Creativity Challenge

Objective: Explore how limiting AI's options (instead of expanding them) often leads to more original, tailored, and useful results.

Time Required: 30–40 minutes

Materials Needed:

- Any AI tool
- A content creation or writing task (email, outline, story, caption, etc.)
- Optional: timer to enforce time limits

Steps:

1. **Choose a Simple Task (5 minutes)**
   Example:
   - Write a social media post
   - Summarize a recent meeting
   - Draft a paragraph for a bio
2. **Write an Open Prompt (5 minutes)**
   Let AI respond with minimal constraints.
   Example: "Write a 200-word bio for a podcast guest."
3. **Apply Layered Constraints (20 minutes total)**
   Run the same task three more times, adding one new constraint each time:
   - **Version 1:** Add tone constraint (e.g., "Make it sound humble but impressive")
   - **Version 2:** Add format constraint (e.g., "Must be 3 short paragraphs with 1 strong hook")
   - **Version 3:** Add content constraint (e.g., "Don't mention job titles or company names")
4. **Compare All Versions (5–10 minutes)**
   - Which was most engaging or useful?
   - Which surprised you?
   - Which constraints were most helpful in getting a good result?

Success Metric: You should discover at least one constraint that consistently improves your outputs—and gain confidence in using "less" to get more.

💡 Try This: Prompt-to-JUDGE Reflection

Objective: Reinforce the human-centered prompting mindset by evaluating AI results using the JUDGE framework.

Time Required: 20–25 minutes

Materials Needed:

- One recent AI-generated response
- A notebook or printed copy of the JUDGE framework
- Highlighters or notes app

Steps:

1. **Pick an Output to Evaluate (2 minutes)**
   Choose any recent AI result you've used (an email, summary, idea list, etc.).
2. **Apply the JUDGE Filter (10–12 minutes)**
   Ask yourself the following for each letter:
   - **J – Judgment:**
     Does this solve my actual problem, or just a generic version?
   - **U – Underpins:**
     What assumptions of mine are influencing how I'm reading this?
   - **D – Decision:**
     Am I using this as input, or relying on it to make the decision?
   - **G – Guidance:**
     How well did I guide the AI in the first place?
   - **E – Evaluation:**
     Would I be confident sharing this publicly or using it professionally?
3. **Document Insights (5 minutes)**
   - What worked?
   - What felt off?
   - How would you revise your original prompt next time?
4. **Bonus (Optional): Meta-Prompt the AI (5 minutes)**
   Ask AI:

"Here's the output you gave me. I'm evaluating it using the JUDGE framework. Can you walk me through where it might fall short and how I might guide you better next time?"

Success Metric: You'll gain two clear takeaways: how well your prompt aligned with your actual goals—and how to adjust future prompts for even stronger results.

8. Using AI Responsibly – Beyond the Hype and Horror Stories

A Human-Centered Guide to Getting It Right

Let's talk about the conversation that's quietly keeping leaders up at night—and loudly filling Slack threads, boardroom agendas, classroom whiteboards, and those late-night kitchen-table debates between entrepreneurs and their coffee mugs:

"How do we use AI without crossing a line—legally, ethically, professionally?"

It's a fair question. But more often than not, it's asked from a place of anxiety, not strategy. From a place of protection, not possibility. Hold this reframe as we move through the chapter:

Using AI responsibly isn't about avoiding disaster. It's about designing excellence. Most organizations treat AI ethics like a game of "Don't Touch the Tripwire," which leads to long lists of rules that are outdated by the time they're laminated. But the smart ones—the ones gaining trust and market share—are thinking like architects, not bomb squad technicians. They're designing workflows where good choices are built in, not bolted on.

And let's be honest: no one wants to babysit every AI-generated sentence or launch 47 compliance checklists every time they prompt ChatGPT to write a subject line. What you need is a way to make AI decisions in flow—a kind of ethical autopilot for your professional judgment.

This chapter will show you how to build that. We're going to explore:

1. What's genuinely at stake when you cut corners with AI.
2. The CARE framework, a decision-making GPS for AI that works in real time.
3. Additional incorporation of the JUDGE principle, a powerful reminder that you are still the brain behind the machine.
4. Systematic safeguards that catch issues early—before they land you in hot water.
5. Team and organizational best practices to create a culture of trust and transparency.

Let's begin with the stakes. Because this isn't just about ethics. It's about your reputation, relationships, and real-world results.

WHAT'S GENUINELY AT STAKE

The Real Costs of Cutting Corners

Let's ditch the hypotheticals for a moment. This isn't about philosophical debates or "What ifs" in a college ethics class. This is about what's already happening to real people—talented, well-meaning professionals—who misused AI tools and paid the price.

When AI Fakes the Facts

Picture this scenario: You're a well-respected public relations director. You've worked hard to build trust in your industry. One day, you use an AI tool to generate some compelling "research" for an upcoming keynote. It sounds smart, it fits your message, and you're on a deadline. You go with it.

The presentation is a hit—until a colleague tries to track down one of the cited studies... and discovers it doesn't exist. The data was made up. Generated. Fabricated by the AI. That's not a scandal you can spin your way out of. Two years later, that PR professional is still clawing her way back into credibility circles.

Now, this isn't just a fluke. Consider what happened when a lawyer submitted an AI-generated legal brief packed with citations to nonexistent cases. The judge (and opposing counsel) did a little digging. What they found? Fiction dressed up as legal precedent. The result? Sanctions. Public embarrassment. A permanently dinged reputation. These are cautionary tales, case studies in professional self-sabotage—unintentional, but devastating.

When Privacy Goes Out the Window

Imagine you're a marketing consultant working with a health organization. You upload client data to a third-party AI platform to segment and analyze it—without checking the platform's terms of service. You assume the platform is secure.

Weeks later, the healthcare client discovers their patient data has been exposed to third parties. Boom: potential HIPAA violations. Contract terminated. Trust shattered. Referrals? Dead in the water. This wasn't malice. It was oversight. And it's all too common.

When Bias Makes the Decisions

Picture an HR manager who leans on AI to screen job applications. The tool, trained on biased data, begins filtering out candidates from certain demographics. Result? A lawsuit. And a reputation that even the slickest employer brand campaign can't repair. Here's the thing: that manager wasn't trying to discriminate. He was trying to save time. But good intentions don't excuse poor design.

When Creativity Crosses the Legal Line

Consider this scenario: A freelance graphic designer builds a gorgeous AI-generated portfolio and starts landing big gigs. Months later, she gets a cease-and-desist letter—turns out her AI art closely resembles copyrighted work. Clients begin to question everything she's created. Her credibility collapses. She didn't know the AI tool was mimicking copyrighted material. But the law doesn't care about ignorance. It cares about ownership.

When the System Catches It—Just in Time

Thankfully, not every story ends in ruin. Picture what happened when one financial firm caught a compliance issue before clients did: multiple advisors were using the same AI tool to write reports, and the outputs were eerily similar. Instead of waiting for a scandal, the firm implemented clear guidelines, enforced transparency, and rebuilt trust before it was broken.

Another time, imagine a pharmaceutical team's human review process flagging a major statistical error in AI-generated trial data. A mistake like that, published, could've altered real-world clinical practices. Instead, they caught it, corrected it, and improved their entire workflow because of it.

The Pattern

The common thread in every story? People weren't trying to be reckless. They were trying to be efficient. Productive. Competitive. They weren't villains. They were professionals moving fast...and skipping checks they didn't realize they needed. The consequences weren't just legal or financial—they were human. Reputations ruined. Trust lost. Opportunities evaporated.

And the good news? Every one of those disasters was preventable. AI ethics isn't about becoming a moral philosopher overnight. It's about having just enough structure to protect your credibility while you innovate. It's time to meet your new decision-making compass.

THE CARE FRAMEWORK

Responsible AI use doesn't mean slowing everything down or second-guessing every choice. What it does require is a decision-making mindset—one that helps you make confident calls in complex situations, even when the rules are still being written.

The CARE framework isn't just a checklist—it's a filter. A fast, flexible, repeatable lens to help you figure out: "Am I doing this the right way—for my role, my values, and the people this affects?" Let's break it down.

C – Context-Aware

Ask: Does this make sense here?

AI isn't good or bad in itself. It's a tool. Like a hammer. And just like you wouldn't use a hammer to do brain surgery (we hope), you shouldn't drop AI into sensitive tasks without thinking through where and why you're using it.

- ✓ What are the stakes if this goes wrong?
- ✓ Who's affected—and how?
- ✓ Are there industry rules or cultural expectations I need to respect?
- ✓ Is this a space where human nuance matters?

Imagine Kevin, a nonprofit director who uses ChatGPT to draft board reports. In that context? Totally fine. Internal communication, no sensitive data, minimal risk.

But when he starts using the same tool to draft grant applications with embedded donor information—without anonymizing the data or reviewing output carefully—it becomes a problem. One draft includes outdated figures and speculative language that makes it into a live submission. The funder flags the inconsistencies and pauses the funding conversation. Same tool. Different context. Different consequence.

Think of context as your altitude check. The higher the stakes, the clearer your decision-making needs to be.

A – Accountable

Ask: Am I ready to own this outcome?

- ✓ What human oversight did I include?
- ✓ Can I explain the logic behind the output?
- ✓ Would I be comfortable having my name on this...forever?
- ✓ If challenged, could I articulate my decision-making process?

This one's simple but powerful: if this AI-generated work showed up in front of your boss, your board, your client—or, let's be real, went viral for all the wrong reasons—could you explain how it came to be? Could you say, "Here's how I verified the data, why I used AI for this task, and what I did to double-check the results"?

Consider this scenario: A high school principal uses AI to draft a sensitive parent newsletter about school policy changes. The tool does a great job making the message clear, even empathetic. But she knows the issue (student surveillance tech) is loaded. So before sending, she asks two colleagues—one tech specialist, one parent rep—to read it.

They help her adjust the tone, add transparency, and clarify what AI had touched. That extra step? It saves her from a district-wide backlash.

Being accountable doesn't mean being perfect. It means being able to say, with clarity and confidence, "I thought this through." You're not just responsible for the task. You're responsible for how the AI shapes the outcome.

R – Respectful

Ask: Who else is affected by this—and have I considered their experience?

Whether you're automating content, generating decisions, or using AI for personalization, respect means thinking about:

- ✓ Direct users: Who's touching this output?
- ✓ Indirectly affected people: Who's affected by decisions downstream?
- ✓ Your profession: Are you raising or lowering the bar?
- ✓ The broader community: What norms are you reinforcing?

This part of the framework might sound "soft," but it's where most AI disasters happen. Not because people meant harm. But because they forgot to zoom out.

Picture a startup founder who uses AI to auto-generate onboarding content for her new marketing team. Time-saving, yes—but she doesn't catch that some of the cultural references in the training materials are U.S.-centric. One staff member—working remotely from Mexico City—is left confused, and feels like the materials weren't made with him in mind. That's a missed opportunity for inclusion—and one that could've been avoided with just a few minutes of reflection.

Are you reinforcing bias? Using language that excludes? Automating something that deserves a human touch? Respect is your empathy engine. It brings humanity into the loop.

E – Explainable

Ask: Could I teach someone else to make this call the way I just did?

Explainability builds credibility. If your process is invisible—even to you—that's a red flag. Checklist for explainability:

- ✓ What steps did I take to check the AI's work?
- ✓ What assumptions did I rely on?
- ✓ Where did I intervene, revise, or reject AI suggestions?
- ✓ Could someone else replicate this process with confidence?

Let's be clear: this isn't about creating a 47-page documentation spreadsheet. (Unless you love that sort of thing. No judgment.) Explainability means being able to narrate the path you took. Think of it as ethical GPS. If someone asked, "How did we end up here?"—could you replay the route?

Consider an educator—an edtech coach named Marcy—who uses AI to help generate quiz questions for her high school science class. Some of the questions are spot on. Others...not so much. A few reference outdated research or phrase answers in ways that could easily trip up students with learning accommodations.

She doesn't scrap the tool. Instead, she adds a short verification checklist and explains to her team how she reviews the questions before publishing. Not only does her team adopt the process, but they also trust her more because she was transparent.

WHY CARE MATTERS
(Even When Nobody's Watching)

The biggest AI risks often don't come from villainous actors or deliberate bad faith. They come from smart people moving fast. The CARE framework slows the decision down just enough to make it smart, not sloppy. It gives you room to assess—not obsess. It's the mindset that separates AI professionals from AI dabblers. And it's the foundation for becoming someone your team (and industry) trusts with tomorrow's most powerful tools.

Different sectors face unique AI ethics challenges.

Here's how to adapt the CARE framework for specific contexts:

Healthcare. Context: Life-and-death decisions require maximum caution. Accountability: Professional liability and patient safety paramount. Respect: Patient autonomy and informed consent essential. Explainability: Medical decisions must be defensible to peers and patients.

Education. Context: Student learning and development at stake. Accountability: Professional standards and institutional policies. Respect: Student growth, academic integrity, and equal opportunity. Explainability: Transparent to students, parents, and administrators.

Legal. Context: Justice system integrity and client representation. Accountability: Professional responsibility rules and client duties. Respect: Due process, client confidentiality, and legal integrity. Explainability: Court requirements and professional standards.

Creative Industries. Context: Originality, artistic integrity, and cultural impact. Accountability: Copyright law and professional reputation. Respect: Other creators' rights and audience expectations. Explainability: Client relationships and artistic community standards.

Financial Services. Context: Client financial wellbeing and regulatory compliance. Accountability: Fiduciary duty and professional licensing. Respect: Client interests and market integrity. Explainability: Regulatory requirements and client relationships.

JUDGE: Human Oversight That Makes the Difference

That's right, we're going to cover the JUDGE framework again – for those of you who skipped right over prompting and dropped in here with ethics. Let's talk about why your brain is still the most important tech in the room. And that doesn't mean you have to have advanced knowledge of training algorithms or JSON or even have a Github account. To be successful using AI, – more than anything—is judgment. Good, human, real-world judgment.

You can't outsource wisdom to an algorithm. You are not just a prompt writer. You are the pilot. The director. The final filter. The JUDGE principle is here to help you own that role.

Let's unpack what it means—not in theory, but in practice, where real decisions get made, real people get affected, and real reputations are on the line.

JUDGE In action

J – Judgment You are the expert. Not the AI. Not the tool. You. Your life experience, your ethics, your professional standards—those are your superpowers.
You get to decide when AI adds value... and when it needs a human override.

U – Underpins Everything comes back to your role as the decision-maker. Whether you're an executive, educator, consultant, or creator, your human insight is the bedrock that keeps everything aligned.

D – Decisions AI doesn't make decisions. It generates options. You make decisions. And sometimes the hardest part is choosing what not to automate.

G – Guidance Envision AI as a skilled novice with incredible potential: alternately razor-sharp and completely off-base. You're required to coach it. Direct its focus. Model what success means in your unique environment.

E – Evaluation AI isn't fire-and-forget. Your job doesn't end when the prompt ends. Every AI-assisted result needs an evaluation step. Not a full audit every time—but enough review to catch what the tool can't see.

When JUDGE Oversight Isn't Optional

Let's talk about when your human judgment isn't just helpful—it's mission critical.

Strategic Decisions. AI can give you options. But it doesn't understand the politics, priorities, or trade-offs unique to your organization. That's your job.

Example: Picture a nonprofit ED asking ChatGPT to generate a donor segmentation strategy. The tool suggests slicing by donation size—but forgets the nuance of long-term engagement, board politics, or major giving cycles. You know those nuances. AI doesn't.

External Communications. AI might write with flawless grammar, but it has no emotional memory. It doesn't remember that a client was frustrated last month or that a policy issue is still raw for your community.

Example: Imagine using AI to draft a public statement after a controversial event. The language is polished—but tone-deaf. You bring in a trusted colleague, rework the message, and avoid a PR disaster. Human sensitivity matters.

People-Impacting Choices Any time a decision affects someone's opportunity, access, or identity, pause. Breathe. Apply judgment. **Example:** Picture an instructional designer using AI to auto-generate assessment questions. The tool favors Western cultural references. A student from a different background misses key points—not from lack of knowledge, but from lack of cultural alignment.

Professional Standards. AI is great at speed. But speed without standards? That's how trust erodes. **Example:** Consider a journalist who uses AI to help write background pieces. One goes live with a misquote that was never verified. The credibility hit isn't just personal—it undermines the publication.

Your field has standards. You are the guardian of them.

A REAL-WORLD WALKTHROUGH

Marketing With Care + Judge

Let's walk through Sarah—the marketing manager who needs to create a campaign targeting parents of teenagers. High stakes, emotionally sensitive. Here's how she applies CARE and JUDGE in practice:

Step 1: Context-Aware This isn't a typical product pitch. The campaign will influence how parents view their kids' behavior—and potentially themselves. That's emotional terrain. Sarah's AI Task: Brainstorm campaign themes and emotional hooks. JUDGE Checkpoint: She filters out anything that preys on parental fear or guilt. She adjusts tone to feel empowering, not alarmist.

Step 2: Accountable Sarah asks herself: "Would I be proud to present this to a parent advocacy group?" Her move: She reviews and documents her verification steps. She makes sure every AI-assisted idea aligns with brand ethics and family values.

Step 3: Respectful She checks the language for bias, stereotypes, or assumptions about parenting styles. Her move: She consults a teen development specialist to ensure the campaign doesn't inadvertently shame or oversimplify teen behavior.

Step 4: Explainable Sarah whips up a little "behind the magic" explainer for her team that breaks down what the AI cranked out, what she fixed, and how her actual human brain saved the day. But here's her brilliant move - she drops this whole transparency bomb right into the campaign proposal itself, basically turning "we used AI responsibly" into a selling point.

Final JUDGE Moment: Sarah reviews the campaign through four lenses: Would I be proud of this as a parent? Would I defend it to a regulator? Would I explain it to a teen? Would I stand behind it as a professional? She can answer "yes" to all four. That's the power of CARE + JUDGE in action.

JUDGE Isn't About Perfection. It's About Ownership.

There's a myth in AI adoption that keeps people frozen: "What if I get it wrong?" Spoiler alert: *you will sometimes.* We all will. AI is moving too fast, and human systems are too messy for perfection to be the goal. The goal is something better: clear, confident, credible decision-making. CARE gives you a way to ask smart questions. JUDGE reminds you that you're still the adult in the room. Together, they let you move fast and stay smart.

SYSTEMATIC SAFEGUARDS

Build the Net Before You Walk the Tightrope

There's something comforting about setting the coffee pot on a timer, or checking that the doors are locked before bed. These are tiny acts of foresight. Routines we don't always notice until we skip them—and then, suddenly, we do. Responsible AI use works the same way. When things go right, it's invisible. When things go wrong, the absence of a safeguard becomes a spotlight.

One of my favorite questions to ask professionals—and increasingly, students, parents, and creatives—is this: "What would it take for you to trust the next decision you make with AI?" Most people don't say, "I want the perfect algorithm." They say something like, "I just want to know I didn't miss something obvious." That instinct—to protect the future with simple, thoughtful steps—is the entire point of this chapter.

Picture this scenario: A well-meaning principal uses AI to draft an email to parents about changes to the district's lunch policy. It's intended to be a clear and empathetic message about allergy accommodations, but the AI-generated language includes phrasing like "cost-cutting" and "streamlining," which parents read as code for "your child's health is less important than our budget." The backlash is immediate—and intense. She hadn't meant to be dismissive; she just hadn't noticed what the AI had inserted. If a second set of eyes—or even a short checklist—had been part of her process, the message would have landed with clarity instead of controversy.

This is what I mean by systematic safeguards: routines that make "doing it right" the easiest, most natural thing in the world. Not because we expect mistakes, but because we're smart enough to know they're possible.

The Two-Pass Process (or: Why You Should Never Trust the First Draft)

Let me take you inside a process that has become second nature. Whether someone is writing a client-facing report or drafting educational content, they almost always start by generating a draft using one of their AI tools. The first pass is about flow, not perfection. They're letting the AI help them think. But once that's done, they make a conscious switch: they reread the output not as its creator, but as its critic.

And here's where the magic happens.

They'll often ask the AI: "Now review this for factual errors, tone misalignment, or anything that would be ethically questionable." Sometimes it catches things they didn't notice. Other times, it gives them bad advice—and that tells them where to dig deeper.

This habit—creating with one mindset, then reviewing with another—has saved countless professionals from publishing incorrect citations, unintentionally biased language, and more than one emotionally tone-deaf metaphor. It takes five minutes. Maybe ten. But it transforms the final product from "good enough" to credible, clear, and trustworthy.

You wouldn't publish the first photo you take on your phone without checking the lighting. Why would you release the first thing your AI gives you without checking the thinking?

What's at Stake? Look at the Room You're In.

Let's shift gears and talk about how to choose how much review is needed. Because the truth is, not everything needs a three-hour audit. The note you generate for your own morning journaling session probably doesn't need a legal disclaimer. But if that journaling prompt becomes part of a mental health course you're developing for teens, the stakes change. The audience changes. And so should your process. This isn't just a business principle. It's a life one.

Picture Rachel, a parenting coach who starts using AI to help her write blog posts about family routines. At first, she just lets the AI run with it. But then she gets an email from a reader: "I loved your post, but the example about screen time sounded like it came from a household with no neurodiverse kids. Any thoughts on that?"

Rachel is stunned. The example the AI had used—a kid earning screen time by completing chores—had come off as tone-deaf to parents of autistic children. Not because it was wrong, but because it ignored a big part of her audience. She hadn't even noticed. Now, she builds a quick review into every post: "Who might this exclude? What assumptions am I making? Is there nuance I'm missing?" That's what a safeguard is: not a punishment. A practice.

MATCHING THE SOLUTION TO THE SITUATION

To keep it practical, here's how to frame the "stakes" of AI use, both personally and professionally: Not everything needs the same level of scrutiny. Match your verification intensity to the stakes involved:

Low stakes is when the output is for you—brainstorming, internal drafts, exploratory content. You're the only one seeing it, and you can make real-time decisions:

- ✓ Basic fact-checking for obvious errors
- ✓ Simple reasonableness test
- ✓ Minimal documentation

Medium stakes is when the output touches other people—client emails, classroom materials, content others will trust as accurate. You don't need a three-hour process, but you do need a thoughtful review: Does this sound like me? Is the tone appropriate? Are the claims accurate?:

- ✓ Two-pass verification process
- ✓ Source verification for key claims
- ✓ Documented review process
- ✓ Clear disclosure of AI assistance where appropriate

High stakes is when the output could have real consequences—financial recommendations, public health messaging, legal guidance, or communication in moments of crisis. Here, safeguards become non-negotiable. Multi-step human review, documentation of your process, and wherever possible, the involvement of an expert—not to question your judgment, but to complement it:

- ✓ Multiple human reviews
- ✓ Expert validation
- ✓ Comprehensive source verification
- ✓ Detailed documentation of decision process
- ✓ Clear protocols for AI limitations

The Checklist Ritual (A Lifesaver in Disguise)

Checklists are incredibly valuable—not because they're bureaucratic, but because in moments of pressure, they save your brain from forgetting something obvious. Here's one that works regularly, whether reviewing an article or a workshop outline:

- ✓ Did the AI introduce claims I haven't verified?
- ✓ Am I assuming this information is true just because it sounds right?
- ✓ Who might feel left out or misrepresented in this narrative?
- ✓ What context is missing that a human would need to make a good decision?
- ✓ Would I feel proud explaining this process to someone I respect?

These questions don't slow things down. They speed up trust in what's about to be shared. They let you hit "publish" or "send" with confidence—not with fingers crossed.

Choosing the Right Tools (and Asking the Right Questions)

Picture working with a therapist who wants to use AI to draft client worksheets. When asked "Which platform should I use?" the better question is: "Which one explains how it handles your client's data?"

Many professionals dive into AI tools without checking the privacy policy, the opt-out options, or the training disclosures. If you're working with sensitive material—whether it's student data, patient stories, or family photos—you have to understand what the tool is doing behind the curtain.

The right tools aren't just about features. They're about values. Choose platforms that make their privacy policies transparent, that give you control over what's stored, and that tell you—not just sell you—their limitations. Because when you know how the tool works, you can use it on purpose.

There's a moment in every AI user's journey where they think, "Can I *really* trust this thing?" Probably not. But you don't have to. You just have to build consistency in your self-checking help you trust *yourself*. Safeguards aren't about becoming paranoid. They're about becoming a pro. The kind of person others rely on—not because you never make mistakes, but because you catch most of them before they cause harm.

It's not glamorous work. It doesn't earn applause. But it's the reason your clients come back. Your team trusts you. Your work makes a difference.

Because what you build quietly—your checklists, your second looks, your curiosity—those are the things that keep your integrity intact when things get fast, loud, or messy. And in a world racing toward faster and faster AI output?

Integrity is the most future-proof system you've got.

BUILDING A CULTURE OF TRUST

What It Means to Lead With AI, Not Just Use It

Picture this moment: You're consulting for a mid-sized education nonprofit, and you've just wrapped a session with the leadership team on integrating AI into their curriculum planning. One of the program directors stays behind after the meeting. She leans in and says, "This all makes sense... but how do I get my team to care?"

That moment is telling. Because what she's really asking is this: How do I build a culture where thoughtful, responsible AI use isn't just my priority—it's everyone's? And the answer isn't a policy binder. It's shared ownership. Conversation. Modeling. Trust. Responsible AI use doesn't happen because someone at the top says it should. It happens when the people in the room feel like they're part of the conversation. When they understand the why, not just the how.

So let's talk about what it looks like to build AI-savvy, ethically grounded teams—without killing curiosity, speed, or innovation.

Step One: Normalize the Conversation.

Picture a small nonprofit where the development team starts using AI to write donor letters. At first, it's just one person experimenting on the side. Then another. Then the marketing lead jumps in. But no one is talking about it. Eventually, a major donor emails to say, "This letter didn't sound like you." That triggers a flurry of behind-the-scenes apologies and awkward justifications.

Now imagine this scenario: what if that team had simply had a standing meeting every quarter to talk about "How we're using AI"? A space to share tools, flag concerns, and set basic norms together?

Transparency doesn't slow you down. It creates alignment. Here are a few questions to start those conversations:

- ✓ What AI tools are we using regularly—and why?
- ✓ Are there tasks we've quietly automated without discussion?
- ✓ Where should human review be non-negotiable?
- ✓ Who's responsible if an AI-generated error causes confusion or harm?

These conversations aren't about enforcing control. They're about building shared clarity. The kind that prevents surprises, protects your brand voice, and makes your team feel smarter—not smaller.

Step Two: Give People Something to Say "Yes" To.

One of the biggest mistakes in AI policy creation is the "no list." No generating resumes. No using AI for analysis. No automating outreach. While there are valid boundaries (especially in education, healthcare, and law), the best cultures don't just say what you can't do—they show you what great looks like.

Picture a private high school in Colorado, where a teacher named Alex creates a simple poster with his students:

- ✓ AI use is welcome in idea generation
- ✓ AI must be cited if it contributes to an assignment
- ✓ Human judgment is always the final step

He doesn't write that policy for them. He writes it with them.

Now his students use AI to brainstorm science fair topics, outline essays, and analyze practice test results—but they're always part of the process. They're not outsourcing learning. They're enhancing it. And because the expectation is clear, no one feels like they're "cheating" when they use the tools thoughtfully.

This same approach works for teams. Instead of listing prohibitions, ask: • What's an example of responsible AI use we can point to? • What templates, checklists, or tools do we want to co-create? • How will we know if something feels off—and what's our plan to address it? People don't need perfect guardrails. They need clear lanes.

Step Three: Talk to Clients & Customers Like They're on Your Team (Because They Are).

Picture a solo consultant who uses ChatGPT to help write client proposals. The tool helps him save hours—until one day, a client asks, "Did you write this?" And he freezes. Not because he'd done anything wrong, but because he wasn't sure what counted as "writing" anymore. Here's a useful rule:

If the use of AI meaningfully shaped the product, disclose it in a way that builds trust.

You don't have to give a transcript of every prompt you typed. But if you're delivering work someone will act on, buy into, or share with others, they deserve to know that a machine was part of its creation—and more importantly, that you reviewed, verified, and stand behind it. Here's an example you can adapt:

> *"We use AI tools as part of our creative and analysis process. Everything you receive is reviewed by a human expert to ensure it meets the quality, accuracy, and tone we're committed to."*

It's not about confessing. It's about transparency. And transparency is a trust accelerator.

Step Four: Plan for When Things Go Wrong (Because They Will).
Consider this very real scenario from a district office: A team of instructional designers had started using AI to help generate lesson content for teachers. One module—about Native American history—included a passage that sounded polished but was historically inaccurate and culturally reductive. A teacher caught it early. The district pulled the lesson, apologized to the class, and reached out to Indigenous community leaders to collaborate on a better version.

It was a hard moment. But because the team had a simple internal "red flag" protocol—catch, report, respond—they avoided a PR nightmare and turned a mistake into a relationship-building opportunity. H When everything goes sideways, your emergency playbook could include:

- ✓ A clear path to report AI-related concerns internally
- ✓ A commitment to notify affected parties quickly and transparently
- ✓ A short list of questions to guide the postmortem: What happened? Why? How can we adjust our tools or process going forward?

Crisis response doesn't start with disaster. It starts with expectation. The expectation that mistakes will be met with honesty and accountability—not denial or panic.

The Real Win? Psychological Safety and Professional Integrity
When teams feel safe saying, "I used AI for this," they're more likely to use it well. When clients know you review everything with care, they trust you more. When students, patients, or partners know you're willing to rethink your process in light of new information, they become part of the learning journey.

This is what responsible AI leadership looks like. It's not about mastering every technical detail. It's about creating an environment where smart, thoughtful decisions are normal, not exceptional.

So whether you're managing a team of fifty, teaching in a classroom of fifteen, or freelancing from your kitchen table—ask yourself: • Where can I model transparency? • Where can I co-create better practices with others? • Where do I need to be clearer—not just about what I expect, but why it matters?

Because the more people you bring into that conversation, the more resilient your work becomes. And in an age of automation, resilience beats speed every time.

RESPONSIBLE AI, UP CLOSE

What It Looks Like in Your World

Because context isn't just important—it's everything. Let's be honest: "responsible AI" sounds like a generic ideal until you apply it to something specific. It's easy to nod along in theory. But what does it look like when you're making decisions that affect students? Patients? Legal clients? Creative collaborators?

That's what this section is about. Not just mapping CARE + JUDGE to industries, but stepping into the shoes of the people doing the work—the nurse practitioner on a tight schedule, the teacher building a lesson before 7am, the graphic designer with a deadline and a copyright clause.

We'll walk through five core sectors—healthcare, education, legal, financial services, and creative work—and explore how responsible AI shifts shape depending on the stakes, standards, and human stories involved.

Healthcare: When Accuracy Isn't Optional

Picture this scenario: A physician assistant named Marisol is preparing a patient summary for a cardiologist consult. She uses an AI tool to summarize lab results and previous notes. It saves her time—twenty minutes she can now spend with another patient. But in the auto-generated summary, a single phrase jumps out: "History of hypertension well-managed with losartan." That's not right. The patient switched to lisinopril two months ago. It's a small detail. But in medicine, small details aren't small at all.

Responsible AI in healthcare means: • Verifying every clinical claim—no exceptions. • Treating AI-generated summaries as a starting point, not a final record. • Never using AI to replace informed consent, diagnosis, or patient communication.

The CARE framework in healthcare means starting with context—is this information being used to inform medical judgment? If so, it must be vetted like any other clinical source. Accountability means documenting that vetting. Respect means considering how AI might overlook cultural, linguistic, or disability-related nuances in a patient's presentation. And explainability? If you can't walk a peer through what the AI contributed and what you corrected, it's not ready for use.

Consider what one nurse practitioner discovered:

"AI can chart faster than I can. But only I can chart what matters."

Education: Where the Stakes Are Human Growth

Let's step into a middle school classroom in Milwaukee. The bell rings. Ms. Thompson is prepping her lesson on the water cycle. She's used AI to help generate an exit ticket—five multiple-choice questions to assess student understanding. One of the questions reads: "Which of the following is not a phase of the water cycle?" The "correct" answer, according to the AI, is "evaporation." She catches it before printing, thankfully. But imagine she hadn't.

In a classroom, one bad AI answer doesn't just risk confusion. It risks reinforcing misinformation. Worse, if students are quietly struggling or in a testing environment, they may never even realize they were misled.

Responsible AI in education means: • Treating students as real people, not just test-takers. • Ensuring AI use supports student agency and inclusion—not just teacher convenience. • Disclosing AI use to parents and administrators when it shapes instruction or feedback.

Picture an elementary art teacher who creates a classroom norm: if a student uses AI to help brainstorm a project, they have to include a one-sentence note explaining how they used it. It creates a natural reflection process and opens powerful conversations about authorship, creativity, and originality. Explainability isn't a burden in education—it's the whole point.

Legal: When Precision Is the Line Between Credibility and Catastrophe

Now let's walk into a small law office in Kansas City. Eric, a junior associate, is helping draft a brief for a workers' compensation case. He uses an AI tool to help him summarize relevant case law. It spits out six precedents that sound perfect—relevant jurisdiction, similar injuries, clean language.

Two of those cases don't exist. They look real. They even have plausible citations. But when his supervising attorney checks the citations manually, she discovers they're AI fabrications—textbook hallucinations.

In law, there's no such thing as "close enough." Responsible AI here isn't just about professional pride—it's about justice, licensing, and sometimes someone's freedom or livelihood. Responsible AI in law includes:

- ✓ Always validating sources with primary legal databases.
- ✓ Never outsourcing case analysis or precedent selection.
- ✓ Documenting exactly how AI was used in research or drafting—and clearly separating it from final legal advice.

Consider how firms integrate AI into their workflow brilliantly—not by replacing legal reasoning, but by speeding up first drafts of memos, generating alternative phrasings for contracts, or simplifying explanations for clients. But every one of those outputs is reviewed by a human attorney. Every one. In court, "I didn't know the AI made it up" isn't a defense. It's a liability.

Financial Services: When Assumptions Cost Real Money

Meet Tasha, a wealth advisor managing retirement portfolios for mid-career professionals. She uses an AI platform to help visualize market trends, summarize portfolio performance, and draft client reports.

One afternoon, the AI summarizes market news and includes this line: "The Fed's decision to raise interest rates has led to immediate market recovery." Except... the Fed didn't raise rates. They held steady. The "recovery" the AI cited was a short-term bump in two isolated sectors.

Tasha catches it and rewrites the section. But she's shaken. That single paragraph—left uncorrected—could have triggered calls, trades, and real emotional reactions from clients nearing retirement. Responsible AI in finance means:

- ✓ Verifying every economic claim against a primary, real-time source.
- ✓ Understanding that AI reflects past data—not market nuance, regulation shifts, or global news interpretation.
- ✓ Never delivering client-facing financial advice based solely on AI output.

CARE in finance means checking whether the context is forward-looking strategy or real-time compliance. Respect means knowing that one inaccurate phrase can erode a client's confidence—not just in your tools, but in you. Picture an advisor who creates a policy where any AI-generated market analysis has to be reviewed by two people: a peer and a compliance officer. Was it slower? Slightly. Did it protect client trust? Absolutely.

Creative Work: When Originality and Ownership Blur

Now we're in a Brooklyn studio apartment. Casey is a freelance illustrator working on a pitch for a children's book series. She uses an AI image generation tool to mock up a few sample pages—mostly as a visual aid for the publisher. The publisher loves the aesthetic. They ask if the AI-generated art will be part of the final product.

Casey hesitates. She's unsure. Some of the images were lightly edited. Others were raw. And a few...well, one looked suspiciously similar to a 1990s European picture book she used to read as a kid. She didn't realize how close it was until someone in her online art group pointed it out. This is the ethical minefield of creative AI.

Ownership. Attribution. Influence. Authorship. It's all suddenly...murky. Responsible AI in creative industries means:

- ✓ Being honest about what's generated, what's referenced, and what's yours.
- ✓ Actively checking for similarity to known works—especially in commercial settings.
- ✓ Ensuring clients understand what they're buying—and how it was created.

Consider a design agency that adds a new line to every contract: "We may use AI tools during the creative process, but all final deliverables are reviewed, verified for originality, and meet industry copyright standards." It's a small line. But it opens big conversations. And those conversations protect both the agency and the artist. Because in creative work, your name is your currency. And transparency is your portfolio.

CARE and JUDGE Flex to Fit the Room You're In

Every field has different thresholds. Different reputational risks. Different definitions of "good enough." But what unites them is the truth that people still matter more than output. Whether you're guiding a legal case, mentoring a student, drafting a treatment plan, or building a brand—AI is just a tool. A powerful one. But the ethics come from you. And the best way to use it responsibly is to make your context part of the conversation.

So here's your question: "What does responsible AI look like in my world—and who do I need to bring into that conversation to get it right?" Because when you ask that, you're not just using AI well. You're leading with it.

Your Next Steps: Move Smart. Stay Human. Lead On.

By now, you've seen the terrain. You've walked through the risk zones, the judgment calls, the frameworks, the real-world stories. You've explored what responsible AI looks like—in theory, in systems, and in the heat of real decisions. But if you're like most professionals—whether they're senior VPs, school leaders, solopreneurs, or creative freelancers—this is the part where the self-doubt creeps in.

"Okay, but can I really do this right?"

"What if I miss something and get it wrong?"

"What if I'm not technical enough to lead this well?"

Let me answer that clearly: You can. And you don't need to be an engineer to do it. Responsible AI isn't about perfection. It's about practice. And the people who will lead this next chapter—ethically, confidently, credibly—are not the ones who never make mistakes. They're the ones who keep showing up with care. You're here. You're paying attention. That already puts you ahead of most.

So let's anchor this moment with something practical. Below, I've outlined your next steps: what you can do this week, this month, and this quarter to make responsible AI use not just a philosophy, but a natural part of your workflow, your leadership, and your legacy.

THIS WEEK: START WITH ONE PRACTICE

Pick something small. This isn't about launching a new policy or writing a manifesto. It's about building one moment of intentionality into how you use AI this week. Here are three simple places to begin:

Use the CARE framework once. Choose one AI-assisted task—an email, a report, a content draft—and pause before you hit "send." Ask: • Does this make sense in this context? • Am I okay owning this outcome? • Who's affected, and have I considered them? • Could I explain how I made this decision?

Run a Two-Pass Review. Create something with AI. Then shift gears. Critique it. Ask, "What would a skeptical expert challenge here?" Even five minutes of reflection can prevent a credibility slip that takes weeks to fix.

Talk about it. Share your AI use with one colleague, student, client, or friend. Not to impress—but to normalize transparency. Ask them how they're using AI. Start a real conversation. Small actions teach your brain—and your team—what "thoughtful" looks like.

THIS MONTH: BUILD A REPEATABLE SYSTEM

Now that you've practiced, it's time to formalize. Not in a rigid way—but in a way that lets good choices become your default.

Here's a practical illustration:

Create a verification checklist for your three most common AI use cases. If you're a teacher, that might be lesson planning, quiz generation, and parent communication. If you're a consultant, maybe it's reporting, pitch decks, and client emails. For each one, write a quick "pre-flight" checklist—2–5 questions to catch bias, tone issues, or factual errors.

Audit one AI tool you rely on. Read the privacy policy. Look at the data sharing defaults. Check for transparency about model limitations. Don't assume safety—verify it. Choose tools that earn your trust, not just your clicks.

Have a transparency conversation with clients or stakeholders. Let them know how (and why) you use AI. Invite their questions. Offer them opt-outs if it makes sense. You don't need legalese. Just clarity and confidence.

Because "I never thought to ask" is how reputational damage starts. "We talked about it early" is how trust begins.

THIS QUARTER: STRENGTHEN YOUR TEAM AND PLAN FOR THE UNEXPECTED

If you're in a position to influence others—whether that's five employees, a classroom, a board of directors, or your own creative team—this is the time to build culture.

Co-create team guidelines. Don't hand down policies like commandments. Invite your team into the process. Ask: • What's working? • Where do we feel uneasy? • What norms will help us move fast and stay smart? You'll get more buy-in, and better ideas than you'd generate alone.

Create a lightweight crisis response plan. It doesn't need to be fancy. Just make sure everyone knows: • How to flag an AI-related issue • Who to notify • What steps to take (pause use, notify stakeholders, review what went wrong) You don't need a problem to justify having a plan. That's the whole point.

Reflect on what's changed. AI is moving fast—but so are you. Take 30 minutes to review: • What risks did I avoid this quarter? • What wins did AI help accelerate? • Where did my values show up in my process? Write it down. Share it with your team if you have one. Keep that insight close.

Because leadership isn't measured by how many tools you use. It's measured by how well you think when no one's watching.

Your Work Matters More Than Ever

The more AI expands, the easier it is to feel like we're being replaced. But the people who will thrive in this new era aren't the ones who compete with machines. They're the ones who collaborate wisely with them. Who stay grounded in human judgment, emotional intelligence, and ethical clarity—no matter how impressive the technology gets.

That's you.

You don't have to be perfect. You just have to be present. Intentional. Willing to slow down, ask better questions, and build the best path that aligns with your values. Because AI might be writing faster, analyzing deeper, or simulating more than ever before.

But it can't care.

It can't take responsibility.

It can't lead with empathy.

Only you can do that.

And in a world that's moving at machine speed, the most powerful thing you can do is show up human—every time. But awareness isn't the destination. It's the launchpad. You've built your ethical foundation. You've mapped your mindset, tools, and processes. Now it's time to move into the most exciting—and often the most overlooked—stage of the journey: Manifest.

This next chapter is where strategy becomes action. Where AI isn't just an idea, but a force for meaningful, measurable change in your workflows, your goals, and your everyday decisions. It's where you learn to bring AI-powered solutions into your life and work—not just responsibly, but boldly and effectively.

Because knowing how to use AI ethically is important.
But knowing how to use it powerfully? That's what makes it yours.

Let's make it real.

Bonus Guide: Building Organizational Capabilities

Individual responsible AI use is important, but organizational capabilities create lasting competitive advantage.

The Competitive Edge
Organizations that master responsible AI use gain several advantages:

Speed with safety: They can adopt new AI capabilities quickly because they have frameworks for managing risk

Stakeholder trust: Clients, partners, and employees trust them to use AI responsibly

Innovation space: They can experiment with cutting-edge applications because they have safeguards in place

Talent attraction: Top professionals want to work for organizations that take AI ethics seriously

Regulatory resilience: They're prepared for evolving regulations because they've built good practices from the start

Team-Level Implementation

Establish clear policies: What AI use is encouraged, required approval, or prohibited?

Create review processes: How will high-stakes AI use be validated?

Build expertise: Who becomes your organization's AI ethics resource?

Foster culture: How do you encourage responsible innovation rather than reckless adoption?

Organizational Risk Management

Assessment frameworks: Regular evaluation of AI use across the organization

Training programs: Ensuring everyone understands both opportunities and responsibilities

Incident response: What happens when AI use goes wrong?

Continuous improvement: How do you learn from mistakes and evolve practices?

Companies that implement thoughtful AI safeguards aren't just protecting themselves from downside risk—they're positioning themselves for sustainable competitive advantage. While their competitors are either avoiding AI entirely or using it recklessly, they're building systematic capabilities that let them move fast while staying smart.

Subject-Specific Checklists

Different types of content carry different risks. Build verification checklists for your most common AI-assisted tasks:

For financial content:

- All figures verified with authoritative external sources
- Risk disclosures included where appropriate
- No specific investment advice without proper disclaimers
- Compliance with relevant regulations checked

For educational content:

- Historical facts and dates verified
- Scientific claims checked against peer-reviewed sources
- Age-appropriate language and concepts confirmed
- Learning objectives clearly met

For healthcare-related content:

- Medical facts verified with authoritative sources
- Appropriate disclaimers about not replacing professional medical advice
- Potential harm from misinformation considered
- Regulatory compliance confirmed

For creative work:

- Originality verified (no unintentional copying)
- Copyright considerations addressed
- Attribution handled appropriately
- Client expectations about AI use clarified

For legal work:

- All case citations verified as real and relevant
- Jurisdictional accuracy confirmed
- Current law reflected
- Professional responsibility rules followed

The Verification Checklist

Build a systematic approach to checking AI outputs:

1. **Immediate review:** Does this make basic sense?
2. **Fact verification:** Are the key claims accurate?
3. **Source validation:** Are references real and relevant?
4. **Bias check:** Are there obvious prejudices or blind spots?
5. **Stakeholder consideration:** Who might be affected, and how?
6. **Professional standards:** Does this meet the quality expected in my field?
7. **Disclosure decision:** Should others know about my AI assistance?

Documentation That Protects You

Keep simple records of your verification process—not for bureaucracy, but for protection. When someone asks "How did you reach this conclusion?" you want to be able to show a thoughtful process.

What to Document

For routine AI use:

- What tools you used for what purposes
- What level of verification you applied
- Any significant concerns or limitations identified

For high-stakes decisions:

- What sources you verified
- What assumptions you made and why
- Where you chose human judgment over AI suggestions
- What alternative approaches you considered
- What experts you consulted

For collaborative work:

- Who knew about the AI assistance
- What disclosure was provided
- How responsibilities were divided
- What review processes were followed

Simple AI Use Verification Log

Use this template to document everyday AI use for transparency and accountability.

Date of AI Use:

Purpose of AI Use:
☐ Brainstorming
☐ Drafting
☐ Data Analysis
☐ Research
☐ Other: ___________________________

Verification Level Applied:
☐ Low Stakes (internal use only)
☐ Medium Stakes (shared with team or clients)
☐ High Stakes (external or public impact)

Key Sources Checked for Accuracy or Validation:

- ______________________________
- ______________________________
- ______________________________

Points Where Human Judgment Was Applied:

- ______________________________
- ______________________________
- ______________________________

Concerns or Limitations Noted (if any):

- ______________________________
- ______________________________

Detailed AI-Supported Decision Record

Use this template for high-impact decisions supported by AI tools.

Problem or Question Being Addressed:

AI Tools and Prompts Used:

- Tool(s): ________________________________
- Prompt(s): ____

Verification and Validation Steps Taken:

- Source comparisons? ☐ Yes ☐ No
- Fact-checking completed? ☐ Yes ☐ No
- Additional methods used: ______________________________

Experts or Stakeholders Consulted (if applicable):

- Name/Role: ___________________________
- Insights or Contributions: ______________________________

Alternative Approaches or Options Considered:

- Option 1: __________________________________
- Option 2: __________________________________
- Reason(s) for selecting the final approach: _______________

Final Decision and Rationale:

Disclosure Provided To (team, client, public):

☐ Yes – Method and sources shared

☐ No – Reason: ________________________________

8. Learning Lab

💡 Try This: CARE Quick-Fire Audit

Objective: Apply the CARE framework under time pressure to build intuitive ethical reflexes before using AI for real work.

Time Required: 10–15 minutes

Materials Needed:

- One current or upcoming AI-assisted task
- Notebook, template, or digital doc
- CARE framework (for reference)

Steps:

1. **Pick a live task** you'll work on this week (e.g., generating marketing copy, internal memo, client summary).
2. **Set a 10-minute timer.**
3. **Answer each CARE question** in 2–3 sentences:
   - Context: What is this for, and who is affected?
   - Accuracy: What assumptions or claims need checking?
   - Responsibility: Who owns the outcome?
   - Explainability: Would I be comfortable explaining this to my client/team?
4. **Highlight weak responses**—any that feel vague or hedged.
5. **Add a concrete action** to strengthen each weak point (e.g., "Run a bias scan," "Link to original data").
6. **Save your audit** to revisit after completing the task and assess how well you followed through.

Success Metric: Your follow-up review should show improved foresight and reduced ethical ambiguity in your AI use.

💡 Try This: Two-Pass Reality Check Drill

Objective: Experience the value of layered review by catching errors, omissions, or bias that may slip through on first pass.

Time Required: 20–25 minutes

Materials Needed:

- AI tool(s) of choice
- A topic or task you regularly publish/share externally
- Optional: alternate AI model for comparison

Steps:

1. **Pass One – First Draft**
    - Prompt your AI to write a 250-word LinkedIn post (or similar task).
    - Save the result without editing.
2. **Pass Two – Critique & Verify**
    - Prompt the same or another model:
      "Act as a devil's advocate. Critique this for inaccuracy, bias, and missing citations."
    - Manually fact-check one concrete claim or stat.
3. **Post-Mortem (5 minutes)**
    - List all issues or gaps the second pass surfaced.
    - Count how many of those you would have missed.
    - Label each one as a **save** (real error) or **false alarm** (nitpicky or stylistic).

Success Metric: Your second pass should uncover at least one substantive issue the first draft missed—demonstrating the necessity of layered validation.

Try This: Build-Your-Own Verification Checklist

Objective: Create a reusable checklist to catch ethical and factual issues specific to your domain and content type.

Time Required: 25–30 minutes upfront; 3 minutes per use

Materials Needed:

- Notebook, template, or doc
- Familiar content type (e.g., newsletter, investor memo, white paper)
- CARE framework reference

Steps:

1. **Pick one recurring content type** you create using AI.
2. **Copy this skeleton into a blank document:**
   [Content Type] Verification Checklist
   - ☐ Data points cross-checked against __________
   - ☐ Claims align with documented capabilities? Y / N
   - ☐ Tone & audience fit confirmed by __________
   - ☐ Disclaimers needed? Where?
   - ☐ CARE red-flags? (C) (A) (R) (E)
   - ☐ Judgment escalation required? (Yes → route to ________)
3. **Customize each blank** with the actual sources, tools, or people you use.
4. **Trial your checklist** on your next AI-assisted draft.
5. **Revise** until it can be completed in under 3 minutes.

Success Metric: You've created a checklist that improves content reliability and ethical clarity—without slowing your workflow.

💡 Try This: JUDGE Roundtable Scenario

Objective: Apply the full JUDGE framework collaboratively (or solo) to practice resolving ethically ambiguous or high-stakes AI scenarios.

Time Required: 45–60 minutes

Materials Needed:

- 2–4 colleagues (or a solo journaling setup)
- JUDGE framework reference
- One scenario involving AI recommendations (real or hypothetical)

Steps:

1. **Choose a gray-area scenario.** Examples: AI-generated hiring shortlist, public health messaging, internal policy generation.
2. **Walk through the JUDGE steps:**
   J – Judgment: What hinges on human values or interpretation?
   U – Underpins: What assumptions and data does this decision rely on?
   D – Decision: What would the AI recommend?
   G – Guidance: What additional inputs (human, policy, lived experience) should inform our approach?
   E – Evaluation: Define success metrics and document rationale.
3. **Debrief as a group (or journal):**
   - Where did your judgment diverge from the AI's?
   - Which biases crept in (automation bias, groupthink, deferral to authority)?
   - What safeguards or escalation steps might be necessary?

Success Metric: Your team or notes should reflect one key insight about where human intelligence must override or refine AI logic.

💡 Try This: Risk-Tier Mapping & Escalation Plan

Objective: Match the level of oversight to the stakes of your AI-assisted tasks—and avoid over- or under-trusting the tech.

Time Required: 30–40 minutes (plus quarterly updates)

Materials Needed:

- Large paper or spreadsheet
- List of 10–15 recurring tasks
- Wall space or pinboard (optional)

Steps:

1. **Draw three columns:**
   - Low Risk | Medium Risk | High Risk
2. **Sort at least 5 tasks into each tier.**
   - Examples:
     - Low: Brainstorming ideas, draft social posts
     - Medium: Client-facing materials, executive summaries
     - High: Regulatory filings, legal docs, public health info
3. **Define minimum safeguards per tier:**
   - **Low**: Spot check + context statement
   - **Medium**: Two-Pass Review + CARE Audit
   - **High**: Peer/legal review + Full documentation trail
4. **Add Escalation Triggers:**
   - Examples:
     - "Circulation > 500 people" → Medium
     - "Includes legal or medical advice" → High
5. **Pin this map near your workspace.**
   - Revisit every quarter to adjust based on evolving projects or risk exposure.

Success Metric:
You can now immediately assign a review protocol based on a task's tier—saving time, avoiding overkill, and improving accountability.

9. Manifest – Bringing AI Ideas to Life

Rebecca stared at her screen like someone who'd just been handed the keys to a Ferrari—and suddenly realized she'd never learned to drive stick.

After three hours with various AI tools, she had a marketing campaign blueprint that was, frankly, brilliant. The AI had suggested personalizing client outreach through dynamic content, automating follow-ups based on engagement patterns, and creating social media campaigns that could practically read minds. It was the kind of strategic gold that would have taken her team weeks to brainstorm. So why did she feel like she was drowning?

The problem wasn't the ideas—it was the yawning chasm between "brilliant AI suggestion" and "thing that genuinely happens in the real world." Rebecca had fallen into what we call the Implementation Gap, that peculiar modern purgatory where great AI insights go to die.

So far, you've learned to achieve **Clarity**—getting crystal clear on what you want for your ideal AI output before you even choose a tool to use. You've mastered **Alignment**—finding the right tool for the job instead of forcing square pegs into round holes. You've developed **Leverage** skills that blend AI capabilities with your own humanness to craft truly ideal outputs. Now comes what may be the most important part: **Manifest**. It's about bringing those AI outputs into the real world effectively and efficiently.

This is where most people stumble. They collect AI insights like some people collect vintage postcards or those little spoons that end up in a display cabinet on the wall—impressive to look at, but not particularly useful for getting anywhere. They bookmark brilliant strategies, screenshot perfect prompts, and save AI-generated plans with the best of intentions. But somehow, those ideas never quite make it from their digital wishlist into their day-to-day reality.

Manifest is about changing that. It's the art of turning AI-generated possibilities into measurable improvements in your work and life. Not through grand transformations or overnight revolutions, but through smart, strategic implementation that builds momentum without burning you out.

Think of Manifest as your translation layer—the skill that takes abstract AI wisdom and converts it into concrete actions that fit your specific situation, your particular constraints, and your unique definition of success. Because here's the thing: AI can generate a thousand brilliant ideas, but only you can decide which ones deserve to exist in the real world.

The "M" in C.A.L.M. isn't about doing everything the AI suggests. It's about doing the right things well, in the right order, with the right expectations. It's about building a sustainable practice of implementation that grows stronger with each small success rather than collapsing under the weight of ambitious plans. So let's talk about how to make that happen.

The Tyranny of Too Many Good Ideas

If you've ever used AI for anything more complex than writing a grocery list, you've probably been here. You ask ChatGPT to help you set up a "life optimization plan" for the next year (yeah, that's a thing), and suddenly you're staring at a 47-point action plan that would require three additional lifetimes to execute. Or on the other hand, you use an AI tool to analyze your customer data, and it spits out insights so profound you wonder if it's been secretly reading your customers' diaries. The ideas are so good they're paralyzing.

This isn't a problem our grandparents had. They weren't drowning in algorithmically generated wisdom about how to revolutionize their corner grocery store. But here we are, living in an age where artificial intelligence can generate more good ideas before breakfast than most humans have in a month—and somehow that's become its own kind of problem.

Rebecca's mentor had once told her something that seemed almost insultingly simple at the time: "The smallest action beats the grandest intention." Sitting there in her overwhelm, she finally understood what he meant.

Instead of trying to implement her AI's entire strategic masterpiece, Rebecca picked exactly one suggestion: personalizing her monthly client progress reports. Not revolutionizing her entire communication strategy. Not automating everything that moved. Just... better progress reports.

The results weren't just surprising—they were embarrassingly simple. Client response rates jumped 40%. The time she saved on drafting could be reinvested in genuine relationship-building. And perhaps most importantly, she'd proven to herself that she could transform all that AI brilliance gathering digital dust in her browser tabs into something real.

This is the secret that separates AI users who get results from those who just get really good at generating ideas: you have to start somewhere small enough that you can't talk yourself out of it, but specific enough that you'll know if it worked.

When Your Brilliant Plan Meets Stubborn Reality

Let's talk about what nobody wants to admit: sometimes your carefully planned AI implementation crashes and burns in spectacular fashion. Not because AI is terrible or you're incompetent, but because the real world has a sense of humor and enjoys humbling our best-laid plans.

Consider Rebecca's colleague, James, who learned this the hard way when he launched his automated follow-up system. He'd spent weeks getting it just right—perfect timing, professional tone, all the elements the productivity blogs said were essential. He hit "activate" feeling like he'd just solved client communication forever.

Two weeks later, he was fielding complaints. Clients were getting follow-ups at weird times—right after they'd already responded, during their stated vacation weeks, in the middle of crisis situations when the last thing they needed was a cheerful "just checking in!" The emails that were supposed to feel personalized instead felt like they were written by an overly enthusiastic robot who'd never heard of reading the room.

James's first instinct was to scrap the whole thing and go back to manually writing every email. But then he realized something: the problem wasn't that automation couldn't work for his business. The problem was that he'd tried to automate a process he didn't fully understand yet.

The Art of Strategic Retreat

Instead of giving up, James did something smarter: he stepped back without stepping away. He turned off the automation but kept using the AI-generated templates manually. This gave him back control while preserving the time-saving benefits that had drawn him to AI in the first place.

For the next month, he paid attention. When did clients genuinely want to hear from him? What kind of follow-ups got responses versus eye-rolls? Which templates felt natural to send, and which ones made him cringe as he hit send?

The patterns became obvious once he was looking for them. Clients preferred follow-ups on Tuesday mornings, not Friday afternoons. They responded better to emails that referenced their specific challenges rather than generic check-ins. And they definitely didn't need follow-ups during busy seasons that James already knew about from previous years.

Armed with these insights, James gradually reintroduced automation—but smarter this time. He set up rules that prevented follow-ups during known busy periods. He personalized templates with client-specific details. He tested timing carefully and adjusted based on response rates.

Six months later, his follow-up system was running smoothly, getting better response rates than his original manual emails. The failure had taught him things about his clients' preferences that he never would have learned if everything had worked perfectly from day one.

Why "Failure" Is Often Just Incomplete Data

James's story illustrates something important about working with AI: what looks like failure is often just the difference between your assumptions and reality. The automation didn't fail because automation is bad—it failed because James's initial assumptions about timing, personalization, and client preferences were incomplete.

This is genuinely good news. It means that most AI implementation "failures" aren't permanent setbacks—they're learning opportunities disguised as frustrations. More often than not, rejection is just redirection.

When your AI-assisted project doesn't work as expected, resist the urge to either abandon it entirely or double down on the exact same approach. Instead, ask yourself: what is reality trying to teach me that I didn't know when I started?

Maybe your audience prefers shorter content than your AI suggested. Maybe your timing assumptions were wrong. Maybe your success metrics were measuring the wrong things. Maybe your clients have unstated preferences that no AI tool could have predicted but that become obvious once you start paying attention.

The Resilient Approach

The most successful AI implementers share a particular mindset: they treat every attempt as an experiment, not a final exam. When something doesn't work, they don't see it as evidence that they're bad at this or that AI can't help them. They see it as data that will make their next attempt more informed. It is not a verdict on their worth; it's a vessel for genius.

This mindset turns setbacks into advantages. Because while your competitors might give up after their first automated campaign flops or their AI-generated content falls flat, you'll be gathering the insights that let you succeed where others have failed.

The real skill isn't avoiding mistakes—it's getting good at extracting value from them quickly and cheaply. Because in a world where everyone has access to the same AI tools, your competitive advantage isn't having perfect implementations. It's having better recovery strategies and more persistence than the people who quit after their first attempt doesn't go perfectly.

So when your brilliant AI plan meets stubborn reality and loses, don't treat it as a failure. Treat it as tuition paid toward understanding how to make these tools work in your specific situation, with your particular audience, solving your unique challenges.

That education is worth more than any perfectly executed plan you copied from someone else.

YOUR REAL-WORLD AI IMPLEMENTATION STORIES

Let me tell you about five people who figured out how to bridge that implementation gap. Their stories might sound familiar—in fact, one of them might be exactly the nudge you need.

The Meeting Whisperer

Imagine Trevor, who had reached his breaking point with meetings. You know the type—those meandering hour-long affairs where everyone talks in circles and nobody quite remembers what they decided by Thursday. His AI assistant suggested the usual suspects: structured agendas, time-boxing, action item tracking. A whole productivity overhaul that would make a consultant weep with joy.

But Trevor didn't try to revolutionize corporate America, unfortunately for some of us working in corporate America. He just created a simple three-part agenda template: Updates, Decisions Needed, Next Steps. That's it. No bells, no whistles, no acronyms that would require a training session.

The transformation was almost stupid in its simplicity. Those hour-long thought-spirals became focused 40-minute sessions. His team knew what they were walking into each week. And Trevor? He got back roughly six hours a month—time he could spend on work that didn't involve explaining what they'd already explained three meetings ago.

The Storytelling Strategist

Picture Natalie, who ran a small sustainable goods company, and her AI had blessed her with approximately 847 different content ideas. Product spotlights! Behind-the-scenes videos! Customer testimonials! Trend analysis! Educational carousels! She could have launched seventeen different content strategies and still had leftovers.

Instead, she picked one thing: storytelling. Three times a week, she'd use AI to generate story angles about her products, then blend them with her own voice and passion. One day, it was the journey of her eco-friendly packaging from concept to compost bin. Another, the 3 AM brainstorm session that led to her bestselling lip balm.

Within a month, her engagement had doubled. More importantly, she'd found a rhythm she could maintain without hiring a content team or sacrificing her sanity to the algorithm gods.

The Communication Optimizer

Consider Marcus, whose client communications were like a game of email tag played in slow motion. Follow-ups, progress reports, check-ins—all the necessary friction that keeps businesses running but makes you question your life choices around 4 PM on Fridays.

He asked his AI for help and got back a comprehensive client communication overhaul plan that would have impressed McKinsey. Instead of implementing the whole thing, Marcus focused on just his monthly progress reports. He created a dynamic template that pulled in relevant metrics and updates for each client, personalizing what had been painfully generic.

The result? Clients started responding to his emails—not just acknowledging them, but engaging with them. They appreciated the personalized touch so much that several mentioned it in renewal conversations. Sometimes the smallest changes create the biggest ripples.

The Data Decoder

Think about Karen, who was spending every Monday morning in spreadsheet purgatory, manually compiling weekly sales reports that her boss needed but nobody particularly enjoyed creating. When she turned to AI for help, it offered to analyze trends and create digestible summaries—basically promising to be her data analyst for free.

But Karen didn't hand over her entire reporting process on day one. She tested the AI on just regional sales performance, letting it generate insights for one section while she kept control of the rest. The results were not only accurate but genuinely insightful—the kind of analysis that usually required three cups of coffee and a minor existential crisis.

That saved hour gave her something she hadn't had in months: time to think strategically instead of just shuffling numbers around. She eventually automated the full report, but only after proving to herself that the AI could handle the basics without turning her data into digital gibberish.

The Launch Coordinator

Finally, imagine Patricia, for whom product launches always felt like juggling flaming torches while riding a unicycle. Marketing plans, customer lists, deadlines—all the moving pieces that separate successful launches from expensive learning experiences.

Her AI suggested a detailed launch plan that was honestly impressive. It had thought of things she'd forgotten and organized them in ways she hadn't considered. But instead of trying to execute a master plan, Patricia picked one task: drafting the customer announcement email.

She used AI to generate several variations, tweaked them to match her brand's voice, and had a polished email ready in half the time it would have taken her to stare at a blank cursor. The results—higher open rates, more pre-orders—gave her the confidence to tackle the next piece: social media posts.

The Pattern Behind the Stories

Notice what didn't happen in any of these stories: nobody tried to implement everything at once. Nobody created a "digital transformation roadmap" or scheduled a company-wide AI training session. They just picked one small, specific thing and did it well.

The magic isn't in the AI tools—it's in the willingness to start somewhere small enough that you can't talk yourself out of it, but meaningful enough that you'll notice when it works.

THE REALITY BRIDGE: HOW IDEAS TRANSFORM INTO THINGS

So what's the thread connecting all these stories? None of these people were AI wizards or productivity gurus with color-coded calendars and morning routines that would make a life coach weep. They were just ordinary humans who figured out how to stop drowning in good ideas and start swimming with them.

The secret sauce isn't in having the perfect AI tool or the most sophisticated prompts. It's in having a bridge—a way to get from "wow, that's a brilliant suggestion" to "hey, look what I did." Let me show you how to build that bridge for yourself.

Step 1: Choose Your Battle (Wisely)
When you're staring at a list of AI suggestions longer than a pharmacy receipt, your brain will try to convince you that you need to tackle everything at once. Your brain is lying. Your brain is also probably the same part of you that thought you could learn Spanish, take up yoga, and start meal prepping all in the same week.

Instead, you need to become ruthlessly selective. Think of yourself as a bouncer at an exclusive club, and most of these ideas aren't getting past the velvet rope. Here's how to choose your VIP idea.

The Two-Question Filter:

- Will this move the needle on something I care about?
- Can I do this without requiring a highly-specialized team or a minor miracle?

Let's say your AI suggested automated follow-ups, personalized social media ads, and targeted client reports. Quick gut check: automated follow-ups might get you immediate responses (high impact), and you can probably set up a basic template this afternoon (low effort). The social media ads sound impressive but would require you to figure out targeting algorithms, budget allocation, and creative testing—basically a part-time job.

The follow-ups win. Not because they're more important in some cosmic sense, but because they're your best shot at getting something done.

Step 2: Make It Stupidly Specific
Once you've picked your idea, you need to break it down until it's so simple that future-you can't weasel out of it. This is where most people go wrong—they keep their plans vague enough to sound impressive but specific enough to be paralyzing.
Instead of "implement automated follow-ups," try:

- Tomorrow: Use AI to draft one follow-up email template
- Day after tomorrow: Send it to five clients who haven't responded in a week
- End of week: Check if more people responded than usual

Notice how none of these steps require you to understand automation software or become an email marketing expert? That's intentional. You're not trying to build the perfect platforms and processes—you're trying to prove that this idea can work for you.

Step 3: Embrace the Beautiful Messiness of Testing

Here's something nobody tells you about implementation: it's going to be weird the first time. Your first AI-generated email might sound like it was written by a very polite robot. Your initial automation might hiccup. Your metrics might be disappointing.

This is not failure—this is data.

Rebecca's first personalized progress reports were, in her words, "aggressively mediocre." But 30% of her clients responded, which was 30% more than her old generic updates. That wasn't a failure; that was permission to keep going.

Start small, expect imperfection, and pay attention to what happens. Did people respond differently? Did the task take longer or shorter than expected? Did your AI-generated content capture your voice, or did it sound like a corporate press release?

Use those insights to tweak your approach. Maybe the AI needs more context about your brand voice. Maybe your success metric was too ambitious. Maybe you discovered that your clients prefer shorter emails to longer ones.

Step 4: Ride the Wave

Once you've got something working—even if it's just working okay—you've earned the right to expand. But here's the crucial part: build on what's already working instead of starting something entirely new.

If your follow-up emails are getting responses, try applying the same template to thank-you notes. If your personalized progress reports are landing well, experiment with personalizing your project proposals. You're not reinventing the wheel; you're just putting it on different vehicles.

This is how you build momentum without burning out. Each success makes the next step feel less risky and more inevitable.

Step 5: Take a Victory Lap (Then Plan Your Next Move)

After you've gotten your first AI implementation humming along, pause and recognize what you've accomplished. You took an abstract suggestion from an algorithm and turned it into something real that affects real people in the real world. That's not nothing.

Then ask yourself: What did I learn about working with AI? What surprised me? What would I do differently next time?

Maybe you discovered that your AI gives better suggestions when you provide more context. Maybe you realized that you need to budget more time for testing than you initially thought. Maybe you found out that your clients have been waiting for more personalized communication and you just never asked.

These insights are more valuable than any productivity hack or AI prompt library. They're your personal playbook for turning ideas into reality.

THE HUMAN ELEMENT

Why Your Weirdness Is Your Superpower

Here's something that might surprise you: the best AI implementations aren't the ones where humans become more robot-like. They're the ones where AI makes humans more human, where the technology amplifies what makes you distinctly you rather than replacing it.

I know that sounds backwards. You'd think that bringing artificial intelligence into your workflow would make everything more... artificial. More template-y. More corporate-speak-y. More like it was written by someone who's never experienced a Monday morning or spilled coffee on their keyboard.

But when you master this approach: AI manages all the mundane framework tasks—the planning, the structuring, the "where do I go from here" freeze—freeing you to concentrate on the uniquely human elements. The parts that make people care about what you're creating.

The Thing AI Will Never Be Able to Fake- A Reminder of Who You Really Are

Let me paint you a picture: Maria runs a small pottery studio. She started using AI to help with her social media content because, frankly, she'd rather be elbow-deep in clay than trying to come up with Instagram captions. The AI would suggest posts about her process, customer stories, behind-the-scenes glimpses—all perfectly reasonable content that any pottery business might post.

But then Maria would take these suggestions and do something the AI couldn't: she'd remember the woman who cried when she picked up the mug Maria made for her late husband's birthday. She'd recall the frustration of the piece that cracked in the kiln after twenty hours of work, and how that failure led to her breakthrough technique. She'd think about the kid who pressed his nose against her studio window every day after school, watching her work.

Those details—the ones that made her audience *feel* something—came from her memory, her relationships, her accumulated years of caring about what she does. The AI gave her the framework, but Maria gave it a soul.

Where Humans Are Still Irreplaceable (And Always Will Be...in case you skipped that chapter)

The question isn't whether AI can generate content that's technically correct or strategically sound. It absolutely can. The question is whether that content will make someone pause their scrolling, lean forward in their chair, or think "yes, exactly" when they read it.

That response happens in the space between logic and emotion, in the details that reveal character, in the choices that show someone understands not just what you need, but why you need it.

When AI suggests three different approaches for your marketing campaign, it's your judgment that recognizes which one will resonate with the client who mentioned their kids during last week's call. When AI drafts a progress report, it's your memory that adds the line about how the project milestone coincided with the client's company anniversary. When AI generates blog topic ideas, it's your understanding of your audience that knows they're tired of the same old advice and hungry for something that challenges their assumptions.

This isn't about being precious or gatekeeping human creativity. It's about recognizing that your accumulated experience—all those moments of trial and error, connection and misunderstanding, success and spectacular failure—creates a kind of judgment that can't be automated.

The Art of Strategic Humanity in Manifest

Here's how to think about the division of labor between you and your AI tools:

Let AI handle the scaffolding. The structure, the organization, the "what goes where" questions that can eat up hours of your day. AI is fantastic at creating outlines, suggesting formats, and providing that initial push when you're staring at a blank page.

You handle the soul. The personal anecdotes that illustrate your points. The humor that reflects your personality. The details that show you've been paying attention to what matters to your audience.

Take customer communications, for example. AI can draft a perfectly professional apology email—proper structure, appropriate tone, all the right elements. But it's your decision to mention that you've implemented a new quality check specifically because of their feedback, or your acknowledgment that this mistake happened during their busy season when they needed everything to go smoothly.

Those details matter because they demonstrate that you see your customers as humans, not ticket numbers.

Your Authentic Voice Is Your Competitive Advantage

The internet is increasingly full of content that sounds like it was written by a very sophisticated, well-trained robot. Which means that content that sounds like it was written by a specific human—with their particular perspective, sense of humor, and way of seeing the world—stands out more than ever.

Your job isn't to compete with AI on efficiency or comprehensiveness. Your job is to be irreplaceably, authentically you. The person who notices things others miss. Who makes connections that seem obvious in retrospect but weren't obvious to anyone else. Who can take a generic AI suggestion and turn it into something that makes your audience think, "This person gets it."

The Sous Chef in Your Creative Kitchen

Think of it this way: AI is like having a really competent sous chef in your creative kitchen. It's fantastic at the prep work—chopping the metaphorical vegetables, measuring ingredients, keeping track of timing. But you're still the one creating the signature dish that people will remember.

Your sous chef doesn't have opinions about whether the sauce needs more acid or if the seasoning captures the feeling you're going for. It doesn't know that your customers prefer their content with a little more edge, or that this particular client always responds better to data than storytelling. Those decisions—the ones that transform competent work into memorable work—still belong to you.

The magic happens when you stop worrying about what AI might replace and start noticing what it makes possible. When you're not spending three hours wrestling with a blank page or formatting a report, what do you do with that recovered time and mental energy?

The answer, if you're doing this right, is that you get to be more thoughtful, more creative, more strategically human than you were before.

How to Bounce Back Without Bouncing Out

When your AI implementation hits a wall, your brain will offer you two equally unhelpful options: panic and abandon ship, or stubbornly double down on the exact same approach while hoping for different results. Both are tempting. Neither will help.

What works is becoming a detective of your own failure. Not in a self-flagellating way, but in a genuinely curious "huh, that's interesting" way. Because buried in every setback is information you couldn't have gotten any other way.

Start With the Real Problem, Not the Obvious One

Consider the tale of Oliver, whose automated social media posts were getting the engagement equivalent of crickets chirping. His first instinct was to blame the AI. "These posts are terrible," he muttered, already mentally drafting his breakup letter to artificial intelligence.

But when he looked at the data—not just the disappointing numbers, but the patterns within them—he noticed something interesting. The posts weren't terrible across the board. The ones that bombed were the generic industry insights and motivational quotes. But the posts that mentioned his specific projects or included behind-the-scenes details were doing fine.

The problem wasn't that AI couldn't write for his audience. The problem was that he'd been asking it to write like every other business account instead of like his business specifically.

The Power of Ridiculously Small Experiments

Once Oliver understood the real issue, he didn't overhaul his entire content strategy. He made one tiny change: instead of asking the AI to generate posts about "entrepreneurship tips," he started asking it to create posts about "lessons from building a small design agency in Denver."

That specificity made all the difference. The AI still provided the structure and initial ideas, but now those ideas were rooted in Oliver's experience rather than generic business wisdom. His engagement rates didn't just improve—they tripled.

The beauty of small experiments is that they're low-risk and high-learning. If Oliver's tweak had failed, he would have lost maybe an hour of time and learned something valuable about what doesn't work. Since it succeeded, he gained a sustainable content approach and confidence to try bigger changes.

Pay Attention to the Surprises

The most valuable insights often come from results you didn't expect. When Natalie's AI-generated email templates started getting responses, she initially credited the improved personalization. But when she dug deeper, she realized that the real game-changer was the subject lines.

Her old subject lines were professional but boring: "Monthly Project Update" or "Progress Report - May." The AI's suggestions were more specific and curiosity-driving: "The design challenge that changed everything" or "Why we're ahead of schedule (and what it means for June)."

Natalie hadn't even been trying to improve her subject lines—that improvement was an accidental side effect of asking the AI to make her emails more engaging overall. But recognizing that surprise insight led her to experiment with subject lines across all her communications, not just the ones where she was using AI.

Building Your Bounce-Back Muscle

The goal isn't to become someone who never has setbacks. The goal is to become someone who recovers from them faster and extracts more value from them when they happen.

Every time you turn an AI failure into a learning opportunity, you're building pattern recognition that will serve you in future implementations. You start to recognize the difference between "this tool doesn't work for my situation" and "I need to adjust how I'm using this tool." You develop intuition about which variables to test first when something isn't working.

Most importantly, you stop taking AI implementation failures personally. They're not evidence that you're bad at this or that these tools aren't for you. They're just part of the process of figuring out how to make powerful tools work in your specific context, with your particular audience, solving your unique challenges.

The people who succeed with AI aren't the ones who get it right immediately. They're the ones who get comfortable with the iteration cycle—try, observe, adjust, try again. They treat each setback as tuition paid toward mastery rather than evidence of inadequacy.

The Best Teacher: "Failure"

Let me tell you about three people who turned their AI disasters into unexpected wins—not through positive thinking or persistence alone, but by getting curious about what went wrong.

The Authenticity Awakening

Picture Jamie, whose AI-generated social media posts were getting the kind of engagement you'd expect from watching paint dry. The content was technically fine—proper hashtags, decent timing, relevant topics. But something was missing, and her audience could sense it.

Instead of blaming the AI or her audience, Jamie started paying attention to which posts got any response at all. The pattern was clear: anything that felt like it could have been written by any business in her industry got ignored. But the rare posts where she'd added a quick personal story or behind-the-scenes detail? Those got comments.

The fix was embarrassingly simple. She kept using AI for structure and ideas, but added one authentic detail to every post—a client success story, a mistake she'd learned from, something that happened in her office that week. Her engagement tripled, and she finally understood why people kept talking about "authentic content."

The Conversation Revolution

Imagine David, whose AI-generated sales scripts were technically perfect and completely ineffective. Prospects would listen politely, give noncommittal responses, and never call back. The scripts covered all the right points but somehow managed to suck the life out of every conversation.

When David listened to his recorded calls, he realized the problem: he sounded like he was reading a telemarketing script, because essentially, he was. The AI had created thorough, professional talking points that addressed every possible objection—and made him sound like a robot.

His adjustment was counterintuitive: he used the AI scripts as research, not scripts. Before each call, he'd review the AI's suggested talking points, then put them away and have a real conversation. The AI had done the heavy lifting of preparation, but David brought the human connection that closed deals.

The Collaboration Catalyst

Consider Selina, whose team meetings had become exercises in agenda compliance rather than genuine collaboration. Her AI-suggested structure was efficient and well-organized, but her team seemed to be going through the motions rather than engaging.

The breakthrough came when she asked her team directly: "What's not working about our meetings?" The answer surprised her. The structured agenda was great, but it didn't leave room for the kind of spontaneous problem-solving that her team enjoyed and excelled at.

Selina's solution was to hybrid her approach: keep the AI-generated structure for the business portion, but always end with ten minutes of unstructured time for whatever was on people's minds. Those ten minutes often produced the best ideas and strongest team buy-in of the entire meeting.

The Real Framework: Curiosity Over Defensiveness

What these stories share isn't a step-by-step process—it's a mindset. When something didn't work, none of these people got defensive about their AI tools or their implementation skills. They got curious.

They asked questions like: What pattern can I spot in what's working versus what isn't? What assumptions did I make that might be wrong? What would the people affected by this change tell me if I asked them?

Most importantly, they treated their setbacks as information rather than verdicts. A failed automation wasn't evidence that AI couldn't help them—it was data about how to use it better.

Your Next Move

The gap between AI suggestion and real-world success isn't a design flaw—it's where the learning happens. It's where you figure out how to take tools that work for everyone and make them work specifically for you, your audience, your particular way of doing business.

Your competitive advantage isn't having perfect implementations. It's having better recovery strategies and more persistence than the people who quit after their first attempt doesn't go perfectly. While your competitors are either avoiding AI because they're afraid of looking incompetent, or giving up after their first attempt doesn't work perfectly, you're developing the skill that will matter most in the long run—the ability to adapt and improve.

Because the AI landscape is changing so rapidly that everyone's best practices will be obsolete within a year or two. The tools will evolve, new ones will emerge, and the strategies that work today won't work tomorrow. But the meta-skill of experimental resilience—the ability to try things, learn from what happens, and adjust quickly—will always be valuable.

So when your next AI implementation doesn't go according to plan—and it probably won't, at least not entirely—remember that you're not failing at using AI. You're succeeding at learning how to use it better. The question isn't whether you'll hit obstacles. The question is what you'll do when you do.

Rebecca eventually implemented most of her AI-generated ideas, but not all at once and not without course corrections along the way. A year later, her agency had increased client retention by 40% and cut campaign development time in half. Not because she was naturally gifted at AI implementation, but because she got comfortable with the process of trying, adjusting, and trying again.

That comfort with iteration, that willingness to start small and build on what works, that curiosity about what reality is trying to teach you—these aren't just skills for using AI. They're skills for thriving in a world where the only constant is change, where the best strategy is often the one that adapts fastest to new information.

The bridge between brilliant AI suggestion and real-world success isn't built once. It's built every time you decide to try something small, pay attention to what happens, and adjust based on what you learn. Every time you choose curiosity over defensiveness, iteration over perfection, progress over paralysis.

8. Learning Lab

Try This: Build Your Reality Bridge

Objective: Turn one overwhelming AI suggestion into a small, meaningful action you can take right now.

Time: 30–40 minutes

Materials: A saved AI suggestion (or generate one on the spot), a notepad or digital doc

Steps:

1. **Capture the Beast (5 min):** Find the AI suggestion that's been haunting your to-do list—something smart, ambitious, and totally paralyzing. Write it down exactly as the AI gave it to you. No polishing, no simplifying. See the monster in full.
2. **Get Honest About the Why (10 min):** Ask yourself: "If this worked perfectly, how would my day-to-day life actually improve?" Write the answer in real-world terms, like you're explaining it to a friend. This step unlocks motivation and anchors the idea in your reality—not the AI's.
3. **Make It Embarrassingly Small (10 min):** Break the idea down until it feels almost laughably easy. Ask, "What's the smallest version of this I could try today without needing new tools, training, or anyone's approval?" Then go smaller.
4. **Define Your Victory Lap (5 min):** Decide how you'll know this first step "worked." Set a low-stakes, measurable outcome like: "If one client replies with a question, that's a win." Clarity beats ambition here.
5. **Plan Your Comeback (2 min):** If the first step flops, what's your next move? Write down Plan B now, before you need it. This turns potential failure into a data point instead of a dead end.

Why This Works: AI doesn't know your limits, bandwidth, or priorities. You do. This activity puts you back in control by converting suggestion into strategy, overwhelm into action, and pressure into progress.

🕵 Try This: Become a Failure Detective

Objective: Turn any AI flop into your next breakthrough.

Time: 10–15 minutes (do this right after something doesn't work)

Materials: A recent AI implementation attempt, reflection space (notes app, journal, or doc)

Steps:

1. Document What Happened (2 min):
   Don't sugarcoat it. What exactly didn't work? Be precise, not dramatic: "Clients didn't open the email," "Post got 2 likes," "Automation fired at the wrong time."
2. Interrogate Your Assumptions (3 min):
   What did you assume that might not be true? Timing? Tone? Audience preference? Tool capability? Write them out—even if they feel obvious.
3. Spot the Outliers (3 min):
   Did *anything* work better than expected? Even if the overall attempt flopped, find the glimmers of insight. A surprising open rate? An unexpected comment? These are breadcrumbs.
4. Extract the Lesson (3 min):
   Imagine you're teaching someone else: What would you tell them *you learned* from this attempt?
5. Set Your Next Micro-Test (3 min):
   What's the tiniest thing you can try next time based on what you just learned? Keep it small and specific. Example: "Test a curiosity-driven subject line" or "Send email on Tuesday morning instead of Friday."

Why This Works: Most people run from failed attempts. You're going to mine them for gold. Every stumble is a signal—not a stop sign—and this exercise trains your brain to decode that signal faster than your competitors can quit.

📅 Try This: The One-Thing Implementation Sprint

Objective: Build confidence and momentum with one small AI win each week.

Time: 10–15 minutes per week for 4 weeks

Materials: AI tool of choice, habit tracker or blank journal page

Steps:

Week 1 – Start Tiny

Pick one AI-generated suggestion and implement the smallest version of it. Just one. Could be an email subject line, a revised meeting agenda, a personalized follow-up message.

Week 2 – Double Down

Don't start something new. Instead, ask: "What's the logical next step based on last week's win?" Build *on* your success—not *around* it.

Week 3 – Apply Laterally

Take the exact same approach you used in Weeks 1 and 2, and apply it to a different part of your work. You're now pattern-matching and replicating what works.

Week 4 – Teach It

Explain your implementation journey to someone else. This could be a peer, a journal entry, a social post, or even a 2-minute voice memo. The act of teaching cements what you've learned.

Why This Works: Momentum isn't magic—it's movement plus memory. This sprint bypasses the perfection trap and gives you proof that real change is possible in less time than your coffee break.

10. The Empowered AI User

I used to think being "empowered" with AI meant having it do everything for me. Write my emails, organize my calendar, draft my reports—the works. I was basically trying to turn myself into a human supervisor of a very sophisticated autocomplete function.

It took about three months of this approach to realize I'd created a strange new kind of helplessness. Sure, I was getting things done faster, but I'd also become weirdly anxious whenever the AI wasn't available. Worse, I started second-guessing my own instincts about everything from email tone to strategic priorities. I'd accidentally trained myself out of thinking.

Real AI empowerment, it turns out, is almost the opposite of what I'd imagined. It's not about handing over your cognitive keys to a digital chauffeur. It's about becoming a better driver yourself—more skilled, more confident, more capable of navigating complex terrain because you've got the right tools and you know exactly when and how to use them.

The empowered AI user isn't someone who's figured out how to get AI to do their job for them. They're someone who's figured out how to do their job better with AI as a thinking partner.

There's a crucial difference, and it shows up in everything from daily productivity to long-term career trajectory. The difference between enhancement and replacement. Between becoming more capable and becoming more dependent. Between using AI as a tool and being used by it.

How Empowered Users Think Differently

The shift happens gradually, then all at once. You start noticing it in small moments—like when a colleague mentions a complex problem and instead of feeling that familiar knot of "how am I going to figure this out," you think, "okay, let me break this down and see what tools might help." But it's not just about having tools available. It's about having developed the judgment to know which tools are right for which problems, and more importantly, which problems don't need tools at all.

Take Fathia, a marketing manager who spent years drowning in campaign data. Every month, she'd face the same dreaded ritual: pulling numbers from six different platforms, trying to spot patterns, and somehow turning it all into actionable insights for her team. The process usually involved a lot of Excel acrobatics, several late nights, and the nagging worry that she was missing something important.

The old Fathia would have approached this with a mix of determination and dread. She'd block out entire afternoons for data wrangling, knowing she'd emerge hours later with tired eyes and a half-coherent summary that never quite captured the full picture.

Now she approaches it completely differently. But here's her boundary: she doesn't have AI dissect every detail and interpret its importance. That would be the dependency trap I fell into. Instead, she uses AI strategically, almost surgically.

She'll have it clean and standardize data formats—the kind of mind-numbing work that used to eat hours and left her too mentally exhausted for genuine analysis. She'll ask it to spot obvious anomalies or trends she might have missed—not because she can't spot them herself, but because having a second set of eyes (even artificial ones) makes her more confident in her conclusions.

But the interpretation? The strategic implications? The decisions about what to test next? The nuanced understanding of how this data fits into the broader competitive landscape and customer journey? That's all her.

The result isn't just faster monthly reports. Fathia told me she's become more curious about the data, more willing to dig into unexpected patterns, more confident in presenting findings to leadership. She's asking better questions because she has the mental energy to think strategically instead of getting bogged down in data formatting.

The AI handles the tedious parts so she can focus on the thinking parts—and her thinking has gotten sharper because she's doing more of it, not less. She's become a better analyst, not just a more efficient one.

AI doesn't replace your brain. It frees your brain to do what only it can do.

This pattern shows up everywhere once you start looking for it. The consultant who uses AI to research industry trends but applies her own frameworks for strategic analysis. The designer who leverages AI for rapid prototyping but maintains full creative control over the final vision. The project manager who automates status updates but personally handles all stakeholder relationship management.

In each case, the empowered user has made deliberate choices about where AI adds value and where human expertise is irreplaceable. They're not trying to automate everything—they're trying to optimize their cognitive resources for maximum impact.

The Productivity Paradox Solved

Here's something counterintuitive about AI and productivity: the people who get the biggest productivity gains aren't the ones using AI for everything. They're the ones who've figured out exactly what not to use it for.

Kris learned this the hard way. When Kris first started using AI tools seriously, they went a little crazy with automation. AI was drafting their emails, organizing their calendar, summarizing their meetings, even generating their to-do lists. Kris felt incredibly productive—for about two weeks.

The illusion was compelling. Kris's output had definitely increased. They were churning through tasks at a pace that felt superhuman. Their inbox was staying clean, their calendar was optimized, and they were producing more content than ever before.

Then Kris hit a wall. They realized they'd stopped thinking about priorities because AI was setting them. They'd lost touch with the nuances of their client relationships because AI was handling the communications. Kris was productive in the same way a very efficient zombie might be productive—lots of output, not much brain activity.

The wake-up call came during a client call when Kris found themselves unable to answer a basic question about their own recommendations. They'd become so accustomed to AI-generated insights that they'd stopped developing their own understanding of the underlying issues. Kris was presenting conclusions they couldn't defend, using language that sounded like them but didn't represent their thinking.

That's when Kris realized they'd confused activity with productivity, automation with empowerment.

The breakthrough came when Kris started thinking about AI productivity in terms of cognitive load rather than task completion. Instead of asking "what can AI do for me," they started asking "what mental energy am I wasting on things that don't require my brain?"

This reframing changed everything. Instead of trying to automate their entire workflow, Kris became selective about where to apply AI assistance. They started protecting their cognitive resources for the work that required their expertise.

Take email, for example. The old Kris would have had AI draft all their responses. The current Kris uses AI differently: they'll have it pull key information from long email threads, or help them find the right tone for a tricky message, but they write their own responses. The AI handles the information processing (what did they ask for?) so Kris can focus on the relationship management (how do I want to respond?).

The difference is subtle but profound. In the first case, Kris was outsourcing the thinking. In the second case, they were using AI to eliminate friction so they could think more clearly.

The result? Kris spends less time on email overall, but their communication is more thoughtful, more personal, and more effective. AI doesn't make you more productive by doing your work for you. It makes you more productive by helping you do your work better.

Understanding What Feels Like Relief

Here's something nobody tells you about getting good with AI: it doesn't feel like becoming a superhuman productivity machine. It feels more like... relief. Relief that you can focus on the parts of your work that require your brain instead of burning mental energy on tasks that don't.

I talked to a consultant who described it perfectly: "I used to spend so much time on research and data gathering that I barely had energy left for the thinking. Now I can spend most of my time on analysis, strategy, and synthesis—the stuff that adds value. It's not that I'm working faster; I'm working on better problems."

That's what real AI empowerment looks like. Not a person who's figured out how to get AI to do their job, but a person who's figured out how to do their job at a higher level because they've offloaded the right tasks to the right tools.

The empowered AI user isn't trying to become redundant. They're trying to become indispensable by focusing on what makes them irreplaceable: judgment, creativity, strategic thinking, and the ability to navigate complex human dynamics. AI handles the information processing. They handle the wisdom.

This relief manifests in different ways for different people. For some, it's the relief of not having to manually format reports anymore. For others, it's the relief of being able to explore more creative options without the time pressure. For many, it's simply the relief of having enough mental energy left at the end of the day to engage thoughtfully with their families.

The transformation isn't dramatic—it's sustainable. Instead of radical productivity gains that burn out after a few weeks, empowered users experience steady improvements in work quality and personal satisfaction that compound over time.

Balancing Efficiency with Empathy

Miranda had been a nurse for twenty-two years, and she could tell you exactly when healthcare stopped feeling like healthcare and started feeling like data entry. It wasn't one dramatic moment. It was the slow accumulation of electronic health records that never talked to each other, handoff reports that read like grocery lists, and the growing realization that she was spending more time staring at screens than looking into patients' eyes.

The breaking point came on a Tuesday night. Mrs. Chen, a 78-year-old woman recovering from hip surgery, had been asking all evening about when she could see her granddaughter. Miranda knew the family had been discussing visiting hours, but somewhere between the shift change chaos and the scattered notes in three different software, that conversation had been lost. When Miranda finally pieced together the story from various charts and nurse comments, she realized Mrs. Chen had been anxious for hours about something that could have been resolved with a simple phone call.

"I used to remember everything about my patients," Miranda told her husband that night. "Now I can barely remember which room needs what medication."

When the hospital announced they'd be piloting AI tools to "enhance patient care coordination," Miranda's first thought was: Great. Another computer program that promises to solve problems it doesn't understand.

But Mrs. Chen's anxious face kept haunting her. Maybe it was time to stop fighting the future and start working with it.

Miranda started with **Clarity**—naming the real problem. It wasn't that she'd gotten bad at her job—it was that her job had become impossible. Shift handoffs were supposed to take 10 minutes per patient but regularly stretched to 30 minutes of hunting through disconnected systems for critical information. By the time she'd gathered the medical facts, she'd lost track of the human details that made care personal.

Alignment was about finding an AI tool that understood healthcare wasn't just about vital signs. Miranda chose a solution designed specifically for nursing handoffs—one that could synthesize information from multiple sources but also preserve the qualitative observations that matter most.

Leverage transformed how Miranda prepared for each shift. Instead of asking the AI to simply "summarize patient status" (too generic), she crafted prompts like: "Create a handoff summary for Mrs. Chen including current medications, mobility restrictions, pain levels, and any family concerns or patient preferences noted in the last 24 hours."

The AI would generate: "Mrs. Chen, Room 312. Post-op day 3 hip replacement. Current pain level 4/10, managed with prescribed schedule.

Limited mobility, requires assistance to bathroom. Family concern: granddaughter's visit timing—patient has been asking repeatedly. Prefers ice chips over water. Responds well to encouragement during physical therapy."

Manifest was where Miranda added her twenty-two years of nursing intuition. She'd review the AI summary, then add her own observations: "Mrs. Chen seems more anxious today—check in about family visit first thing. She mentioned feeling dizzy yesterday when standing—monitor closely during mobility."

The first time Miranda walked into Mrs. Chen's room armed with this complete picture, something magical happened. "Good morning, Mrs. Chen. I know you've been wondering about when your granddaughter can visit. Let me check with the charge nurse about extending visiting hours today."

Mrs. Chen's face lit up. "You remembered."

The transformation wasn't just about efficiency—though handoff time did decrease by 45%. It was about getting back to why Miranda became a nurse in the first place. When you're not spending mental energy trying to piece together fragmented information, you have a lot more left over for noticing that Mrs. Chen seems anxious, or that Mr. Rodriguez lights up when you ask about his grandson's baseball games.

Three months later, Miranda received her first patient satisfaction comment in years: "My nurse Miranda knew exactly what I needed before I even asked. It felt like she saw me as a person, not just a diagnosis."

Building Sustainable Learning Habits

The worst advice about staying current with AI is to "keep up with everything." I see people trying to follow every AI newsletter, test every new tool, and read every "game-changing" announcement. They burn out within months, overwhelmed by the pace of change and convinced they're falling behind.

From witnessing numerous people wrestle with this dilemma, I've realized: the aim isn't to stay current with AI developments. It's to develop a sustainable approach to learning that helps you get better at the work that matters to you.

The difference is subtle but crucial. Instead of trying to master every AI tool that emerges, you're developing judgment about which developments are worth your attention and which ones you can safely ignore.

The most common mistake people make with AI learning is treating it like software training. They think staying current means learning to use the latest tools, so they spend their time on tutorials and feature updates rather than developing deeper understanding of when and how AI can help with their work.

I know a designer who was exhausting herself trying to stay current with AI image generation tools. Every week brought news of some amazing new capability—better photorealism, new artistic styles, faster rendering. She felt like she had to test everything to stay competitive.

The breakthrough came when she shifted focus from tools to principles. Instead of asking "What can the latest AI image tool do," she started asking "What kinds of visual problems am I trying to solve, and how might AI help with those specific challenges?" This led her to focus deeply on a smaller set of tools that enhanced her creative process, rather than superficially exploring everything new. She became more capable, not less, by learning less.

The key insight was that tool mastery is less valuable than problem-solving mastery. When you understand your core challenges deeply, you can quickly evaluate whether new tools address those challenges. When you're just chasing new tools, you end up with a collection of solutions looking for problems.

Effective AI learning looks different from the frantic "keep up with everything" approach:

Start with Your Problems. Instead of learning AI tools in the abstract, identify specific challenges in your work where AI might help. This gives you a clear framework for evaluating new developments—does this help with problems I face, or is it just interesting in theory?

Focus on Patterns, Not Features. When you do explore new AI capabilities, pay attention to underlying patterns rather than specific features. How does this tool handle context? What kinds of tasks does it excel at versus struggle with? These insights transfer across tools and help you make better decisions about future AI applications.

Develop a Learning Budget. Just like financial budgeting, learning requires conscious allocation of time and attention. Decide how much time you want to spend on AI learning each week—maybe it's an hour, maybe it's fifteen minutes—and stick to it. This prevents the endless scroll through AI updates from consuming your productive time.

Practice Productive Ignorance. This might be the most important skill: learning to deliberately ignore most AI developments. Unless something directly relates to your core work or represents a fundamental shift in AI capabilities, it's probably safe to skip. The fear of missing out on the latest AI tool is usually much worse than missing out.

FIVE STORIES OF C.A.L.M. IN ACTION

Let me show you how the C.A.L.M. framework looks when it's working in the real world. These aren't theoretical examples—they're the messy, human stories of people who figured out how to turn abstract principles into concrete improvements.

The Overwhelmed Event Planner

Kathleen had reached that special kind of panic that comes with organizing a 500-person conference when half your vendors decide to change their requirements three weeks before the event.

She was drowning in a sea of emails, spreadsheets, and conflicting information. The catering company needed final headcounts. The venue wanted updated room layouts. The speakers were asking about A/V requirements. The registration application was sending her reports that might as well have been written in ancient Greek. Meanwhile, her phone kept ringing with questions she couldn't answer because she couldn't find the information fast enough.

Kathleen started with **Clarity**: What did she need to happen? Not "plan a perfect conference" (too vague) but "ensure every vendor has the specific information they need to execute their part without last-minute surprises." The real goal wasn't perfection—it was preventing chaos.

For **Alignment**, Kathleen chose an AI tool designed for project coordination rather than general planning. She needed something that could parse vendor requirements, cross-reference information, and flag potential conflicts—not something that would try to redesign her entire event.

Leverage meant crafting very specific prompts. Instead of "help me organize my conference," she asked: "Review these vendor emails and create a checklist of all outstanding requirements, organized by deadline and dependency." The AI pulled requirements from seventeen different email threads and organized them into a clear action plan with dependencies mapped out.

Manifest was where Kathleen's seven years of event planning experience made the difference. The AI had flagged a potential issue: the A/V company needed room layouts before the catering company could finalize table arrangements, but the venue couldn't provide final layouts until they knew the catering setup. That circular dependency could have killed her timeline.

Kathleen solved it by scheduling a three-way call between all parties to work through the interdependencies together—something the AI couldn't have suggested but that she knew would work from experience.

The conference ran smoothly, but more importantly, Kathleen wasn't a stress-induced zombie by opening day. She'd preserved her mental energy for the human problems that inevitably arise—like when the keynote speaker's flight got delayed and she had to completely reorganize the morning schedule on the fly.

The Struggling Therapist

Leanne loved helping people heal, but she was drowning in treatment plan documentation that left her too exhausted to do her best work with clients. Every session required detailed notes, treatment plan updates, insurance documentation, and progress reports. By the time she'd finished writing about therapy, she barely had energy left for doing therapy. She was spending two hours on paperwork for every hour with clients—a ratio that made her question whether she was still helping people or just feeding bureaucracy.

Clarity helped Leanne distinguish between documentation that served her clinical work and documentation that just satisfied administrative requirements. Her real need wasn't "better paperwork"—it was "preserving mental energy for the therapeutic relationship while meeting professional obligations."

Alignment led her to an AI tool specifically designed for mental health documentation that understood clinical language and therapeutic frameworks. This wasn't general-purpose writing assistance—it was built for people who needed to document progress in ways that both insurance companies and clinical supervisors would accept.

Leverage transformed how Leanne approached session notes. Instead of staring at blank templates after each session, she'd speak her observations into her phone immediately after clients left: "Client showed increased emotional regulation when discussing family conflict. Used grounding techniques successfully during anxiety spike. Homework assignment completed partially—explored barriers."

The AI would transform these verbal notes into properly formatted documentation: "Client demonstrated improved emotional regulation strategies during family-focused discussion, particularly when implementing previously learned grounding techniques during mild anxiety activation. Partial completion of between-session homework provided opportunity to explore implementation barriers and adjust therapeutic approach."

Manifest was where Leanne's clinical judgment remained essential. The AI could format her observations and ensure proper clinical language, but only she could determine whether a client's subtle change in body language indicated progress or concern, or decide when to adjust therapeutic approach based on what wasn't being said.

The result wasn't just time savings—though she did cut documentation time by 60%. Leanne found herself more present during sessions because she wasn't mentally composing notes while clients were talking. She could focus entirely on listening, understanding, and responding therapeutically.

Six months later, Leanne's supervisor noted that her treatment plans had become more detailed and her progress notes more insightful. "It's like you've found a way to capture the nuances of your therapeutic work better," her supervisor observed.

Leanne smiled. "I just stopped letting paperwork steal energy from the actual work."

The Data-Driven Marketing Director

Connor inherited a marketing department with great intuition and terrible measurement. His team could create campaigns that felt right, but nobody could prove what was working or why. When the CEO started asking for "data-driven decision making," Connor realized he needed to transform his approach without destroying his team's creative spirit.

The problem wasn't lack of data—they were drowning in it. Google Analytics, social media metrics, email campaign reports, sales attribution data—they had numbers coming from everywhere, but no coherent story about what any of it meant.

Clarity helped Connor define what "data-driven" realistically meant for his team. Not "make decisions based purely on numbers" but "use data to inform creative decisions and measure what matters for business growth." The goal was enhancing intuition with evidence, not replacing creativity with spreadsheets.

Alignment led Connor to an AI tool that specialized in marketing attribution and could connect data from multiple sources without requiring a data science degree to interpret. He needed something that could spot patterns across channels and campaigns while still allowing for human interpretation of what those patterns meant.

Leverage meant asking the right questions of the data. Instead of "tell me what's working," Connor crafted prompts like: "Analyze the relationship between email open rates, social media engagement, and sales conversions for our last three campaigns. Identify which creative elements correlate with higher conversion rates."

The AI revealed that their most successful campaigns shared three characteristics: they used customer testimonials in the subject lines, included behind-the-scenes content in the body, and were sent on Tuesday mornings. But it also flagged something interesting—campaigns that performed poorly on traditional metrics sometimes generated the highest customer lifetime value.

Manifest was where Connor's marketing experience became crucial. The AI could identify correlations, but only he and his team could understand why Tuesday morning testimonials worked (their audience was small business owners who checked email first thing) and why some "failed" campaigns generated valuable long-term customers (they attracted people who needed more time to make purchasing decisions but became loyal advocates).

This insight led to a complete shift in how they measured success. Instead of optimizing for immediate conversions, they started tracking engagement quality and customer lifetime value. Their campaigns became more sophisticated, targeting different audiences with different success metrics.

A year later, Connor's department had increased customer lifetime value by 35% while maintaining creative campaign quality. More importantly, his team felt empowered rather than constrained by data—they were using numbers to validate their creative instincts rather than replacing them.

The Time-Strapped Small Business Owner

Tim ran a specialty coffee roasting business that had grown beyond his ability to manage everything personally, but not large enough to hire full-time help for every function. He was trying to be the master roaster, customer service representative, inventory manager, marketing director, and bookkeeper all at once.

The breaking point came when he realized he was spending more time managing the business than roasting coffee—the craft that had inspired him to start the company in the first place. His days were consumed by responding to customer emails, tracking inventory, updating the website, and managing social media. By evening, he was too mentally exhausted to focus on developing new roast profiles or improving his existing blends.

Clarity helped Tim distinguish between tasks that required his expertise as a master roaster and tasks that just required competent execution. His real goal wasn't "manage everything myself" but "preserve time and mental energy for the work that only I can do while ensuring customers receive excellent service."

Alignment led Tim to several AI tools: one for customer service that could handle routine inquiries, another for inventory prediction based on sales patterns, and a third for social media content generation. He chose tools that could handle the routine work while escalating complex issues to him.

Leverage meant training the AI on his specific business context. For customer service, he provided examples of how he liked to respond to different types of inquiries—warm and personal, but informative. For inventory, he explained seasonal patterns and special events that affected coffee consumption. For social media, he shared his brand voice and the stories behind different coffee origins.

The AI customer service could handle questions about shipping, brewing instructions, and product recommendations, but escalated complex complaints or special requests to Tim. The inventory program predicted when he'd run low on green beans and suggested reorder quantities based on seasonal trends. The social media tool generated posts about coffee education and brewing tips, which Tim would personalize with stories from his roasting experience.

Manifest was where Tim's coffee expertise remained irreplaceable. The AI could predict that he'd need more Ethiopian beans based on sales trends, but only he could decide which specific farms to source from based on cup quality. The AI could generate educational content about pour-over brewing, but only he could add the personal insights that came from years of experimentation and customer conversations.

Six months later, Tim had returned to spending 60% of his time on roasting and product development, up from 20%. Customer satisfaction scores increased because routine inquiries were handled faster, while complex issues got Tim's full attention. Most importantly, he'd launched three new seasonal blends—the kind of creative work that had made him fall in love with coffee in the first place.

The Burned-Out Project Manager

Dennis managed software projects for a consulting firm, and he was drowning in status meetings, progress reports, and the constant task of translating between technical teams and business stakeholders who seemed to speak entirely different languages.

His days were consumed by meetings where developers would explain complex technical challenges using jargon that made clients' eyes glaze over, followed by other meetings where clients would express concerns in business terms that made developers frustrated. Dennis spent most of his time playing translator, but he wasn't particularly good at it—he'd often leave both sides feeling misunderstood.

Meanwhile, his project timeline tracking was a disaster. He had spreadsheets, Gantt charts, and project management software, but none of them talked to each other. By the time he'd updated all his tracking elements, the project status had changed again.

Clarity helped Dennis identify his core value as a project manager: ensuring that complex technical projects delivered business value on time and budget. The real challenge wasn't managing tasks—it was managing communication and expectations across different types of expertise.

Alignment led Dennis to AI tools that specialized in translation and synthesis rather than just project tracking. He needed something that could take technical status updates and convert them into business-focused summaries, and vice versa.

Leverage meant crafting prompts that bridged different perspectives. When developers submitted technical updates, Dennis would ask the AI: "Translate this technical update into business language, focusing on timeline impact, budget implications, and risk factors." When clients raised concerns, he'd prompt: "Convert this business concern into specific technical requirements and questions for the development team."

For a typical project update, the AI would take developer input like "Completed API integration for user authentication module, identified performance bottleneck in database queries requiring optimization before load testing" and convert it to: "User login functionality is complete and working. The team discovered that the application runs slowly with large numbers of users and is fixing this before final testing. This may add 3-5 days to the timeline but will prevent serious problems after launch."

Manifest was where Dennis's project management experience remained crucial. The AI could translate between technical and business language, but only he could read between the lines when a developer said something was "straightforward" (usually meaning complicated) or when a client said they were "flexible on timeline" (usually meaning the opposite). His job became less about managing information and more about managing relationships and expectations.

The transformation was dramatic. Project stakeholders started commenting on how much clearer communication had become. Developers felt heard by business stakeholders, and clients felt confident that the technical team understood their concerns. Dennis's stress levels dropped significantly because he was spending less time frantically trying to keep everyone informed and more time overseeing project risks and opportunities. It's like finally hiring a town crier so you can stop running around the village shouting updates and actually focus on making sure the castle isn't about to fall into the moat.

A year later, Dennis's project completion rate had improved by 40%, and client satisfaction scores were consistently high. More importantly, he'd rediscovered what he'd originally loved about project management—helping different types of expertise combine to create something valuable.

What These Stories Reveal

Notice what didn't happen in any of these stories: nobody became superhuman, and nobody had AI solve their problems entirely. Instead, each person figured out how to combine AI capabilities with their own expertise to become better at what they were already good at.

Kathleen didn't become an event planning genius—she became better at the strategic thinking that prevents conference disasters. Leanne didn't become a perfect therapist—she preserved her mental energy for the therapeutic relationships that were her real strength. Connor didn't become a data scientist—he learned to use data to enhance rather than replace his team's creative instincts.

The C.A.L.M. framework worked because it forced each person to think clearly about their actual goals, choose appropriate tools for their specific context, optimize for quality rather than automation, and measure results that mattered to their real work.

But perhaps most importantly, each person maintained agency over their professional identity. They didn't let AI tools redefine what their work meant—they used AI tools to do their work better.

That's what empowerment looks like in practice. Not becoming dependent on AI, but becoming more capable of independent thinking because you're not wasting mental energy on tasks that don't require your expertise.

The Confidence That Comes from Systems

Real AI confidence doesn't come from knowing you can prompt ChatGPT to write a perfect email. It comes from knowing you can systematically approach any challenge and determine what combination of human thinking and AI assistance will produce the best outcome.

This is a different kind of empowerment than most people expect. It's not the thrill of discovering a magical new tool that solves all your problems. It's the quiet satisfaction of having a reliable process for tackling complex work, whether AI is involved or not.

When new AI tools emerge—and they will, constantly—you don't feel pressure to immediately master them. You can evaluate them calmly against your existing process. Does this help with clarity, alignment, leverage, or manifest? If so, how? If not, you can safely ignore it without worrying that you're falling behind.

When AI tools fail or change—and they will, frequently—you don't lose your footing. Your core process remains intact. You might need to find new tools or adjust your workflows, but the systematic thinking that makes AI useful doesn't disappear.

Perhaps the most significant change is that you become more intentional about when to use AI and when not to. Instead of defaulting to AI for everything or avoiding it entirely, you make deliberate choices based on clear thinking about what each situation requires.

Sometimes that means using AI heavily—when you need to process large amounts of information, generate multiple options quickly, or handle routine tasks that don't require your expertise. Sometimes it means using AI minimally—when the work requires deep domain knowledge, sensitive human judgment, or creative insights that emerge from your unique perspective.

And sometimes it means not using AI at all—when the process of thinking through a problem yourself is more valuable than the output you'd get, when the stakes are too high for any risk of error, or when the human connection is the point of the work.

The C.A.L.M. framework gives you a navigable way to make these choices rather than just going with your gut or following the latest productivity trend.

Your Next Chapter

The gap between AI suggestion and real-world success isn't a design flaw—it's where the learning happens. It's where you figure out how to take tools that work for everyone and make them work specifically for you, your audience, your particular way of doing business.

Your competitive advantage isn't having perfect implementations. It's having better recovery strategies and more persistence than the people who quit after their first attempt doesn't go perfectly. While your competitors are either avoiding AI because they're afraid of looking incompetent, or giving up after their first attempt doesn't work perfectly, you're developing the skill that will matter most in the long run—the ability to adapt and improve.

Because the AI landscape is changing so rapidly that everyone's best practices will be obsolete within a year or two. The tools will evolve, new ones will emerge, and the strategies that work today won't work tomorrow. But the meta-skill of systematic thinking—the ability to approach problems clearly, choose appropriate tools, optimize for quality, and measure what matters—will always be valuable.

The professionals who thrive as AI becomes more powerful won't be those who learned to use 2025's AI tools most effectively. They'll be those who developed strategic, process-based approaches to thinking about when and how to augment human capabilities with technological assistance.

That's a meta-skill that transfers across tools, technologies, and even career changes. The specific AI models you're using today will be obsolete in a few years. But the ability to think clearly about outcomes, match tools to tasks, optimize for quality, and measure what matters—those capabilities will become more valuable, not less. When you've mastered C.A.L.M., you're not just better at using AI. You're better at the kind of strategic thinking that makes technology useful in service of human goals.

The empowered AI user isn't someone who's memorized the perfect prompts. They're someone who's learned to think clearly about outcomes, context, and measurement—and can apply that thinking whether they're working with AI or without it.

That comfort with systematic thinking, that willingness to start small and build on what works, that curiosity about what reality is trying to teach you—these aren't just skills for using AI. They're skills for thriving in a world where the only constant is change, where the best strategy is often the one that adapts fastest to new information.

The future belongs to people who can think clearly about complex problems and use whatever tools are available to solve them effectively. The C.A.L.M. framework isn't just about AI—it's about becoming that kind of person.

Your move.

Signs You're an Empowered AI User

- ☑ You can explain why you chose not to use AI for a specific task
- ☑ You feel confident tackling challenges even when your preferred AI tools aren't available
- ☑ You focus more on the quality of your thinking than the sophistication of your prompts
- ☑ You help colleagues think through problems rather than just showing them tools
- ☑ You make deliberate choices about when to use AI vs. when to stay fully human
- ☑ You measure AI success by business outcomes, not just time saved
- ☑ You're curious about AI limitations, not just capabilities
- ☑ You can work effectively without AI but choose to use it strategically
- ☑ Your expertise has grown stronger since you started using AI tools
- ☑ You sleep better at night knowing your core value doesn't depend on any specific technology

10 Learning Lab

💡 Try This: The AI Enhancement Reality Check

Objective
Learn to distinguish between using AI as a thinking partner versus using it as a substitute for your own thinking, building confidence in your irreplaceable value while maximizing AI's benefits.

Time Required

- Setup: 20 minutes
- Daily practice: 15 minutes per day
- Total commitment: 4 days

Materials Needed

- Simple tracking document (digital or paper)
- Access to your preferred AI tool
- Three work tasks you can experiment with
- Timer or stopwatch

The Process

Day 1: Setup (20 minutes)

Step 1: Choose Your Test Tasks (10 minutes) Select three different work tasks you'll complete this week:

- One analytical task (data review, competitive analysis, research summary)
- One creative task (presentation design, content creation, strategy development)
- One communication task (email responses, meeting prep, stakeholder updates)

Step 2: Create Your Tracking System (10 minutes) Set up a simple document with these columns:

- Task & Date
- Approach Used (Enhancement vs. Replacement)
- Time Spent
- Would I present this to my manager? (Yes/No)
- Energy level after (1-10)

Days 2-4: Testing Both Approaches (15 minutes daily reflection)

For Each Task, Try Both Methods:

Method A: AI Enhancement (Your target approach)

1. Start with your objective: Define what you want to achieve before opening AI
2. Identify your unique value: What parts need your expertise, judgment, or context?
3. Use AI strategically:
    - Data gathering and initial research
    - Generating multiple options or first drafts
    - Formatting and organizing information
    - Checking for gaps or errors
4. Apply your expertise:
    - Analysis and interpretation
    - Strategic decisions and recommendations
    - Customization for specific stakeholders
    - Final quality control

Method B: AI Replacement (For comparison)

1. Give AI the complete task with minimal guidance
2. Edit only for obvious errors or formatting
3. Use the output essentially as-is

Daily Reflection Questions (5 minutes after each task):

- Which approach gave me more confidence in the result?
- What did I learn about the subject matter with each approach?
- If AI disappeared tomorrow, which approach prepares me better?
- Which result would I be more comfortable defending?

Day 5: Analysis and Framework Creation (20 minutes)

Step 1: Review Your Data (10 minutes) Look for patterns in your tracking:

- Which tasks benefited most from each approach?
- When did enhancement feel natural versus forced?
- Where did your energy levels differ significantly?

Step 2: Create Your Personal Enhancement Rules (10 minutes) Write down your guidelines:

- "I use AI for ______ but always handle ______ myself"
- "I know I'm enhancing (not replacing) when ______"
- "Warning signs that I'm over-relying on AI: ______"

💡 Try This: The AI Learning Budget Challenge

Objective

Develop disciplined, strategic habits around AI learning that focus on practical application rather than endless information consumption.

Time Required

- Week 1: 5 minutes daily tracking
- Week 2: 30 minutes total learning + 5 minutes daily logging
- Week 3: 20 minutes analysis and planning
- Total commitment: 3 weeks

Materials Needed

- Timer app or stopwatch
- Simple log (digital notepad or paper)
- Calendar for scheduling learning time
- List of your current work challenges

The Process

Week 1: Baseline Reality Check

Daily Tracking (5 minutes setup, then ongoing) For five workdays, log every minute spent on AI-related learning:

- Reading AI newsletters, articles, or social media
- Watching AI tutorials or demos
- Testing new AI tools or features
- Attending AI webinars or listening to podcasts

Weekend Analysis (15 minutes) Calculate your total time and categorize:

- High-value: Directly applicable to current work challenges
- Medium-value: Useful for potential future applications
- Low-value: General AI news, speculation, or casual browsing

Week 2: The 30-Minute Budget

Monday Planning Session (10 minutes)

1. Review your biggest work challenge that AI might help solve
2. Set your learning priority for the week
3. Allocate your 30-minute budget:

    - 20 minutes: Focused learning on your priority
    - 10 minutes: Quick scan of developments in your field

Daily Execution

- Set a 30-minute timer when you begin any AI learning
- Stop immediately when the timer hits zero, even mid-article
- Log what you learned and how it relates to your work challenge

Resistance Tracking When you want to continue past 30 minutes:

1. Write down what you wanted to keep exploring
2. Rate its relevance to your current challenges (1-10)
3. Note your emotional response (FOMO, curiosity, frustration)
4. Save this list for next week's planning

Week 3: Optimization and System Design

Mid-Week Analysis (10 minutes)

- Did the constraint improve your learning focus?
- What "urgent" AI news proved unimportant?
- Which sources provided the highest value?

Create Your Sustainable System (10 minutes) Design your ongoing approach:

- Weekly budget: Your optimal time allocation
- Priority framework: How you'll decide what deserves attention
- Source curation: Your list of high-signal resources
- Review schedule: Monthly reassessment plan

💡 Try This: The Human-First Boundary Setting

Objective

Identify and protect the areas of your work that should remain fully human, building confidence in your irreplaceable professional value while using AI strategically elsewhere.

Time Required

- Week 1: 30 minutes setup + 10 minutes daily
- Week 2: 5 minutes daily tracking + 15 minutes mid-week check
- Final analysis: 20 minutes
- Total commitment: 2 weeks

Materials Needed

- Work activity inventory list
- Daily tracking template (provided below)
- Calendar for scheduling reflection time
- Feedback from one trusted colleague (optional)

The Process

Week 1: Discover Your Unique Value

Days 1-2: Map Your Work (20 minutes total) Create a comprehensive list of your regular activities:

- Daily tasks (emails, planning, analysis, meetings)
- Weekly responsibilities (reports, project management, team coordination)
- Monthly work (strategy, reviews, presentations, relationship building)

Days 3-4: Find Your Boundaries (10 minutes total) For each activity, ask:

1. Does this require understanding of relationships, politics, or context that only I have?
2. Is my unique perspective or judgment the primary value?
3. Would I lose important skills or insights by delegating this to AI?
4. Does this involve confidential information or sensitive decisions?

Day 5: Select Your Three Boundaries (10 minutes) Choose three types of work to keep fully human. Strong boundaries often include:

- Strategic decisions affecting team members
- Relationship-building communications
- Creative work where your voice is the value
- Analysis requiring deep domain knowledge
- Confidential or politically sensitive situations

Week 2: Practice and Validation

Daily Boundary Practice Morning Intention (2 minutes):

- Review your three boundaries
- Identify today's boundary tasks
- Set intention to proceed without AI assistance

Moment of Choice Recognition: When you encounter a boundary task:

1. Pause before opening any AI tool
2. Remind yourself: "This is my unique value zone"
3. Choose deliberately to proceed without AI
4. Complete the task using your human judgment

Daily Tracking Template

Date: ________

Boundary Tasks Today:

1. Task: ________________

-Tempted to use AI? (Y/N)

-Maintained boundary? (Y/N)

-Outcome satisfaction (1-10):

-What I learned/reinforced:

Key Insight: What did I notice about my work when I couldn't rely on AI shortcuts?

Mid-Week Check-in (15 minutes)

- Are your boundaries realistic and sustainable?
- Which boundary feels most important to maintain?
- When have you been tempted to compromise, and why?

Final Analysis: Refine Your Approach

Boundary Assessment (10 minutes) For each boundary:

1. Impact: Did human-only work produce noticeably different results?
2. Development: What skills did you practice by avoiding AI?
3. Satisfaction: How did it feel to maintain full control?
4. Validation: Would stakeholders notice if you used AI instead?

Create Your Personal AI Ethics Statement (10 minutes) Write 2-3 sentences describing:

- What work you commit to keeping fully human and why
- How these boundaries strengthen your professional confidence
- What you've learned about your irreplaceable value

11. The Scale-Up Framework for Organizations

Sal thought she was being progressive when she announced that everyone at the Brightwater Community Foundation could start using AI tools like ChatGPT. "We need to embrace the future," she told her team during their Monday staff meeting. "Use this technology to work smarter, not harder."

What happened next was like watching a well-intentioned social experiment go spectacularly sideways.

Within a week, David from Sal's development was using ChatGPT to write thank-you letters that read like they'd been composed by an overly polite robot. "We are deeply grateful for your generous donation and hope you will consider supporting our mission again in the future," every letter concluded, regardless of whether the donor had given $50 or $5,000, whether they were longtime supporters or first-time contributors.

Meanwhile, Marissa in programs started using AI to write grant applications, but since she hadn't learned to provide proper context, the proposals were impressively professional and completely generic. One funder called to ask why their application for youth mentoring funding included three paragraphs about environmental conservation.

The marketing team discovered they could generate social media content in seconds, so they flooded their channels with AI-produced posts about "community impact" and "transformative change" that said absolutely nothing about what the foundation did or why anyone should care.

But the real disaster came during grant reporting season. The team had used AI to help write their quarterly impact reports, and everything looked great on paper—until their biggest funder called with concerns. The reports were beautifully written but fundamentally hollow. They described programs in glowing terms without connecting activities to actual outcomes. They used impressive language to disguise the fact that no real analysis had been done.

"It feels like you're telling us what you think we want to hear rather than what's happening," the program officer said during a tense phone call. "These reports could have been written about any nonprofit in the country."

Six months after Sal's AI announcement, the foundation had lost two major grants, their donor retention rate had dropped 30%, and their social media engagement had flatlined. They were producing more content than ever before, but none of it was meaningful, personal, or strategic.

"We're using AI," Sal told me when she called for advice, "but somehow everything we create feels... fake. Like we've lost our voice."

That's when I realized Sal's team had fallen into the classic organizational AI trap: they'd given people powerful tools without any framework for using them effectively. They were getting outputs, but not the right ones. They weren't leveraging AI for the things that could transform their work—improving donor personalization, enhancing strategic planning, optimizing grant applications, or analyzing program effectiveness. Instead, they were using sophisticated technology to create bland, generic content that made them sound like every other nonprofit using the same approach.

The problem wasn't the technology. It was the complete absence of systematic thinking about when, how, and why to use it.

If only someone had advised Sal prior to rolling out AI across her enterprise: methodologies provide value, but they're not instant solutions. You can't just wave C.A.L.M. at a team and expect transformation to happen overnight.

But when you apply it thoughtfully—with genuine humans in mind, not just processes—something interesting happens. The same principles that helped you navigate your personal AI journey become a roadmap for helping others find theirs.

But when you apply it thoughtfully—with genuine humans in mind, not just processes—something interesting happens. The same principles that helped you navigate your personal AI journey become a roadmap for helping others find theirs.

Clarity: The "What Are We *Actually* Trying to Fix?" Phase

Scaling starts with getting brutally honest about what's legitimately broken. Not what feels broken or what you think should be improved, but what's genuinely making people's lives harder. Scaling starts with getting brutally honest about what's legitimately broken. Not what feels broken or what you think should be improved, but what's genuinely making people's lives harder.

I learned this when I assumed our biggest problem was "inefficient communication." Sounds important, right? Except when I got around to talking to people, the real issue was that our project updates were so dense and jargon-heavy that nobody read them. The solution wasn't better communication tools—it was helping people write updates that humans wanted to read.

The clarity phase isn't about hosting a brainstorming session where everyone lists every pet peeve they've ever had. It's about finding the one thing that, if you fixed it, would make everyone's Tuesday significantly better.

The questions that actually matter:

- What's the task that makes people groan when it lands on their desk?
- Where do we keep making the same mistakes over and over?
- What would happen if we could give people back five hours a week?

Take Jennifer's team in customer service. They thought their problem was "too many support tickets." But when we dug deeper, the real issue was that 60% of tickets were asking variations of the same five questions—questions that were technically answered in their knowledge base, but buried in corporate speak that nobody could decipher.

The clarity wasn't "handle more tickets faster." It was "make our existing answers helpful."

Alignment: The "Not Every Tool Is Your Tool" Reality Check

This is where most scaling efforts go to die: the everything-bagel approach. Someone discovers AI can do amazing things, so they try to use it for everything all at once. It's like deciding to renovate your entire house because you successfully changed a light bulb.

The alignment phase is about matchmaking, not maximizing. You're pairing specific tools with specific problems for specific people. Revolutionary? No. Effective? Absolutely.

Remember Jennifer's customer service team? We didn't implement a comprehensive AI customer service platform with sentiment analysis and predictive routing. We started with one simple AI assistant that could rewrite their existing knowledge base articles in plain English, then generate three different versions of common responses—formal, friendly, and "I'm having a ridiculously bad day but still trying to help you."

The tool did one thing well instead of ten things poorly. Six"m'nths later, their ticket resolution time dropped by 40%, not because they were handling tickets faster, but because they were preventing them in the first place.

The alignment test: If you can't explain what the tool does and why it matters in one sentence, you're likely not ready to scale it.

Leverage: When the Magic Happens

When it comes to leveraging at scale, it's not about everyone becoming an AI expert. It's about creating strategic systems where people can get AI-level results without needing AI-level expertise. Think of it like driving a car. You don't need to understand internal combustion to get to work, but you do need to know what the brake pedal does.

The breakthrough came when we stopped trying to teach people to be prompt engineers and started building what I call "conversation templates"—basically, fill-in-the-blank prompts that anyone could customize for their specific situation.

Instead of teaching everyone to craft the perfect prompt for rewriting knowledge base articles, we created a template: "Rewrite this [type of content] for [target audience] in a [tone] that addresses [specific concern]." People could plug in their own values and get consistently good results.

For Jennifer's team, it looked like this: "Rewrite this technical support article for frustrated customers in a helpful tone that addresses their urgency to solve the problem quickly." The magic wasn't in the AI—it was in making the

AI accessible to people who had better things to do than become prompt engineers.

Manifest: The "Small Wins Build Big Changes" Approach

I used to think manifestation at scale meant rolling out grand initiatives with company-wide launches and training programs. Turns out, it's the opposite: finding the smallest possible success and then helping it spread naturally.

Jennifer's team didn't transform overnight. It started with one person, Lisa, who volunteered to try the new approach with just the five most common support questions. She spent one afternoon rewriting those articles using AI, then tested them with the next week's tickets.

The result? Those five questions generated 80% fewer follow-up tickets. Word spread. Not because we sent out an announcement, but because Lisa's colleagues noticed she wasn't staying late anymore to handle the endless stream of "I still don't understand" responses.

Within a month, the entire team was asking to try the approach. Within three months, other departments were asking how they could do something similar.

The manifest principle: Success spreads faster than mandates.

What scaling looks like when it works: it's not about implementing AI everywhere. It's about creating a culture where people feel confident experimenting with tools that might make their specific jobs easier.

You'll know you're succeeding when people start coming to you with their own discoveries instead of waiting for you to teach them everything. When they say things like, "I tried using AI to help with [random task you never thought of] and it worked pretty well." That's when you realize you haven't just scaled AI tools—you've scaled AI thinking. And that's when the real transformation begins.

Let me show you what this looks like in practice.

The Education Foundation That Found Its Voice

Veronica remembers the exact moment she realized everything had shifted at the Riverside Education Foundation. She was sitting in their monthly board meeting, listening to program updates that used to make her cringe.

For three years, these presentations had followed the same soul-crushing pattern: read statistics from grant reports, mention a few generic success stories, field polite questions that everyone knew the answers to. Board members would nod thoughtfully and move on to budget discussions.

But something was different this time. Marcus, their youth mentor coordinator, was describing their high school program, and the board was leaning forward. They were asking follow-up questions. Real questions.

"Tell me more about what you mean when you say the students became advocates for their own learning," said Dr. Chen, the board chair who usually spent meetings checking her phone.

Marcus didn't just answer—he painted a picture. He talked about Jessica, a junior who'd been failing three classes and convinced she was "too stupid for school," who had started tutoring freshmen in math after discovering she could explain concepts in ways that made sense to struggling students.

As Marcus answered with specific examples and thoughtful analysis, Veronica realized she wasn't watching a program update anymore. She was watching strategic thinking in real time.

After the meeting, she cornered Marcus. "That was incredible. How did you prepare for that presentation?" Marcus looked surprised. "The same way I always do? I just had a conversation with ChatGPT about what I wanted to communicate, then refined it until it felt right."

The Framework in Action: How They Applied C.A.L.M.

The transformation at Riverside didn't happen overnight, and it didn't start with a strategic plan. It began with Veronica's personal frustration with grant reporting and spread through what she now recognizes as a textbook application of organizational C.A.L.M.

Clarity: Finding the Real Problem The breakthrough came when Veronica stopped asking "How can we write better grant reports?" and started asking "What are these reports supposed to accomplish?"

The real purpose wasn't checking boxes for funders—it was demonstrating genuine impact in ways that would inspire continued support and better programming decisions. Their reports were failing because they buried impact under layers of nonprofit jargon and standardized metrics that satisfied requirements but inspired no one.

> *Key insight for organizations: Clarity at scale requires distinguishing between what you think the problem is and what the problem is. This usually requires talking to the people who are doing the work, not just the people who manage it.*

Alignment: Choosing Tools That Match the Mission

Instead of generic writing assistance, Veronica chose AI tools designed specifically for nonprofit storytelling. She needed technology that could help extract compelling narratives from program data while maintaining analytical rigor.

This wasn't about finding the most powerful AI tool—it was about finding the right AI tool for their specific context and constraints.

> *Implementation guidance: Don't choose AI tools based on capabilities; choose them based on how well they address your specific challenges. A specialized tool that does one thing excellently will outperform a general tool that does everything adequately.*

Leverage: Creating Scalable Conversations

Veronica developed what she called "story extraction conversations" with AI. Instead of asking it to write reports, she'd describe specific program interactions and ask for help framing them within broader impact narratives.

Her typical prompt structure:

1. Context setting: "I'm writing a grant report for our youth mentoring program"
2. Specific example: "A teacher told me about Maria, a seventh-grader who hadn't turned in homework all semester but started participating actively after we introduced peer tutoring"
3. Strategic framing request: "How can I tell this story in a way that illustrates our program's approach to engaging disengaged students?"

Scaling strategy: Create prompt templates that anyone can customize rather than training everyone to become prompt engineers. The goal is consistent quality, not individual expertise.

Manifest: Spreading Success Through Results

The approach spread organically when other staff members noticed that Veronica's reports were generating genuine engagement from funders—not just approval letters, but real questions about expanding successful approaches.

Marcus started applying similar thinking to his youth program documentation. Priya, their family outreach coordinator, began using AI conversations to identify which intervention approaches worked best with different family challenges.

> *Cultural insight: Success spreads faster through demonstrated value than through mandates. When people see their colleagues getting better results, they naturally want to understand the approach.*

The Compound Effect: What Happened Next

Six months later, the foundation had increased its funding by 35%, but the numbers didn't capture the real transformation. Their team meetings had shifted from administrative logistics to strategic discussions about program effectiveness.

The process of explaining their work clearly to AI had helped staff recognize patterns they'd been too close to see. They discovered that their most effective interventions shared characteristics they hadn't consciously designed for, leading to program improvements that made their work more impactful.

Veronica learned that AI adoption at the organizational level isn't absolutely about technology—it's about creating human-centered approaches to thinking clearly about work that matters.

The Music Store's Digital Awakening

Dmitri had owned Harmony Corner Music for fifteen years, and he could tell you exactly when he realized the internet was winning.

It wasn't when his sales numbers started declining—that had been happening gradually for years. The moment that hit him was watching Mrs. Patterson, a regular customer, standing in his store with her phone out, comparing prices on the exact guitar he'd just spent twenty minutes helping her understand.

"I immensely appreciate your help," she said, not quite meeting his eyes. "I'm just going to think about it for a while." They both knew she was going home to order it online for sixty dollars less.

Dmitri understood the economics. He couldn't compete on price with warehouse retailers. But he also knew he offered something Amazon couldn't: the ability to spend an hour helping a parent find the right beginner guitar for their child, considering the kid's hand size, musical interests, and family budget.

The problem was that all this expertise lived in his store, trapped in conversations that happened once and were never shared with anyone else.

The Framework in Action: Scaling Personal Expertise

Dmitri's transformation illustrates how C.A.L.M. can help small businesses leverage their core strengths in digital environments without losing what makes them special.

Clarity: Identifying the Unique Value The breakthrough came when Dmitri stopped trying to compete on price and started competing on expertise. His real value wasn't selling instruments—it was solving musical problems that parents and students didn't know how to solve themselves.

> *Strategic question for small businesses: What do you do in person that your competitors can't replicate online? How can that expertise become your digital differentiator?*

Alignment: Tools for Expertise Sharing Instead of generic social media management tools, Dmitri chose AI platforms that could help him create educational content that felt like conversations rather than marketing.

He needed tools that could help him scale his personal touch, not replace it—technology that could turn his daily customer interactions into shareable wisdom.

> *Tool selection principle: Choose AI that amplifies your existing strengths rather than trying to make you good at things you're not naturally good at.*

Leverage: Converting Conversations to Content Dmitri developed a brilliant approach to documenting customer interactions, using AI to help him transform specific problem-solving conversations into generally useful content.

His process:

1. Document the customer challenge: "Parent came in worried that their 8-year-old wants drums but they live in an apartment"
2. Explain his solution: "I recommended electronic drums with good headphone capabilities and explained how to set practice boundaries"
3. Ask AI to help generalize: "How can I turn this into helpful content for other parents facing the same dilemma?"

Content strategy: Use AI to help you recognize the patterns in your expertise that you're too close to see. Your daily problem-solving contains more valuable content than you realize.

Manifest: Building Digital Community

Instead of just posting content, Dmitri used his expertise-sharing approach to build genuine relationships with customers online. Parents started commenting with their own musical challenges. Local teachers began sharing his posts. Musicians started asking questions they'd never felt comfortable asking in person.

> *Community building insight: Authentic expertise shared consistently creates more engagement than polished marketing content. People want to learn from real experts, not perfect presentations.*

The Unexpected Business Impact

Six months later, Dmitri's online engagement had increased by 400%, but more importantly, people were driving from neighboring cities because they'd read about his approach to helping customers. His website had become a resource that demonstrated his expertise rather than just listing inventory.

The process also revealed something unexpected: when Dmitri had to explain his decision-making process to AI, he became more conscious of the expertise he'd been taking for granted. This made him a better advisor to customers and helped him train his part-time staff to provide similar thoughtful guidance.

His business model shifted from "local store competing with online prices" to "recognized expert who happens to have a physical location." The difference in both profitability and job satisfaction was remarkable.

The Training Revolution That Started Small

Cassandra had been developing corporate training programs for eight years, and she'd gotten very good at creating content that checked all the required boxes while putting participants into a meditative trance.

The wake-up call came during a harassment prevention session when she noticed Bob from accounting had perfected the art of looking attentive while clearly thinking about spreadsheets. After the session, she overheard him tell a colleague, "Well, that's another hour of my life I'll never get back. But at least we're covered if anyone asks whether we had the training."

That night, Cassandra found herself questioning everything about her approach. Adults learn by connecting new information to their existing experience, but her training modules felt like academic lectures with no connection to workplace reality.

The Framework in Action: Personalizing Learning at Scale

Cassandra's transformation shows how C.A.L.M. can solve the fundamental challenge of corporate training: how to make required content feel relevant and actionable for different types of learners.

Clarity: Redefining Training Success

The breakthrough came when Cassandra stopped measuring success by completion rates and started focusing on behavior change. The real question wasn't "Did people attend the training?" but "Are people applying what they learned?"

This shift revealed that her training failed because it treated all learners identically, despite the fact that a new supervisor, seasoned manager, and front-line employee brought completely different perspectives to every topic.

Training strategy: Define success by post-training behavior change, not participation metrics. This forces you to design learning experiences that stick rather than just satisfy requirements.

Alignment: Tools for Adaptive Learning

Instead of generic presentation software, Cassandra chose AI tools designed for personalized learning experiences. She needed technology that could adapt explanations, examples, and exercises based on individual roles and experience levels.

Technology selection: Look for AI tools that can dynamically adjust content based on user input, not just deliver the same material more efficiently.

Leverage: Creating Role-Specific Scenarios

Cassandra developed what she called "adaptive conversation frameworks" that generated different versions of the same core content tailored to specific audiences.

For harassment prevention training, instead of generic presentations about inappropriate behavior, she created role-specific scenarios:

For team leads: "You notice that jokes in your department are making some people uncomfortable, but the joker is your highest performer and claims they're just building team morale. Your manager has commented positively on your team's 'great chemistry.' How do you address this?"

For HR representatives: "An employee reports that their manager makes comments about their appearance that feel inappropriate, but the manager claims they're just being friendly. The employee doesn't want to 'make a big deal' but is clearly uncomfortable. How do you investigate while protecting everyone involved?"

Scenario development principle: Create training situations that feel like actual work challenges rather than theoretical exercises. People engage when they recognize their own professional dilemmas.

Manifest: Measuring Real Impact

The true test came when Cassandra started tracking workplace behavior changes rather than just training completion. Harassment incident reports decreased by 60% over the following year—the first time their training had demonstrated measurable impact on workplace culture.

More importantly, participants started approaching her with real questions about workplace challenges, treating her as a resource for ongoing problem-solving rather than just a presenter of required content.

Impact measurement: Track downstream outcomes that matter to your organization, not just training metrics. Real learning shows up in changed behavior, not perfect test scores.

The Optimal Transformation

Cassandra applied the same approach to all their learning initiatives. Safety training became about recognizing and responding to actual risk situations rather than memorizing procedures. Leadership development moved beyond theoretical frameworks to practicing real-world scenarios new managers would face immediately.

The success came from using AI to create training that felt like problem-solving rather than information transfer, helping employees develop skills they could immediately apply rather than knowledge they might eventually need.

Within a year, training satisfaction scores increased dramatically, but more importantly, the business impact was measurable across all their programs. They'd solved the fundamental challenge of corporate learning: making required content genuinely useful.

The Course Creator's Scaling Solution

Natalie had built exactly the business she'd dreamed of: teaching small business owners how to develop marketing strategies that felt authentic rather than sleazy. Her courses were well-regarded, her students got results, and she'd reached comfortable income levels.

But success had created an unexpected problem. Every time she tried to scale beyond her current student base, something crucial got lost—the personal connection and customized guidance that made her courses effective.

The breaking point came when she received two student emails on the same day. Jennifer, a marriage counselor, wrote: "I understand your framework for building trust with prospects, but how does that apply when people don't want to admit they need therapy?"

Marcus, a business coach, wrote: "Your content creation strategies make sense, but my target audience is burned out executives who don't have time to read lengthy blog posts. How do I demonstrate expertise without adding to their information overload?"

Both students had absorbed her content thoroughly, but they needed completely different guidance about applying the same principles to their specific situations.

The Framework in Action: Personalizing Guidance at Scale

Natalie's challenge represents the core scaling dilemma for expertise-based businesses: how to provide personalized guidance without personally guiding everyone.

Clarity: Defining Scalable Value

The insight came when Natalie realized her real value wasn't in the frameworks she taught—it was in helping people apply those frameworks to their unique circumstances. Students didn't just need marketing knowledge; they needed help customizing that knowledge for their specific situations.

> *Business model insight: In expertise-based businesses, the scalable value often lies in application guidance rather than information transfer. People can learn frameworks anywhere; they need help making those frameworks work in their specific context.*

Alignment: Tools for Contextual Coaching

Instead of course creation platforms, Natalie chose AI tools that could provide personalized feedback and adaptive guidance. She needed technology that could understand student contexts and provide the kind of customized advice she would give personally.

Platform selection: Look for AI tools that can maintain context and provide personalized responses, not just deliver content efficiently. The goal is scaling personalization, not just scaling delivery.

Leverage: Building Conversation Architectures

Natalie created what she called "contextual coaching conversations"—structured AI interactions that could provide guidance tailored to individual business situations.

Students would input details about their business, target audience, and marketing challenges, and the AI, trained on Natalie's coaching methodology, would help them apply her frameworks to their specific context.

Example conversation structure:

1. Context gathering: "I'm a marriage counselor who wants to reach couples before they're in crisis"
2. Challenge articulation: "Marketing therapy feels awkward because people don't like to admit they need help"
3. Framework application: "How can I apply Natalie's trust-building framework to reach people who need my services but won't actively search for them?"

Coaching at scale: Create structured conversation frameworks that can be personalized rather than trying to anticipate every possible variation. The structure ensures consistency while the personalization ensures relevance.

Manifest: Improving Outcomes Through AI Support

The results surprised everyone. Students weren't just implementing Natalie's frameworks more effectively—they were developing independent problem-solving skills. The AI forced them to articulate their challenges more clearly, which helped them understand their own businesses better.

Unexpected benefit: Well-designed AI interactions can improve student thinking skills, not just provide answers. The process of explaining their situation clearly often helps people understand their challenges better.

The Business Transformation

Natalie's revenue increased by 300% over eighteen months, but more importantly, her students' success rates improved dramatically. They were receiving more consistent, personalized support than she could have provided through traditional methods. It was like cloning herself but giving each clone a perfect memory and the ability to be in seventeen places at once without needing coffee breaks.

Marcus, the business coach, discovered that his real strength wasn't creating content for burned-out executives—it was helping them identify which marketing activities would generate results without adding overwhelm. Jennifer, the marriage counselor, realized her discomfort with traditional marketing was an asset, leading her to develop workshops on communication skills that positioned her as someone who helped relationships thrive.

The AI coaching hadn't just scaled Natalie's business—it had helped her students achieve breakthrough clarity about their own unique value propositions.

The App Developer's Mirror Moment

Kai had started Phoenix Labs to solve AI problems for other businesses, but eighteen months in, he faced an embarrassing irony: despite being AI experts, their own company operations were held together with digital duct tape and prayer.

The wake-up call came during a client presentation when Kai realized he couldn't answer a basic question about project timeline because he genuinely didn't know which team member was working on what phase of implementation.

"We'll get back to you on that," he told the client, maintaining professional composure while internally cringing at how disorganized they sounded. After the meeting, Kai gathered his team for what he later called their "mirror moment." They were brilliant at solving operational challenges for other companies while completely ignoring their own.

The Framework in Action: Practicing What You Preach

Phoenix Labs' transformation demonstrates how organizations can apply their own expertise systematically to their internal challenges—and why this often requires the same disciplined approach they use for client work.

Clarity: Admitting the Real Problem

The breakthrough came when Kai admitted that their operational problems weren't technical—they were systematic. They'd grown from three people to fifteen without developing scalable systems for coordination and communication.

Elena, their project manager, was manually tracking project status across multiple clients using spreadsheets and determination. When clients asked for updates, she'd spend hours gathering conflicting information from different team members.

> *Organizational insight: Rapid growth often creates operational problems that feel technical but are systematic. The solution isn't better tools—it's better processes that tools can support.*

Alignment: Building Internal Tools That Match External Expertise

Instead of implementing off-the-shelf project management software, Phoenix Labs decided to build internal AI systems that addressed their specific coordination challenges—the same way they would approach client problems.

They developed AI assistants for client communication that maintained project context across team members, ensuring consistent responses regardless of who was available. They created project planning tools that analyzed past project data to provide accurate time estimates.

Strategic approach: Apply the same problem-solving rigor to internal challenges that you apply to external client work. Don't accept suboptimal internal processes just because they're "internal."

Leverage: Creating Compound Intelligence

The most innovative solution was their knowledge management system that captured problem-solving approaches and technical solutions as they were developed, making the company's collective intelligence accessible rather than trapped in individual expertise. When Violet, their lead developer, went on vacation, her projects continued smoothly because her technical decisions and reasoning had been systematically documented and were accessible to other team members.

> *Knowledge capture: Build systems that capture not just what decisions were made, but why they were made. This creates institutional intelligence rather than just institutional memory.*

Manifest: Turning Internal Success into External Advantage

The operational improvements became a competitive advantage in client sales. They could demonstrate AI's business impact through their own example rather than just theoretical case studies.

Better internal operations meant higher-quality client work, which attracted better clients, which provided more interesting challenges that attracted better developers—creating a virtuous cycle of improvement.

Business development insight: Internal operational excellence becomes a powerful sales tool. Clients want to work with companies that successfully apply their own expertise.

The Cultural Shift

Within a year, Phoenix Labs had reduced administrative overhead by 50% while increasing client satisfaction and project profitability. But the real change was cultural: they became a company that practiced what they preached.

The team developed confidence in their ability to solve any operational challenge systematically, using the same AI approaches they recommended to clients. This created a culture of continuous improvement and systematic problem-solving that made them more effective consultants.

Kai learned that the most convincing AI advocacy isn't telling people what's possible—it's showing them what you've made possible for yourself.

Scaling Principles That Work

Watching these organizations transform taught me something crucial about scaling AI: success spreads through demonstrated value, not through mandates or training programs. Each of these transformations followed similar patterns, despite occurring in completely different contexts.

THE THREE-PHASE PATTERN

Most organizations approach AI implementation backwards—starting with strategy documents and enterprise rollouts instead of letting solutions emerge organically. But the most successful transformations follow a predictable three-phase pattern that begins with individual problem-solving and grows into systematic change.

Phase 1: Individual Discovery Every successful organizational transformation started with one person solving a specific problem using AI. Veronica improving grant reports. Dmitri creating better customer content. Cassandra developing engaging training scenarios. These weren't grand strategic initiatives—they were personal responses to individual frustrations.

Phase 2: Organic Spread The approach spread when colleagues noticed improved results and got curious about the methods. Not because anyone mandated adoption, but because people naturally want to understand why their colleague's work suddenly got better.

Phase 3: Integration Once multiple people were experimenting successfully, organizations developed shared frameworks and support systems. But these emerged from proven practices rather than being imposed from above.

THE CULTURAL PREREQUISITES

Organizations that succeed with AI scaling share certain cultural characteristics:

→ **Psychological Safety for Experimentation** People need to feel comfortable trying things that might not work. The most successful organizations created informal cultures of curiosity rather than formal programs of AI adoption.

→ **Focus on Problems, Not Tools** Successful scaling started with specific challenges that mattered to people's daily work, not with AI capabilities looking for applications.

→ **Celebration of Intelligent Failure** Organizations that sustained their AI initiatives celebrated learning from failed experiments rather than only recognizing successful implementations.

→ **Systematic Sharing of Discoveries** The best transformations included regular opportunities for people to share what they'd learned—both successes and failures—without formal presentation requirements.

The Leadership Approach That Works. The leaders who successfully scaled AI shared a particular approach to change management:

→ **They Started Small and Specific** Rather than launching comprehensive AI strategies, they identified one specific problem that AI might help solve and started there.

→ **They Supported, Don't Managed, Experimentation** Instead of trying to control how AI was adopted, they created conditions for successful experimentation and let people discover what worked for their specific roles.

→ **They Measured Outcomes, Not Activities** They tracked improvements in work quality and mission outcomes rather than AI usage metrics or training completion rates.

→ **They Connected AI Success to Organizational Values** They helped people understand how AI tools could help them do work they already cared about more effectively, rather than asking them to care about AI for its own sake.

YOUR ORGANIZATION'S AI FUTURE

The organizations you've met in this chapter didn't become AI companies. They became better versions of themselves, with AI quietly amplifying what they were already good at.

The Riverside Education Foundation became better at articulating their impact. Harmony Corner became better at sharing expertise. Pinnacle Corp became better at facilitating learning. Natalie became better at providing personalized guidance. Phoenix Labs became better at practicing their own expertise.

This is what successful organizational AI adoption looks like: not dramatic transformation, but steady improvement in how people think about and approach their work.

Your organization's AI story will be unique because it will emerge from your specific culture, challenges, and values. But the C.A.L.M. framework provides a reliable way to approach any AI opportunity systematically:

- **Clarity** helps you identify which problems to prioritize for AI solutions rather than trying to automate everything.
- **Alignment** ensures you choose tools that enhance your organization's existing strengths rather than forcing you to work in unnatural ways.
- **Leverage** enables you to create systems where anyone can get good results with AI, not just the technically sophisticated.
- **Manifest** helps you build on small successes rather than betting everything on comprehensive transformations.

The organizations that thrive with AI won't be the ones with the most sophisticated tools. They'll be the ones with the clearest thinking about when and how to use whatever tools are available to do work that matters.

That future starts with one person, one problem, and one small experiment. The C.A.L.M. framework gives you the roadmap. Your organization's curiosity and commitment will determine where it leads. The quiet revolution is happening one Tuesday at a time.

11- Learning Lab

Try this: The Real Problem Dig

Sometimes what looks like an AI problem is actually a communication or process problem in disguise. This exercise helps you identify the root issue before jumping to solutions.

Step 1: Identify Your "Obvious" Problem

Write down one work challenge that seems straightforward. Examples:

- "We get too many emails"
- "Meetings run too long"
- "Reports take forever to create"
- "Client communications are inconsistent"

Your obvious problem:

Step 2: Ask "Why?" Three Times

For each answer, dig deeper by asking "why" again. This reveals the underlying issues.

Why is this a problem?

Why does that happen?

Why is that the case?

Step 3: Identify the Real Problem

Based on your three "whys," what's the actual issue that needs solving?

The real problem is:

Step 4: Reframe for AI Solutions

Now that you know the root cause, how might AI help address it?

AI could help by:

💡 Try This: The Alignment Matrix

This visual tool helps you match problems with appropriate AI solutions and spot opportunities you might have missed.

Step 1: List Your Top Problems

In the left column, write 4-5 work challenges you face regularly.

Step 2: List Available AI Tools

Across the top, write AI tools you have access to or could easily try.

Step 3: Fill the Matrix

For each problem/tool combination, rate the potential fit:

- ✓✓ = Excellent match
- ✓ = Could help
- ? = Uncertain
- X = Poor fit

Problems	Tool 1: ________	Tool 2: ________	Tool 3: ________	Tool 4: ________
1. ________________				
2. ________________				
3. ________________				

Step 4: Analyze Patterns

Which problems have the most ✓✓ marks?

Which tools seem most versatile?

What gaps do you notice?

Step 5: Plan Your Next Experiment

Based on your matrix, which problem-tool combination will you try first?

I will test: ________________________________ **Expected outcome:**

____

💡 Try This: The Template Challenge

Turn your AI successes into reusable resources that others can benefit from.

Step 1: Choose Your Success Story

Think of one time AI helped you accomplish something useful. Write a brief description:

What you accomplished:

AI tool used:

Why it worked well:

Step 2: Break Down Your Approach

What specific steps did you take? Include your prompts or process:

Step 1:

Step 2:

Step 3:

Step 4:

Step 3: Create the Template

Turn your specific example into a fill-in-the-blank template others could use:

Template:

Step 4: Test with Someone Else

Find a colleague who could benefit from this approach.

Who will you test with:

Their reaction:

What you'll adjust:

Step 5: Refine and Share

Based on the test, how will you improve the template?

Final template:

💡 Try This: The Success Virus

Turn your AI wins into learning opportunities for others—and track how knowledge spreads.

Step 1: Document Your Success

What did you accomplish with AI?

How long did it save you?

What surprised you about the result?

Step 2: Choose Your First "Infection"

Who would benefit from knowing about this?

Why them specifically?

Step 3: Share Immediately

Within 24 hours of your success, tell them about it.

How you shared it: (email, conversation, demo, etc.)

Their initial reaction:

Step 4: Offer to Show Them

Don't just tell—offer to demonstrate or help them try it.

Did you offer to help? Yes / No

If yes, what happened?

Step 5: Track the Spread

Follow up to see if they've used it or shared it with others.

Week 1 follow-up:

Week 4 follow-up:

Who else learned about it?

Step 6: Reflect on Virality

What made this knowledge spread (or not spread)?

What would you do differently next time?

Try This: The Failure Collection

Learn from AI experiments that didn't go as planned—and help others avoid the same pitfalls.

Step 1: Document Three Failures

Think of times AI didn't work as expected. For each one, fill out:

Failure #1

What you tried:

What you expected:

What actually happened:

What you learned:

Failure #2

What you tried:

What you expected:

What actually happened:

What you learned:

Failure #3

What you tried:

What you expected:

What actually happened:

What you learned:

Step 2: Find the Patterns

What common themes do you notice across your failures?

Which type of problem seems most challenging for you?

Step 3: Share One Failure Story

Choose the most instructive failure and share it with someone.

Who did you share with:

How did you frame it:

What was their reaction:

Did they share a similar experience:

Step 4: Create Prevention Tips

Based on your failures, what advice would you give to someone just starting with AI?

Top 3 things to avoid:

1.
2.
3.

Step 5: Turn Failure into Wisdom

How will you approach similar challenges differently in the future?

Your new strategy:

12. Thriving in the AI Era – Writing Your Success Story

Elena was halfway through her usual Tuesday morning latte when she heard it—that particular brand of frustrated muttering that comes from someone wrestling with technology that refuses to cooperate. At the table next to her, a twenty-something guy in a wrinkled startup hoodie was staring at his laptop screen like it had personally offended him.

"This is useless," he was saying to no one in particular. "I've tried five different ways to ask this thing for help with my pitch deck, and it keeps giving me generic garbage."

Six months ago, Elena would have minded her own business, maybe even felt a little smug about someone else's tech troubles. But something had shifted. She recognized that look of defeat—the same expression she'd worn in this very coffee shop when she first tried to make sense of AI prompts. Before she could second-guess herself, she was leaning over. "Mind if I take a look?"

What happened next surprised them both. Elena didn't just help him fix his prompt—she watched his entire approach transform. Instead of throwing vague requests at the AI like darts at a board, she showed him how to think through what he needed.

"You're asking it to 'make your pitch better,'" she explained, "but better how? For who? What specific outcome are you hoping for?" Within ten minutes, he had a pitch deck outline that made him sit back and whistle.

"How did you know to do that?" he asked.

Elena paused, her coffee cup halfway to her lips. How had she known? The answer came to her slowly: she'd stopped thinking about AI as a mysterious black box and started treating it like what it really was—a thinking partner that needed clear direction.

That moment—watching understanding dawn on a stranger's face over lukewarm coffee—was when Elena realized she'd crossed an invisible line. She wasn't just someone who used AI anymore. She'd become someone who understood it.

More importantly, she'd become someone who could help others understand it too.

When the Framework Becomes Second Nature

Here's what's probably happened to you, whether you've fully recognized it or not: the C.A.L.M. framework has stopped being a set of steps you follow and started being how you naturally think about problems.

Clarity used to be a conscious process—sitting down and asking yourself, "What exactly am I trying to accomplish here?" Now? You probably find yourself automatically zeroing in on the heart of any challenge, the way a seasoned editor instinctively spots the real story buried in a rambling first draft.

Alignment has evolved from "Which tool should I use?" to something more like conducting an orchestra. You're not just picking instruments anymore; you're hearing how they'll sound together before you even start playing.

Leverage has transformed from crafting individual prompts to designing entire conversations. Remember when getting a useful response felt like luck? Now you shape interactions the way a skilled interviewer draws out exactly the insights they need.

Manifest isn't just about implementing solutions anymore—it's about creating change that lasts. You're not just using AI; you're quietly reshaping how the people around you think about what's possible.

This evolution isn't just personal growth—it's the foundation of something bigger. You've developed what we might call "AI wisdom," and like all forms of wisdom, it's almost impossible to keep to yourself.

The Accidental Mentor

Jennifer never set out to become her department's unofficial AI guide. She was just a marketing manager who'd gotten comfortable using AI for content creation and campaign analysis. Nothing revolutionary—just solid, practical applications that made her work better.

But word spreads quickly in most organizations, especially when someone finds a way to make Tuesdays less terrible.

When Tom from sales was stuck on a client presentation, someone suggested he "ask Jennifer—she's good with that AI stuff." When the finance team needed help making sense of customer data trends, Jennifer's name came up again. Not because she was the designated AI person, but because she had a reputation for being helpful and practical.

"I started noticing people would swing by my desk more often," Jennifer told me. "At first I thought it was just coincidence. Then I realized they were coming to me with problems that weren't precisely about AI at all—they were about thinking through challenges more clearly. AI just happened to be part of the solution."

What's fascinating about Jennifer's evolution is how natural it felt. She wasn't teaching people to use specific tools so much as helping them develop a different way of approaching problems. Someone would describe what they were trying to accomplish, and Jennifer would ask the kinds of questions that helped them see the situation more clearly:

- What's the real goal here?
- What would success look like?
- Where are the bottlenecks?
- What information do you need versus what you think you need?

The AI recommendations almost became secondary to this deeper shift in thinking. Jennifer had accidentally become what every organization needs but rarely plans for: a bridge between what technology can do and what humans need it to do.

The Questions That Transform Everything

Jennifer cracked the code on AI mentorship, and it's deliciously counterintuitive: forget memorizing every shiny new tool or obsessing over prompt perfection. The real superpower? Becoming a question whisperer. When someone comes to you frustrated with AI results, resist the urge to immediately fix their prompt. Instead, try this sequence:

The Clarity Check

"Before we dive into the AI piece, help me understand what you're really trying to accomplish here."

Most people start with tool problems ("My AI isn't working") when they have outcome problems ("I'm not sure what good would look like"). Get to the real goal first.

The Context Probe

"Tell me about who needs this and how they'll use it."

AI outputs that seem perfectly reasonable in isolation often fail because they don't fit the actual context. Understanding the human side of the equation is crucial.

The Constraint Reality

"What are you working with in terms of time, resources, and approval processes?"

The most elegant AI solution in the world is useless if it requires three levels of approval and a budget increase. Better to find something that works within real constraints than something perfect that never gets implemented.

The Success Picture

"How will you know if this is working?"

This question forces people to get specific about outcomes and often reveals that they need something different from what they initially requested.

Only after working through these questions do you start talking about specific AI approaches. By then, both of you understand the real problem, and the technical solution becomes much clearer.

The Multiplication Effect

Here's where things get interesting. The people Jennifer helped didn't just solve their immediate problems—they started approaching other challenges differently. Tom began using similar thinking in his sales process, which caught the attention of other sales team members. The finance team started asking better questions about their data analysis across multiple projects.

Within six months, Jennifer noticed something unexpected: people were solving problems she'd never heard about using approaches similar to what she'd shown them. Her influence had multiplied beyond her direct interactions.

This is the compound effect of wisdom sharing in action—not just passing along specific techniques, but transmitting a mindset that people can apply broadly.

THE THREE LEVELS OF AI INFLUENCE

As your unofficial mentorship develops, you'll probably notice it happens at three distinct levels:

Level 1: Tool Troubleshooting

"This prompt isn't working. Can you help me fix it?"

This is where most people start—they have a specific technical problem and need immediate help. You show them how to get better results, and they walk away with a working solution.

Level 2: Approach Coaching

"I'm trying to figure out if AI can help with this project. What do you think?"

Here, people are starting to see you as someone who can help them think strategically about AI applications. They're not just looking for technical fixes—they want guidance on whether and how to apply AI to new challenges.

Level 3: Thinking Partnership

"I'm stuck on this problem and not sure how to approach it. Can we brainstorm?"

This is when you know you've crossed into true influence territory. People aren't just coming to you for AI help—they're coming to you because they trust your judgment about problem-solving in general. AI might be part of the conversation, but it's not the focus.

Each level requires different skills and offers different rewards. Tool troubleshooting is quick and gives immediate satisfaction. Approach coaching helps you understand different parts of your organization and builds your reputation for practical wisdom. Thinking partnership is where you have the most impact on how people work and think.

The Cultural Catalyst

The most successful informal AI mentors discover something surprising: their real influence isn't in making people better at using AI. It's in creating permission for thoughtful experimentation.

Marcus, a high school biology teacher, experienced this firsthand. He'd started using AI to help create personalized review materials for struggling students, then began sharing his approach with colleagues. But the real transformation came when other teachers started developing their own AI applications that Marcus had never thought of.

"I realized I wasn't teaching people to copy what I did," Marcus told me. "I was showing them that it was safe to try things, fail safely, and learn from the results. Once people felt that permission, they became incredibly creative."

The Permission-Giving Behaviors

What Marcus discovered is that certain behaviors create psychological safety for experimentation. When you:

Share Failures as Openly as Successes "I tried using AI to generate quiz questions last month, and they were terrible—way too easy and repetitive. But then I realized I could use it to create the raw material and refine it myself." This kind of honest sharing removes the pressure to get everything right the first time and makes experimentation feel safer.

Frame AI as Enhancement, Not Replacement "This isn't about AI doing your job—it's about AI helping you do your job better by handling the parts that drain your energy."

When people understand that the goal is augmentation rather than automation, they're more likely to engage thoughtfully rather than defensively.

Ask for Their Expertise "You know your students better than any AI ever will. If we could get AI to handle the busywork, what would you do with that extra time and mental energy?"

This positions AI as a tool that serves their expertise rather than challenges it.

Model Systematic Thinking "Let me walk you through how I think about this—first I figure out what success looks like, then I identify where the bottlenecks are, then I consider whether AI might help with any of those specific issues."

When people see your thinking process, they can adapt it to their own challenges rather than just copying your solutions.

Becoming the Translator

Perhaps your most valuable role as an informal AI mentor is becoming fluent in two different languages: the language of AI possibility and the language of human reality.

You've probably developed this skill without realizing it. When vendors demo "revolutionary automated insights," you can translate that into plain language: "This tool is good at spotting patterns in large datasets, but you'll need clean data and someone who understands your business context to interpret the results meaningfully."

More importantly, you can translate in the other direction. When colleagues describe their frustrations or aspirations, you can often see the AI applications they can't—not because you're smarter, but because you've developed pattern recognition for where AI adds genuine value.

The Translation Framework

Here's a systematic way to help others bridge the gap between their needs and AI capabilities:

Step 1: Decode the Human Need Listen for the frustration behind the request. When someone says "I need AI to write better emails," they might technically mean "I need help communicating complex ideas clearly" or "I don't have time to craft thoughtful responses to routine requests."

Step 2: Map to AI Strengths AI is excellent at: processing large amounts of information, generating multiple options quickly, maintaining consistency, and following complex but defined patterns.
AI struggles with: understanding unstated context, making judgments that require human experience, handling truly novel situations, and navigating sensitive interpersonal dynamics.

Step 3: Design the Hybrid Approach The best solutions combine AI efficiency with human judgment. AI might generate draft emails, but you choose which tone to use based on your relationship with the recipient. AI might analyze data patterns, but you interpret what those patterns mean for your specific business context.

Step 4: Start Small and Iterate Help people begin with low-stakes experiments that can prove the concept before scaling to more complex applications. Success builds confidence, and confidence enables bigger experiments.

THE RESPONSIBILITY OF INFLUENCE

As your influence spreads, something subtle but important happens: you start feeling a different kind of responsibility. Not the formal accountability that comes with an official role, but the organic responsibility that comes from knowing people trust your judgment.

This changes how you approach your own learning and experimentation. You become more thoughtful about testing new approaches, more careful about the advice you give, more conscious of modeling good practices.

THE THREE RESPONSIBILITIES OF INFORMAL LEADERSHIP

Intellectual Honesty When someone asks about a capability you haven't explored, resist the urge to bluff your way through an answer. "I haven't tried that, but here's how I'd think about testing it" is more valuable than overconfident speculation.

Practical Wisdom Help people separate what's theoretically possible from what's practically useful in their specific context. Your role isn't to get people excited about AI's potential—it's to help them make good decisions about what's worth their time and attention.

Sustainable Development Encourage approaches that build capability rather than create dependency. The goal isn't to become the person everyone comes to for AI solutions—it's to help others develop their own judgment and confidence.

The Network Effect

The most powerful impact of your informal mentorship isn't the direct help you provide—it's the network of thoughtful practitioners you help create.

When Jennifer helps Tom, and Tom adapts that approach to help someone else, and that person discovers a new application that helps Jennifer—you've created a web of mutual learning rather than a one-way flow of information.

These networks tend to be remarkably resilient and adaptive. When new AI capabilities emerge, they don't require formal retraining programs. The network naturally explores, experiments, and shares discoveries. Knowledge flows to where it's most needed, adapts to specific contexts, and evolves based on real-world application.

NURTURING THE NETWORK

You can't create these networks through force or formal structure, but you can create conditions that make them more likely to emerge:

Make Sharing Easy Create low-friction ways for people to share discoveries. Maybe it's a Slack channel, maybe it's five minutes at the beginning of team meetings, maybe it's just making yourself available for informal conversations.

Celebrate Learning, Not Just Success When someone tries something with AI and it doesn't work perfectly, treat that as valuable information rather than failure. "What did you learn?" is often more useful than "What went wrong?"

Connect People to Each Other When two people are working on similar challenges, introduce them. Some of the best AI innovations come from combining insights from different contexts.

Stay Curious Even as you become someone others come to for advice, maintain beginner's mind about new developments. Your willingness to say "I don't know, but let's figure it out together" keeps the network dynamic and adaptive.

The Quiet Revolution

Looking back at Elena's coffee shop moment, it's clear that something significant was happening. Not just one person helping another with a technical problem, but the transmission of a way of thinking that makes technology serve human purposes.

This is how real change spreads—not through mandates or formal programs, but through people like you who model thoughtful practice and help others develop their own capabilities.

You're part of a quiet revolution in how humans and artificial intelligence work together. Not the dramatic revolution of science fiction, where AI either saves us or destroys us, but the practical revolution of everyday people learning to use powerful tools wisely.

Every time you help someone think more clearly about their challenges, you're advancing this revolution. Every time you demonstrate that AI can enhance human capability without replacing human judgment, you're proving what thoughtful adoption looks like. Every time you share both your successes and your failures, you're creating the psychological safety that others need to experiment confidently.

The ripples from your influence spread further than you know, creating workplaces where people use AI not because they have to, but because they've learned to see opportunities that others miss. Where new capabilities are evaluated thoughtfully rather than adopted frantically. Where technology serves human judgment rather than replacing it.

This isn't just about becoming better at AI—it's about becoming the kind of person who helps others navigate technological change with wisdom and confidence. And in a world where the pace of change continues to accelerate, that's exactly the kind of influence we need more of.

The coffee shop conversation continues, one helpful interaction at a time. Your Tuesday is waiting.

12. Learning Lab

💡 Try This: The Ripple Tracker

Purpose: Make visible the influence you're already having on others regarding AI and technology decisions.

Time Required: 5 minutes daily for one week, plus 15 minutes for reflection

Step-by-Step Instructions

Day 1 Setup (5 minutes)

1. Create a simple tracking sheet with these columns:
    - Date/Time
    - Who asked
    - What they asked
    - How I responded
    - Follow-up needed?

2. Set a daily reminder on your phone or calendar for end-of-day logging

Days 1-7: Daily Tracking (2-3 minutes each day)

1. At the end of each workday, review your interactions

2. Record any instance where someone:
    - Asked you about AI tools or capabilities
    - Sought your opinion on a tech solution
    - Wanted help with a digital process
    - Referenced something you'd previously shared about AI
    - Asked "how would you approach this?" for a problem that might involve AI

3. Be specific in the "What they asked" column:
    - Instead of "AI question" write "How to use AI for email responses"
    - Instead of "tech help" write "Which tool for data visualization"

4. In "How I responded," note:
    - Did you provide direct advice?
    - Did you ask clarifying questions first?
    - Did you suggest an experiment or approach?
    - Did you connect them with another resource?

Week-End Reflection (15 minutes)

1. Count total interactions tracked

2. Identify patterns:
    - What types of questions come up most?
    - Which colleagues seek you out repeatedly?
    - How has your response style evolved during the week?

3. Complete these reflection prompts:
    - "I was surprised by..."
    - "I didn't realize people saw me as..."
    - "The most common theme in questions was..."
    - "My typical response approach is..."

Action Planning (5 minutes) Based on your tracking, identify:

- One area where you want to be more helpful
- One type of question you'd like to get better at answering
- One relationship where you could proactively offer assistance

💡 Try This: The Curiosity Filter

Purpose: Develop a personal framework for evaluating new AI developments without getting overwhelmed by every announcement.

Time Required: 30 minutes for framework creation, plus ongoing testing

PHASE 1: FRAMEWORK CREATION (30 MINUTES)

Step 1: Identify Your Context (10 minutes)

1. Write down your primary work responsibilities:
    - What are your top 3 daily/weekly tasks?
    - What are your biggest current frustrations?
    - What outcomes matter most in your role?

2. List your current AI comfort zone:
    - Which AI tools do you use regularly?
    - What types of AI applications do you understand well?
    - Where do you feel confident giving advice to others?

Step 2: Create Your Filter Questions (15 minutes)

Choose 3-5 questions from this list, or create your own based on these examples:

Problem-Focused Questions:

- "What specific problem does this solve that I regularly encounter?"
- "Do I know someone who has this exact frustration?"
- "Would this address one of my top 3 work challenges?"

Readiness Questions:

- "Is this legitimately available to use, or just announced/demoed?"
- "Are there case studies from organizations similar to mine?"
- "What's the likely learning curve vs. potential benefit?"

Integration Questions:

- "How would this fit with tools I already use effectively?"
- "Would this replace something I do well, or enhance it?"
- "Can I test this in a small, low-risk way?"

Resource Questions:

- "Do I have time to properly evaluate this in the next month?"
- "What would I need to stop doing to properly explore this?"
- "Is this worth 30 minutes of experimentation right now?"

Step 3: Set Your Filtering Criteria (5 minutes)

1. Write your chosen 3-5 questions on a reference card or digital note
2. Decide your scoring approach:
    - Simple: Yes/No to each question (need 3+ Yes answers to proceed)
    - Detailed: 1-5 scale for each question (need 15+ total points to proceed)
3. Set your threshold for moving from "ignore" to "investigate"

PHASE 2: TESTING YOUR FILTER (ONGOING)

Step 1: Apply to Current Opportunities (10 minutes)

1. Identify 2-3 AI developments you've recently heard about
2. Apply your filter questions to each
3. Note which ones pass your threshold and which don't
4. Adjust your questions if the results don't feel right

Step 2: Track Effectiveness (Weekly, 5 minutes) For the next month, when you encounter new AI capabilities:

1. Apply your filter before investigating further
2. Track your decisions:
   - What passed your filter?
   - What did you ignore?
   - Were you happy with these decisions a week later?

Step 3: Refine Your Filter (Monthly, 10 minutes)

1. Review your tracking results
2. Adjust questions that led to poor decisions
3. Consider whether your threshold is too high or too low
4. Update your filter based on what you've learned

💡 Try This: The Culture Catalyst

Purpose: Propose one small but meaningful change to improve how your team approaches AI experimentation.

Time Required: 45 minutes for preparation, plus implementation time

PHASE 1: CURRENT STATE ASSESSMENT (15 MINUTES)

Step 1: Observe Current Patterns (10 minutes) Document how your team currently handles new technology:

1. How are AI tools typically introduced? (Top-down mandate? Individual discovery? Vendor demos?)
2. What happens when someone tries something new? (Encouraged? Ignored? Criticized if it fails?)
3. How is information shared about what works/doesn't work?
4. Who makes decisions about adopting new tools?

Step 2: Identify Friction Points (5 minutes) Circle the biggest obstacles you observe:

- Fear of failure or looking incompetent
- Lack of time for experimentation
- No clear process for testing new approaches
- Successes aren't shared effectively
- Failures are seen as personal shortcomings
- Too many tools introduced at once
- No criteria for evaluating what's worth pursuing

PHASE 2: SOLUTION DESIGN (15 MINUTES)

Step 1: Choose Your Focus Area (5 minutes) Select ONE friction point to address. Consider:

- Which obstacle affects the most people?
- What's within your sphere of influence to change?
- What would have the highest impact with minimal resistance?

Step 2: Design a Small Change (10 minutes) Create a specific, actionable proposal. Examples:

For "Fear of Failure":

- Monthly "Learning from Experiments" sharing session where people present both successes and failures
- "Failure Resume" exercise where team members share valuable lessons from things that didn't work

For "No Clear Process":

- Simple "Test Small First" protocol: 30-minute exploration → decision to continue/stop → 2-week pilot → team evaluation
- "AI Experiment Template" with standard questions: Problem being solved? Success criteria? Time limit? What we learned?

For "Successes Not Shared":

- Weekly 5-minute "What's Working" round-robin in team meetings
- Shared document where people log useful discoveries

For "Too Many Tools at Once":

- "One Tool Per Month" rule where team focuses on mastering one new capability before exploring others

PHASE 3: PROPOSAL DEVELOPMENT (15 MINUTES)

Step 1: Write Your Proposal (10 minutes) Structure your proposal with:

1. **Current Challenge:** "I've noticed that..."
2. **Small Solution:** "What if we tried..."
3. **Expected Benefit:** "This could help us..."
4. **Easy Start:** "We could test this by..."
5. **Success Measure:** "We'd know it's working if..."

Step 2: Anticipate Objections (5 minutes) Consider potential concerns:

- "We don't have time for this"
- "This seems like extra work"
- "We've tried similar things before"
- "Leadership won't support it"

For each concern, prepare a brief response that acknowledges the concern and explains how your proposal addresses it.

PHASE 4: IMPLEMENTATION PLANNING

Step 1: Choose Your Approach (Consider your workplace culture)

- Formal proposal to your manager
- Suggestion during team meeting
- Pilot with a few willing colleagues first
- Informal conversation with team lead

Step 2: Start Small

- Propose a 30-day trial rather than permanent change
- Volunteer to coordinate the first few iterations
- Begin with people who are already interested

Step 3: Track Results

- Set specific measures for success
- Check in after 2 weeks and 1 month
- Be prepared to adjust based on what you learn

Conclusion

Your AI Empowerment Journey Continues

Remember that first day? When AI felt like staring into the cockpit of a fighter jet—all those buttons and screens, and you're just hoping you don't accidentally launch something into orbit?

Maybe you saw yourself in Rebecca, wrestling with that 500-square-foot design challenge, wondering how she'd ever make AI understand the difference between "cozy" and "cramped." Or perhaps you were like Miranda, the nurse who just wanted to remember what Mrs. Chen needed without drowning in disconnected health records. Either way, you probably felt like you were standing at the edge of a very deep pool, wondering if you'd sink or swim.

Well, look at you now.

You're not just treading water anymore—you're doing laps. The C.A.L.M. framework has become less like a life preserver and more like muscle memory. You reach for it the way a chef reaches for their favorite knife, without thinking, because it's become part of how you work.

The Transformation You Didn't See Coming

The funny thing about real learning is that it sneaks up on you. One day you're fumbling with prompts like you're trying to ask directions in a language you don't speak. The next, you're crafting conversations with AI that feel more natural than most meetings you attend.

Remember those breakthrough moments?

That first time a prompt hit exactly right, delivering something so useful you did a little victory dance at your desk (don't worry, we've all been there). The day you realized AI wasn't replacing your thinking—it was amplifying it, like having a research assistant who never sleeps, never judges your weird ideas, and never asks for a raise.

The moment you helped someone else get unstuck with AI, and suddenly you weren't just a user anymore—you were a teacher, a translator, a bridge between possibility and practice.

These weren't just wins. They were the moments you stopped being someone who uses AI and started being someone who thinks with it. Let me tell you what happened to some of the people we met along the way, because their stories might remind you of your own transformation.

Where They Are Now

Rebecca doesn't design 500-square-foot apartments anymore—she's moved on to larger projects. But something fundamental changed in how she approaches any design challenge. Last month, when a client wanted to renovate a historic building with impossible spatial constraints, Rebecca didn't panic. She started with Clarity about what the space needed to accomplish, found the right AI tools for spatial analysis, crafted prompts that helped her explore solutions she'd never considered, and manifested a design that preserved the building's character while making it functional for modern use. The project won an architecture award, but more importantly, Rebecca can't imagine working without her AI thinking partnership.

Miranda is still a nurse, still caring for patients with the same compassion that drew her to healthcare twenty-two years ago. But now she spends her time looking into patients' eyes instead of staring at disconnected screens. The AI-assisted handoff application she helped develop has spread to three other hospitals. Last week, a nursing student asked her about "the Miranda Method" for patient communication. Miranda laughed—there's no method, she said. Just using technology to do what nurses have always done: see patients as complete human beings, not just medical conditions.

Elena from the jewelry business has scaled beyond her wildest dreams, but she still makes every piece by hand. The difference is that AI handles the inventory predictions, customer service templates, and social media scheduling, freeing her to focus on the work that drew her to metalworking in the first place. She told me recently that she's never been more creative—not because AI made her creative, but because it gave her back the mental space to think about what silver wants to become.

Veronica at the Riverside Education Foundation just received a call from a funder who'd read one of their impact reports. "This is the first grant report I've ever read that made me want to increase our support instead of just renew it," the program officer said. Veronica smiled, remembering the days when writing those reports felt like torture. Now they're strategic conversations about how to serve students better, with AI helping her tell the stories that matter most.

Each of these people would tell you the same thing: AI didn't change what they care about. It just made them better at caring about it.

Your Framework, Your Superpower

The C.A.L.M. AI Navigator isn't just a method you learned—it's become your operating system. Like learning to drive, where you stop thinking about the mechanics and start thinking about where you want to go.

Clarity taught you that AI without direction is like a Ferrari without a steering wheel—impressive, but not particularly useful. You learned to ask better questions, not just louder ones. You discovered that the most powerful prompts aren't the cleverest—they're the clearest.

Alignment showed you that the best AI strategy isn't about having the fanciest tools—it's about having the right tools for the right job at the right time. You learned to resist the everything-bagel approach and embrace focused solutions that functionally solve real problems.

Leverage transformed you from someone who asks AI to do things into someone who collaborates with it. You discovered that the magic isn't in the prompt—it's in the conversation. You learned to have discussions with AI that feel more productive than most human meetings.

Manifest proved that insights without action are just expensive entertainment. You learned to turn AI outputs into real-world results that matter to the people who sign your checks and the people your work serves.

The beautiful reality of what went down? You grew some serious wisdom muscles. Not just the tech-savvy stuff, but that golden intuition about when to lean in and when to pump the brakes, when to let the AI run wild and when to trust that little voice in your head, when to automate the hell out of something and when to keep it gloriously, messily human.

That judgment is your superpower, and it's transferable to whatever comes next.

The Paradox of Mastery

Here's the beautiful paradox of getting really ridiculously good at stuff: wisdom is basically a never-ending rabbit hole of "wait, there's more?" moments. But plot twist—that constant state of "huh, interesting" isn't a design flaw, it's the entire game.

Six months ago, when you didn't know what you didn't know, every new AI development felt overwhelming. Now that you understand the landscape better, you can evaluate new tools quickly and ignore most of them confidently. Counterintuitively, expertise makes you more selective, not less. You've developed what I call "productive ignorance"—the ability to deliberately ignore most AI developments because you know they won't solve problems you have. This isn't being behind; this is being strategic.

Every AI expert started exactly where you started. Every breakthrough began with someone staring at a blinking cursor, wondering what to type next. The difference isn't that they knew more—it's that they kept going when it felt uncertain, and they learned to trust their developing judgment.

The AI landscape will keep evolving. New tools will emerge, old ones will disappear, and the whole field will probably look completely different in five years. But the fundamentals you've learned—how to think clearly about problems, how to communicate effectively with machines, how to turn possibilities into realities—those don't expire.

Your Daily Practice (Without the Guilt)

Growth doesn't require grand gestures or perfect habits. It requires showing up, even when you don't feel like it. But let's be honest about what sustainable practice looks like.

You don't need to read every AI newsletter, try every new tool, or keep up with every development. That's a recipe for burnout, not mastery. Instead, try this approach that's worked for dozens of successful AI practitioners:

The Monday Momentum Check Start each week by asking: "What's one frustrating task I could tackle differently this week?" Not ten things. One thing. Maybe it's that monthly report that always takes too long. Maybe it's the client emails that never sound quite right. Maybe it's the data analysis that makes your eyes glaze over.

The Friday Reflection End each week by noticing: "What did I learn about working with AI?" This isn't about accomplishments (though celebrate those too). It's about insights. Maybe you discovered that morning is your best time for crafting complex prompts. Maybe you realized that AI works better for your writing when you're tired than when you're fresh. Maybe you learned that your best AI conversations happen when you treat the tool like a slightly formal colleague rather than a magical oracle.

The Monthly Experiment Once a month, try something new. Not because you have to stay current, but because curiosity keeps your skills sharp. Maybe it's a different approach to a familiar task. Maybe it's helping a colleague with their AI challenge. Maybe it's testing whether a new tool solves a problem you have. It's like trying on shoes to see if they prevent blisters on your weird-shaped feet, not because they match your favorite outfit.

This rhythm—weekly focus, weekly reflection, monthly exploration—creates sustainable growth without the pressure of constant optimization.

The Ripple Effect You're Creating

The most powerful thing about mastering AI isn't what it does for you—it's what it does through you.

Think about Elena in that coffee shop, helping a stranger fix his pitch deck. She didn't set out to become an AI mentor that morning. She just recognized someone struggling with something she'd learned to navigate. But that ten-minute conversation probably changed how that founder approaches problem-solving, which will affect how he builds his company, which will influence how his employees think about technology.

That's the ripple effect in action.

Every time you help someone see AI as an ally instead of a threat, you're changing the conversation. Every time you solve a problem that seemed impossible, you're expanding what people think is possible. Every time you approach a challenge with curiosity instead of fear, you're modeling a different way of being in the world.

You're not just becoming better at using AI. You're becoming someone who makes AI better for everyone around you.

Jennifer from the marketing department told me something last week that stuck with me: "I realized I'm not just solving my own problems anymore. I'm solving problems I would have had, which frees me up to work on problems I actually want to have."

That's what mastery looks like—moving from reactive problem-solving to proactive opportunity-creation.

What Happens Next

Closing this book doesn't end your story—it just turns the page. But unlike most conclusions that leave you with vague inspiration, let me tell you exactly what happens next, because I've watched this pattern play out dozens of times.

In the next month, you'll probably help someone else with an AI challenge. It might be a colleague who's frustrated with a tool, a friend who's curious about what you've learned, or a family member who's heard you talking about AI and wants to understand what the fuss is about. When this happens, you'll realize how much you've learned by trying to explain it to someone else.

In the next three months, you'll likely encounter an AI capability that didn't exist when you started reading this book. Instead of feeling behind or overwhelmed, you'll find yourself evaluating it through your C.A.L.M. lens: What problem does this solve? How does it align with my needs? How would I test it safely? This confidence in your ability to assess new developments is one of the most valuable skills you've developed.

In the next six months, someone will probably ask you to lead or advise on an AI initiative at work. Not because you're the designated AI person, but because you've developed a reputation for thoughtful implementation. You'll discover that your real value isn't technical expertise—it's the ability to bridge the gap between what's possible and what's practical.

In the next year, you'll look back on problems that used to frustrate you and realize you've been solving them automatically, without conscious effort. The monthly report that used to take all afternoon now takes an hour. The client communications that used to drain your energy now feel effortless. The data analysis that used to require a degree in statistics now fits into your normal workflow.

Here's the most important prediction: you'll find yourself working on more interesting problems. Not because AI solved all your boring problems (though it helped), but because you freed up mental energy for the kind of thinking that only humans can do—creative problem-solving, strategic planning, relationship building, and figuring out what matters most.

The Question That Matters

The future isn't about whether you're ready for what comes next. You've already proven you can adapt to powerful new tools and integrate them thoughtfully into meaningful work. The question is: what do you want to create now that you have these capabilities?

What problems have you been avoiding because they seemed too complex, too time-consuming, or too overwhelming? What opportunities have you been ignoring because you didn't have the bandwidth to pursue them? What impact could you have if you weren't spending all your time on tasks that artificial intelligence can handle?

Rebecca is designing spaces that seemed impossible to create.

Miranda is providing patient care that feels more human than ever.

Elena is creating art while running a thriving business.

Veronica is telling stories that change how people think about education.

What's your version of that transformation?

Your AI Journey Continues

The truth is, you're not finishing an AI course or completing a training program. You're continuing a journey that started with curiosity and uncertainty, led through strategic, systematic learning and growing confidence, and now opens into possibilities you couldn't have imagined when you started.

The tools will keep evolving. Your judgment will keep developing. The problems you solve will get more interesting, the impact you create will get more meaningful, and the confidence you've built will keep growing.

You've learned to think with artificial intelligence, but more importantly, you've learned to think better about problems that matter. You've developed skills that transfer across tools and technologies. You've built habits of experimentation and reflection that will serve you regardless of what comes next.

The C.A.L.M. AI Navigator was your training wheels, but now you're riding without them. You've developed your own sense of balance, your own intuition about when to lean in and when to pull back, your own ability to navigate whatever terrain comes next.

So go ahead. Take that next step. Ask that bigger question. Try that wild idea. Help that colleague who's struggling. Lead that initiative that could make a difference. Share what you've learned with someone who needs to hear it.

The tools are in your hands, the knowledge is in your head, the judgment is in your bones, and the future is wide open.

More importantly, you're ready for it.

Your AI empowerment journey continues, one thoughtful decision at a time.

Bonus Resources

AI Prompt Templates for Chapter Concepts

For Self-Reflection and Growth

Personal Evolution Assessment

"Help me analyze my professional growth in [specific area]. Over the past [time period], I've experienced these changes: [list 3-5 specific examples]. What patterns do you see in this evolution? What capabilities does this suggest I've developed? What might be logical next steps for continued growth?"

Skill Gap Analysis

"I'm effective at [current capabilities] but want to develop [desired capability]. Given my background in [context], what would be a realistic progression plan? Break this into small, practical steps I could take over the next 3 months."

For Helping Others

Problem Clarification Template

"A colleague described this challenge: [describe situation]. Before suggesting solutions, help me ask better questions to understand: 1) What they're trying to accomplish, 2) What constraints they're working with, 3) What success would look like to them, 4) What they've already tried."

Advice Framing Template

"I want to help a colleague with [specific problem]. They have [background/experience level] with technology. How can I explain [concept/solution] in a way that's helpful but not overwhelming? Give me 2-3 different approaches based on their comfort level."

For Evaluation and Decision-Making

Tool Assessment Template

"I'm considering [specific AI tool/capability] for [specific use case]. Help me evaluate this systematically: What questions should I ask about readiness, integration, learning curve, and potential ROI? What are common failure modes for this type of implementation?"

Experiment Design Template

"I want to test [specific AI application] for [specific problem]. Help me design a small, low-risk experiment. What would be appropriate success criteria, time limits, and evaluation methods? How can I structure this to learn regardless of whether it succeeds?"

For Organizational Change

Change Proposal Template

"I want to propose [specific small change] to improve how my team approaches [specific challenge]. Help me structure this proposal to address potential concerns about time, resources, and risk. How can I frame this as a low-commitment experiment?"

Culture Building Template

"I want to encourage more [specific behavior/mindset] in my workplace around technology adoption. Given that people currently [current behavior], what small actions could I take to model a different approach? How can I influence culture without being pushy?"

Usage Tips for These Templates

1. **Be Specific:** Replace bracketed placeholders with concrete details from your situation

2. **Iterate:** Use follow-up prompts to refine the AI's responses based on your specific context
3. **Adapt:** Modify the templates based on what works best for your communication style
4. **Document:** Save particularly useful responses to reference later or share with colleagues

More Prompt Templates to Get You Started

These 50 prompts—25 for daily tasks and 25 for business-specific needs—are designed to give you a head start in building your AI prompt playbook. Start experimenting with them, adapt them to your unique needs, and watch as your workflows become smoother, faster, and more impactful. Ready to try your first one? Let's see what you can create!

Quick-Start Framework

"I need help with [specific task] for [audience/context]. The outcome should be [desired result] with a [tone/style] approach. Key constraints: [limitations/requirements]. Most important: [primary objective]."

Daily Life & Organization

1. Smart Reminders

Prompt: "Create a reminder process for [event/task] on [date/time]. Include context about [why it matters], preparation needed [specific prep steps], and follow-up actions [what happens after]."

Example: "Create a reminder process for my quarterly review meeting on Thursday at 2 PM. Include context about why performance metrics matter, preparation needed like gathering project examples, and follow-up actions like scheduling development goals discussion."

2. Strategic Shopping List

Prompt: "Design a shopping list for [event/goal] considering [budget/dietary restrictions]. Prioritize by [urgency/importance] and include alternatives for [specific items]."

Example: "Design a shopping list for a healthy meal prep week considering a $75 budget and gluten-free restrictions. Prioritize by nutritional value and include alternatives for expensive proteins."

3. Adaptive Recipe Generator

Prompt: "Create a [meal type] recipe using [available ingredients] that serves [number] people. Accommodate [dietary needs] and provide [skill level] instructions with [time constraint]."

Example: "Create a dinner recipe using leftover chicken and vegetables that serves 4 people. Accommodate dairy-free needs and provide beginner instructions with 30-minute time constraint."

4. Dynamic Calendar Management

Prompt: "Schedule [event] for [date/time] with [duration]. Consider [scheduling conflicts/preferences], include [preparation buffer], and set [reminder sequence]."

Example: "Schedule client presentation for next Tuesday at 10 AM with 2-hour duration. Consider my morning energy peak, include 30-minute preparation buffer, and set reminder sequence at 1 day, 2 hours, and 15 minutes before."

5. Personalized Fitness Planning

Prompt: "Design a [workout type] routine for [timeframe] targeting [specific goals]. Consider [current fitness level], [available equipment], and [physical limitations]. Include progression plan."

Example: "Design a strength training routine for 45 minutes targeting muscle building. Consider intermediate fitness level, home gym equipment, and lower back sensitivity. Include 4-week progression plan."

Travel & Lifestyle

6. Smart Packing Strategy

Prompt: "Create a packing list for [destination] trip lasting [duration] during [season]. Include items for [specific activities], consider [luggage constraints], and optimize for [priorities]."

Example: "Create a packing list for Tokyo business trip lasting 5 days during spring. Include items for client meetings and weekend sightseeing, consider carry-on only constraint, and optimize for versatility."

7. Intelligent Meal Prep

Prompt: "Plan [number] days of [meal type] that meets [dietary goals]. Consider [time constraints], [cooking skills], and [ingredient preferences]. Include storage and reheating instructions."

Example: "Plan 5 days of lunches that meets high-protein goals. Consider 2-hour Sunday prep time, intermediate cooking skills, and preference for Mediterranean flavors. Include storage and reheating instructions."

8. Thoughtful Gift Curation

Prompt: "Suggest gift ideas for [person] celebrating [occasion]. Consider their [interests/hobbies], [relationship dynamic], and [budget range]. Include personalization options."

Example: "Suggest gift ideas for my sister celebrating her promotion. Consider her love of photography and travel, our close relationship, and $50-100 budget range. Include personalization options."

Productivity & Growth

9. Strategic To-Do Management

Prompt: "Create a to-do list for [project/goal] with [timeline]. Prioritize by [criteria], break down [complex tasks], and include [accountability measures]."

Example: "Create a to-do list for launching my freelance business with 3-month timeline. Prioritize by revenue impact, break down legal setup tasks, and include weekly progress check-ins."

10. Curated Learning Resources

Prompt: "Recommend learning resources for [topic] suitable for [current level]. Focus on [learning style], consider [time availability], and include [practice opportunities]."

Example: "Recommend learning resources for data analysis suitable for beginner level. Focus on visual learning style, consider 5 hours weekly availability, and include hands-on practice opportunities."

11. Comprehensive Budget Planning

Prompt: "Create a budget for [goal/event] with [total amount]. Break down by [categories], include [contingency planning], and suggest [cost-saving strategies]."

Example: "Create a budget for home renovation with $15,000 total. Break down by room priorities, include 15% contingency planning, and suggest DIY cost-saving strategies."

12. Optimized Time Management

Prompt: "Design a daily schedule for [primary goal] that accommodates [constraints]. Include [energy management], [buffer time], and [flexibility measures]."

Example: "Design a daily schedule for writing productivity that accommodates part-time job constraints. Include peak creativity hours, 15-minute buffer time, and flexibility for unexpected calls."

13. Structured Skill Development

Prompt: "Create a learning plan for [skill] within [timeframe]. Consider [current knowledge], [available resources], and [practice opportunities]. Include milestones and assessment methods."

Example: "Create a learning plan for public speaking within 3 months. Consider current anxiety level, available online courses, and local Toastmasters opportunities. Include weekly milestones and self-assessment methods."

Entertainment & Wellness

14. Tailored Movie Experience

Prompt: "Plan a movie night for [audience] with [mood/theme]. Consider [viewing preferences], [snack options], and [discussion elements]."

Example: "Plan a movie night for family with nostalgic theme. Consider mixed age preferences, healthy snack options, and post-movie discussion questions."

15. Comprehensive Pet Care

Prompt: "Provide pet care guidance for [pet type] during [situation]. Consider [pet's personality], [environmental factors], and [available resources]. Include prevention and emergency tips."

Example: "Provide pet care guidance for anxious rescue dog during thunderstorms. Consider her fear triggers, apartment living constraints, and limited budget. Include prevention and emergency calming techniques."

16. Guided Meditation Design

Prompt: "Create a [duration] meditation session for [specific goal]. Consider [experience level], [environment], and [preferred techniques]. Include preparation and integration steps."

Example: "Create a 15-minute meditation session for work stress relief. Consider beginner experience, office environment, and preference for breathing techniques. Include desk preparation and return-to-work integration."

17. Professional Event Planning

Prompt: "Draft event materials for [event type] including [specific elements]. Consider [audience expectations], [logistics], and [follow-up requirements]."

Example: "Draft event materials for networking mixer including invitations and agenda. Consider professional audience expectations, venue logistics, and contact exchange follow-up."

Problem-Solving & Creativity

18. Troubleshooting

Prompt: "Diagnose and solve [specific problem] with [device/system]. Consider [symptoms], [recent changes], and [available tools]. Include prevention strategies."

Example: "Diagnose and solve slow internet connection with home network. Consider intermittent symptoms, recent router update, and basic diagnostic tools. Include future prevention strategies."

19. Mood-Based Playlist Curation

Prompt: "Create a [duration] playlist for [specific activity/mood]. Include [genre preferences], [energy progression], and [personal significance]. Consider [listening context]."

Example: "Create a 60-minute playlist for morning workout motivation. Include electronic and rock preferences, building energy progression, and songs with personal achievement memories. Consider gym environment acoustics."

20. Holistic Morning Routine

Prompt: "Design a morning routine for [primary goal] within [time limit]. Consider [personal rhythms], [non-negotiables], and [seasonal adjustments]. Include flexibility options."

Example: "Design a morning routine for mental clarity within 45 minutes. Consider slow-wake personality, meditation non-negotiable, and seasonal light adjustments. Include rushed-day flexibility options."

21. Sustainable Cleaning

Prompt: "Create a cleaning schedule for [space] over [timeframe]. Consider [lifestyle factors], [available time], and [cleaning preferences]. Include maintenance and deep-cleaning cycles."

Example: "Create a cleaning schedule for small apartment over monthly cycles. Consider busy work schedule, 20-minute daily availability, and preference for natural products. Include weekly maintenance and seasonal deep-cleaning."

22. Engaging Social Media Content

Prompt: "Write a [tone] social media post for [content type]. Consider [audience], [platform specifics], and [engagement goals]. Include [call-to-action] and [hashtag strategy]."

Example: "Write an inspiring social media post for career milestone announcement. Consider professional network audience, LinkedIn platform specifics, and networking engagement goals. Include connection invitation and industry hashtag strategy."

23. Creative DIY Project Guide

Prompt: "Create a step-by-step guide for [project] using [materials]. Consider [skill level], [available tools], and [customization options]. Include troubleshooting and finishing touches."

Example: "Create a step-by-step guide for building floating shelves using reclaimed wood. Consider intermediate skill level, basic power tools, and size customization options. Include wall-mounting troubleshooting and staining finishing touches."

24. Immersive Travel Planning

Prompt: "Plan a [duration] itinerary for [destination] focusing on [travel style]. Consider [budget], [interests], and [local context]. Include flexibility for spontaneous discoveries."

Example: "Plan a 4-day itinerary for Barcelona focusing on cultural immersion. Consider moderate budget, architecture interests, and local festival context. Include flexibility for spontaneous neighborhood discoveries."

25. Personalized Self-Care Design

Prompt: "Create a self-care plan for [specific need] considering [time availability]. Include [preferred activities], [environmental factors], and [sustainability measures]. Add progress tracking."

Example: "Create a self-care plan for creative burnout recovery considering 30-minute daily availability. Include nature-based activities, home environment setup, and weekly sustainability check-ins. Add energy level progress tracking."

Strategic Framework
"Analyze [business challenge/opportunity] for [organization context]. Consider [market conditions], [stakeholder perspectives], and [resource constraints]. Deliver [specific outcome] with [success metrics] and [implementation roadmap]."

Strategic Planning & Analysis

1. Comprehensive SWOT Analysis

Prompt: "Conduct a detailed SWOT analysis for [business/project] within [market context]. Include [external factors], [competitive landscape], and [timeline considerations]. Provide strategic recommendations and risk mitigation strategies."

Example: "Conduct a detailed SWOT analysis for launching a B2B SaaS platform within the post-pandemic remote work market. Include economic uncertainty factors, competitive landscape with established players, and 18-month timeline considerations. Provide strategic recommendations and risk mitigation strategies."

2. Data-Driven Customer Persona Development

Prompt: "Create a comprehensive customer persona for [product/service] targeting [specific segment]. Include [psychographic data], [behavioral patterns], [pain points], and [buying journey]. Add persona validation methods and marketing activation strategies."

Example: "Create a comprehensive customer persona for AI-powered project management software targeting mid-market IT directors. Include decision-making psychographics, software adoption patterns, budget approval pain points, and 6-month buying journey. Add persona validation methods and LinkedIn marketing activation strategies."

3. Strategic Business Proposal Development

Prompt: "Develop a compelling business proposal for [specific initiative] addressing [stakeholder concerns]. Include [ROI projections], [implementation timeline], [resource requirements], and [success metrics]. Add risk assessment and change management considerations."

Example: "Develop a compelling business proposal for implementing AI customer service chatbots addressing executive cost concerns. Include 18-month ROI projections, phased implementation timeline, technical resource requirements, and customer satisfaction metrics. Add integration risk assessment and staff change management considerations."

4. Consultative Sales Pitch Architecture

Prompt: "Create a consultative sales pitch for [solution] targeting [specific role/industry]. Focus on [business outcomes], include [objection handling], and provide [proof points]. Add discovery questions and follow-up sequences."

Example: "Create a consultative sales pitch for cybersecurity consulting targeting healthcare CFOs. Focus on compliance cost reduction outcomes, include budget objection handling, and provide HIPAA penalty avoidance proof points. Add financial discovery questions and 14-day follow-up sequences."

5. Integrated Marketing Campaign Strategy

Prompt: "Design a multi-channel marketing campaign for [product/service] targeting [audience segment]. Include [channel mix], [budget allocation], [content themes], and [measurement framework]. Add competitor response scenarios and optimization triggers."

Example: "Design a multi-channel marketing campaign for enterprise software renewal targeting existing customers. Include email/LinkedIn/webinar channel mix, 70/20/10 budget allocation, value reinforcement content themes, and NPS measurement framework. Add competitor poaching scenarios and churn prevention optimization triggers."

Market Intelligence & Competition

6. Strategic Competitor Analysis

Prompt: "Conduct competitive intelligence analysis on [competitor] versus [your position]. Evaluate [market positioning], [pricing strategies], [customer feedback], and [innovation pipeline]. Identify competitive advantages and strategic opportunities."

Example: "Conduct competitive intelligence analysis on Slack versus our team communication platform. Evaluate enterprise market positioning, freemium pricing strategies, G2 customer feedback patterns, and AI integration pipeline. Identify our workflow automation advantages and SMB market opportunities."

7. Actionable Meeting Documentation

Prompt: "Create structured meeting documentation for [meeting type] including [participant roles], [decision frameworks], and [accountability measures]. Add progress tracking and escalation procedures."

Example: "Create structured meeting documentation for cross-functional product roadmap reviews including engineering/product/sales participant roles, priority scoring frameworks, and feature owner accountability measures. Add sprint progress tracking and executive escalation procedures."

8. Outcome-Based Training Program Design

Prompt: "Develop a comprehensive training program for [skill/topic] targeting [audience level]. Include [learning objectives], [assessment methods], [practical applications], and [reinforcement strategies]. Add ROI measurement and continuous improvement processes."

Example: "Develop a comprehensive training program for consultative selling targeting junior sales reps. Include revenue impact objectives, role-playing assessment methods, real deal practical applications, and manager coaching reinforcement strategies. Add deal conversion ROI measurement and quarterly improvement processes."

Content & Communication Strategy

9. Brand-Aligned Social Media Strategy

Prompt: "Create a strategic social media content plan for [brand/campaign] across [specific platforms]. Include [content pillars], [engagement strategies], [influencer partnerships], and [conversion funnels]. Add crisis management and performance optimization protocols."

Example: "Create a strategic social media content plan for B2B fintech product launch across LinkedIn and Twitter. Include thought leadership/product demo/customer success content pillars, executive engagement strategies, industry analyst partnerships, and free trial conversion funnels. Add regulatory compliance crisis management and engagement rate optimization protocols."

10. Conversion-Optimized Product Descriptions

Prompt: "Write high-converting product descriptions for [product] targeting [buyer persona]. Include [emotional triggers], [technical specifications], [social proof], and [urgency elements]. Add A/B testing variations and SEO optimization."

Example: "Write high-converting product descriptions for enterprise security software targeting IT directors. Include data breach fear triggers, compliance technical specifications, Fortune 500 social proof, and limited-time pricing urgency elements. Add headline A/B testing variations and cybersecurity keyword SEO optimization."

11. Media Relations & PR Strategy

Prompt: "Develop a press release strategy for [news/launch] targeting [media outlets]. Include [newsworthy angles], [spokesperson positioning], [media kit elements], and [follow-up sequences]. Add crisis communication protocols and media relationship building."

Example: "Develop a press release strategy for AI startup funding announcement targeting tech trade publications. Include job creation newsworthy angles, CEO thought leader positioning, demo video media kit elements, and journalist relationship follow-up sequences. Add investor privacy crisis protocols and reporter relationship building."

Operations & Human Resources

12. Strategic Employee Onboarding Journey

Prompt: "Design a comprehensive onboarding experience for [role/department] focusing on [cultural integration], [skill development], and [performance acceleration]. Include [milestone checkpoints], [mentorship programs], and [feedback loops]. Add retention metrics and experience optimization."

Example: "Design a comprehensive onboarding experience for remote software developers focusing on company culture integration, coding standard skill development, and 90-day productivity acceleration. Include weekly milestone checkpoints, senior developer mentorship programs, and 360-degree feedback loops. Add 12-month retention metrics and virtual experience optimization."

13. Executive Financial Reporting

Prompt: "Create an executive financial summary for [report/period] highlighting [key metrics], [variance analysis], and [strategic implications]. Include [trend analysis], [forecast adjustments], and [action recommendations]. Add board presentation formatting and stakeholder communication."

Example: "Create an executive financial summary for Q3 performance highlighting recurring revenue metrics, customer acquisition cost variance analysis, and market expansion strategic implications. Include 12-month trend analysis, Q4 forecast adjustments, and investment reallocation recommendations. Add board presentation formatting and investor communication."

14. Professional Development & Training

Prompt: "Develop a structured webinar program for [topic/audience] including [engagement strategies], [content delivery], and [follow-up conversion]. Add participation metrics and continuous improvement protocols."

Example: "Develop a structured webinar program for enterprise sales training including interactive polling engagement strategies, case study content delivery, and CRM implementation follow-up conversion. Add attendance/completion metrics and monthly content improvement protocols."

15. Customer Experience Optimization

Prompt: "Create a customer feedback strategy for [touchpoint/experience] targeting [customer segment]. Include [feedback collection methods], [analysis frameworks], and [improvement implementation]. Add customer journey mapping and satisfaction benchmarking."

Example: "Create a customer feedback strategy for SaaS onboarding experience targeting enterprise customers. Include post-setup survey collection methods, sentiment analysis frameworks, and UX improvement implementation. Add user journey mapping and industry satisfaction benchmarking."

Event & Relationship Management

16. Integrated Event Marketing Strategy

Prompt: "Design a comprehensive event marketing strategy for [event type] targeting [audience segment]. Include [pre-event promotion], [engagement tactics], [lead capture], and [post-event nurturing]. Add ROI measurement and relationship building protocols."

Example: "Design a comprehensive event marketing strategy for industry conference targeting C-suite prospects. Include LinkedIn thought leadership pre-event promotion, interactive demo engagement tactics, qualified lead capture systems, and personalized post-event nurturing. Add pipeline ROI measurement and executive relationship building protocols."

17. Quality Assurance & Process Improvement

Prompt: "Develop a comprehensive review framework for [process/proposal] ensuring [quality standards], [compliance requirements], and [stakeholder alignment]. Include [checkpoints], [approval workflows], and [continuous improvement]. Add error prevention and efficiency optimization."

Example: "Develop a comprehensive review framework for client proposal development ensuring brand consistency standards, legal compliance requirements, and sales/legal stakeholder alignment. Include peer review checkpoints, executive approval workflows, and win-rate continuous improvement. Add common error prevention and template efficiency optimization."

18. Customer Retention & Growth Strategy

Prompt: "Create a strategic customer retention program for [business type] addressing [churn factors]. Include [engagement tactics], [value delivery], [loyalty programs], and [expansion opportunities]. Add predictive analytics and personalization strategies."

Example: "Create a strategic customer retention program for subscription software addressing feature adoption churn factors. Include user success engagement tactics, ROI demonstration value delivery, enterprise tier loyalty programs, and cross-sell expansion opportunities. Add usage predictive analytics and account-specific personalization strategies."

Product & Project Management

19. Strategic Product Launch Planning

Prompt: "Develop a comprehensive product launch strategy for [product/service] including [market preparation], [stakeholder coordination], [risk management], and [success measurement]. Add competitive response planning and post-launch optimization."

Example: "Develop a comprehensive product launch strategy for AI-powered analytics feature including beta customer market preparation, sales/marketing/support stakeholder coordination, data privacy risk management, and user adoption success measurement. Add competitor feature response planning and usage pattern post-launch optimization."

20. Customer Education & Support Content

Prompt: "Create comprehensive FAQ and support content for [product/service] addressing [user challenges]. Include [self-service solutions], [escalation paths], and [continuous improvement]. Add user behavior analytics and content optimization strategies."

Example: "Create comprehensive FAQ and support content for enterprise integration software addressing API implementation challenges. Include code example self-service solutions, technical support escalation paths, and documentation continuous improvement. Add search behavior analytics and content effectiveness optimization strategies."

21. Customer Service Excellence Framework

Prompt: "Develop customer service protocols for [situation type] including [resolution procedures], [escalation management], and [customer satisfaction]. Add quality assurance metrics and team performance optimization."

Example: "Develop customer service protocols for subscription cancellation requests including retention conversation procedures, supervisor escalation management, and satisfaction recovery measurement. Add call quality assurance metrics and agent performance optimization."

Performance & Development

22. Comprehensive Performance Management

Prompt: "Create a performance evaluation framework for [role/team] including [objective metrics], [subjective assessments], and [development planning]. Add career progression pathways and performance improvement protocols."

Example: "Create a performance evaluation framework for sales team including quota achievement metrics, client relationship subjective assessments, and skill development planning. Add account management career progression pathways and performance improvement protocols."

23. Internal Communication Strategy

Prompt: "Develop internal communication templates for [communication type] ensuring [message clarity], [stakeholder engagement], and [action orientation]. Add feedback mechanisms and communication effectiveness measurement."

Example: "Develop internal communication templates for organizational change announcements ensuring transparent message clarity, all-level stakeholder engagement, and clear action orientation. Add employee feedback mechanisms and communication effectiveness measurement."

24. Brand Voice & Messaging Architecture

Prompt: "Create comprehensive brand voice guidelines for [company/product] including [personality traits], [messaging frameworks], [content examples], and [application guidelines]. Add brand consistency monitoring and evolution protocols."

Example: "Create comprehensive brand voice guidelines for B2B fintech platform including trustworthy/innovative personality traits, value proposition messaging frameworks, various content channel examples, and cross-team application guidelines. Add brand consistency monitoring and voice evolution protocols."

25. Strategic Talent Acquisition

Prompt: "Design a comprehensive recruitment strategy for [position] including [candidate profiling], [attraction methods], [assessment criteria], and [onboarding integration]. Add diversity considerations and hiring success metrics."

Example: "Design a comprehensive recruitment strategy for senior product manager including technical/leadership candidate profiling, LinkedIn/referral attraction methods, case study assessment criteria, and team onboarding integration. Add diversity pipeline considerations and 90-day hiring success metrics."

💰 *How to Pay Off Debt Really Comically Fast*

1. Debt Avalanche Accelerator
Prompt: "Create a debt elimination strategy for [total debt amount] across [number] accounts with [monthly available amount]. Use the avalanche method but include [side hustle opportunities] and [expense reduction tactics]. Show month-by-month payoff timeline with motivation milestones."
Example: "Create a debt elimination strategy for $45,000 across 6 credit cards with $800 monthly available. Use the avalanche method but include weekend gig opportunities and subscription audit tactics. Show month-by-month payoff timeline with celebration milestones."

2. Income Explosion Plan
Prompt: "Design a 90-day income boost plan using [current skills/job] to generate an extra [target amount] monthly for debt payoff. Include [time constraints], [available resources], and [risk tolerance]. Add specific action steps and income tracking methods."
Example: "Design a 90-day income boost plan using my graphic design skills to generate an extra $1,500 monthly for debt payoff. Include evening/weekend constraints, laptop and Adobe Suite resources, and low-risk tolerance. Add specific client acquisition steps and invoice tracking methods."

3. Expense Elimination Audit
Prompt: "Conduct a ruthless expense audit to find [target savings amount] monthly for debt acceleration. Analyze [spending categories], identify [painless cuts vs. lifestyle changes], and create [alternative solutions]. Include psychological tricks to maintain motivation."
Example: "Conduct a ruthless expense audit to find $600 monthly for debt acceleration. Analyze dining/entertainment/subscriptions categories, identify

coffee shop cuts vs. gym membership changes, and create home workout alternatives. Include visual progress tracking tricks to maintain motivation."

4. Debt Consolidation Calculator
Prompt: "Evaluate debt consolidation options for [debt details] considering [credit score] and [income]. Compare [consolidation methods], calculate [interest savings], and assess [qualification likelihood]. Include pros/cons and hidden fee analysis."
Example: "Evaluate debt consolidation options for $32,000 credit card debt considering 680 credit score and $65,000 income. Compare personal loan/balance transfer/HELOC methods, calculate 5-year interest savings, and assess qualification likelihood. Include pros/cons and origination fee analysis."

5. Side Hustle Debt Destroyer
Prompt: "Match my [skills/interests] with high-paying side hustles that can generate [target amount] monthly. Consider [time availability], [startup costs], and [income timeline]. Rank by effort-to-income ratio and provide launch strategies."
Example: "Match my writing skills and social media interests with high-paying side hustles that can generate $1,200 monthly. Consider 15 hours weekly availability, $200 startup budget, and 30-day income timeline. Rank by effort-to-income ratio and provide client acquisition strategies."

🛒 *How to Pay Less for Groceries*

6. Strategic Shopping System
Prompt: "Create a grocery budget reduction plan to cut spending from [current amount] to [target amount] monthly. Include [family size], [dietary restrictions], and [time constraints]. Add meal planning, coupon stacking, and store optimization strategies."
Example: "Create a grocery budget reduction plan to cut spending from $800 to $500 monthly. Include family of 4, gluten-free restrictions, and busy schedule constraints. Add batch cooking meal planning, app-based coupon stacking, and multi-store optimization strategies."

7. Bulk Buying Calculator
Prompt: "Analyze bulk buying opportunities for [household size] to maximize savings on [frequently purchased items]. Consider [storage space], [expiration dates], and [upfront costs]. Calculate annual savings and payback periods."
Example: "Analyze bulk buying opportunities for 2-person household to maximize savings on cleaning supplies, rice, and frozen vegetables. Consider small apartment storage, 1-year expiration limits, and $300 upfront budget. Calculate annual savings and 6-month payback periods."

8. Store Loyalty Mastery
Prompt: "Optimize rewards programs across [available stores] to maximize savings on [grocery budget]. Include [credit card rewards], [store-specific benefits], and [seasonal promotions]. Create a shopping rotation schedule and reward tracking system."
Example: "Optimize rewards programs across Kroger, Target, and Costco to maximize savings on $400 monthly grocery budget. Include Chase Freedom credit card rewards, Kroger fuel points benefits, and Target Circle promotions. Create weekly shopping rotation and point tracking system."

9. Meal Prep Cost Analysis
Prompt: "Design a meal prep system to reduce grocery costs by [percentage/amount] while maintaining [nutritional goals]. Include [prep time constraints], [storage solutions], and [recipe variety]. Calculate cost-per-meal and time savings."
Example: "Design a meal prep system to reduce grocery costs by 40% while maintaining high-protein goals. Include 3-hour Sunday prep constraints, freezer storage solutions, and 20-recipe rotation variety. Calculate cost-per-meal and weekly time savings."

10. Garden-to-Table Savings
Prompt: "Plan a container garden for [living situation] to grow [expensive grocery items] and save [target amount] annually. Consider [climate], [space limitations], and [gardening experience]. Include startup costs and harvest timeline."

Example: "Plan a balcony container garden for apartment living to grow herbs, lettuce, and tomatoes and save $300 annually. Consider zone 7 climate, 6x4 balcony space, and beginner gardening experience. Include $150 startup costs and seasonal harvest timeline."

✈️ *How to Spend Less on Travel*

11. Travel Hacking Blueprint

Prompt: "Create a travel rewards strategy to fund [dream destination] trip costing [estimated amount]. Include [current credit score], [spending habits], and [timeline]. Map out credit card applications, point accumulation, and redemption strategies."

Example: "Create a travel rewards strategy to fund Japan trip costing $4,000. Include 720 credit score, $3,000 monthly spending, and 18-month timeline. Map out Chase Sapphire/Amex Gold applications, category bonus optimization, and transfer partner redemption strategies."

12. Off-Season Adventure Planner

Prompt: "Plan [destination] trip during off-peak times to save [percentage] on costs. Consider [weather acceptability], [activity availability], and [crowd preferences]. Include flight/hotel pricing patterns and alternative timing options."

Example: "Plan Caribbean trip during hurricane season to save 60% on costs. Consider September weather acceptability, snorkeling activity availability, and moderate crowd preferences. Include historical pricing patterns and October alternative timing options."

13. Budget Accommodation Optimizer

Prompt: "Find alternative accommodations for [destination] trip that cost [percentage] less than hotels. Include [comfort requirements], [safety priorities], and [social preferences]. Compare Airbnb, hostels, house-sitting, and local options."

Example: "Find alternative accommodations for European backpacking trip that cost 70% less than hotels. Include private room requirements, central location safety priorities, and meeting travelers preferences. Compare Airbnb monthly discounts, upscale hostels, and home exchange options."

14. Transportation Cost Cutter
Prompt: "Minimize transportation costs for [trip type] by comparing [available options]. Consider [time flexibility], [comfort needs], and [luggage requirements]. Include booking timing strategies and alternative routes."
Example: "Minimize transportation costs for cross-country family trip by comparing flights, trains, and road trips. Consider 2-week flexibility, comfort for kids needs, and 4 suitcases requirements. Include Tuesday booking strategies and multi-city route alternatives."

15. Local Living Travel Strategy
Prompt: "Design a 'live like a local' travel experience for [destination] that reduces costs by [amount/percentage]. Include [cultural interests], [food preferences], and [activity priorities]. Add local transportation, markets, and free attraction strategies."
Example: "Design a 'live like a local' travel experience for Barcelona that reduces costs by 50%. Include architecture interests, tapas preferences, and nightlife priorities. Add metro pass strategies, La Boqueria market shopping, and free Gaudí walking tour options."

How to Get Fit Without Exercising

16. Lifestyle Integration Fitness
Prompt: "Create a fitness plan that integrates into [daily routine] without dedicated workout time. Include [current activity level], [physical limitations], and [lifestyle constraints]. Focus on habit stacking and micro-movements throughout the day."
Example: "Create a fitness plan that integrates into desk job routine without dedicated workout time. Include sedentary activity level, lower back issues, and 10-hour workday constraints. Focus on hourly movement habits and desk exercise micro-movements throughout the day."

17. Gamified Daily Movement

Prompt: "Design a gamified movement system using [available technology] to increase daily activity by [target amount]. Include [motivation triggers], [reward systems], and [social accountability]. Add progress tracking and level-up challenges."

Example: "Design a gamified movement system using smartphone and smartwatch to increase daily steps by 8,000. Include achievement motivation triggers, weekend treat rewards, and friend challenge accountability. Add weekly progress photos and monthly distance challenges."

18. Environmental Fitness Hacks

Prompt: "Modify [living/work environment] to naturally increase physical activity and calorie burn. Consider [space constraints], [budget limitations], and [aesthetic preferences]. Include standing desk alternatives, active furniture, and movement cues."

Example: "Modify small apartment and home office to naturally increase physical activity by 300 calories daily. Consider 800 sq ft space, $200 budget, and modern aesthetic preferences. Include adjustable desk alternatives, stability ball seating, and visual movement reminder cues."

19. Transportation-Based Fitness

Prompt: "Transform [daily commute/errands] into fitness opportunities that burn [target calories] weekly. Include [transportation options], [weather considerations], and [time constraints]. Add route optimization and seasonal adaptations."

Example: "Transform 15-minute car commute into fitness opportunities that burn 1,500 calories weekly. Include bike/walk options, year-round weather planning, and cannot-be-late constraints. Add scenic route optimization and winter indoor alternatives."

20. Social Fitness Integration

Prompt: "Design social activities that combine [relationship goals] with physical activity, burning [target calories] monthly. Consider [friend/family interests], [budget constraints], and [scheduling challenges]. Add fun alternatives to traditional exercise."

Example: "Design social activities that combine family bonding with physical activity, burning 2,000 calories monthly. Consider teenage kids' interests, weekend budget constraints, and busy scheduling challenges. Add hiking alternatives to traditional gym sessions."

How to Get a Raise/Promotion

21. Performance Documentation System

Prompt: "Create a promotion portfolio documenting [role achievements] over [time period] to justify [target raise/position]. Include [quantifiable results], [skill development], and [value creation]. Add presentation strategy and timing recommendations."

Example: "Create a promotion portfolio documenting marketing coordinator achievements over 18 months to justify senior marketing manager position. Include campaign ROI results, Google Ads skill development, and client retention value creation. Add quarterly review presentation strategy and annual planning timing."

22. Market Value Research

Prompt: "Research salary benchmarks for [current role] in [industry/location] to support [target compensation]. Include [experience level], [skill sets], and [company size] factors. Add negotiation talking points and alternative compensation options."

Example: "Research salary benchmarks for software developer role in Austin tech scene to support $95,000 target. Include 4-year experience level, React/Node.js skills, and startup company factors. Add remote work negotiation points and equity compensation alternatives."

23. Skill Gap Acceleration

Prompt: "Identify and rapidly develop [missing skills] for [target role] within [timeline]. Include [learning resources], [practice opportunities], and [demonstration methods]. Add skill acquisition schedule and visibility strategies."

Example: "Identify and rapidly develop leadership and project management skills for team lead role within 6 months. Include Coursera learning resources, volunteer practice opportunities, and team presentation methods. Add weekend learning schedule and mentor visibility strategies."

24. Value Creation Proposal

Prompt: "Design a proposal showing how [your contribution] can generate [value amount] for the company, justifying [desired compensation]. Include [implementation plan], [resource requirements], and [success metrics]. Add ROI calculations and risk mitigation."

Example: "Design a proposal showing how automating client reporting can save $50,000 annually, justifying $15,000 raise. Include Python automation implementation, software license requirements, and time-saving metrics. Add 6-month ROI calculations and training risk mitigation."

25. Strategic Networking Plan

Prompt: "Create a networking strategy to build [internal/external] relationships that support [career goal]. Include [target contacts], [value exchange], and [relationship building]. Add LinkedIn optimization and informational interview scripts."

Example: "Create internal networking strategy to build C-suite relationships supporting director-level promotion. Include VP-level target contacts, project collaboration value exchange, and coffee chat relationship building. Add executive LinkedIn engagement and strategic questioning scripts."

How to Get Rich Legendarily Fast Using Skills You Already Have

26. Skill Monetization Audit

Prompt: "Analyze [existing skills/experience] to identify high-income opportunities within [timeline]. Include [market demand], [competition analysis], and [pricing strategies]. Rank by profit potential and time-to-revenue."

Example: "Analyze marketing and writing skills to identify $10,000 monthly income opportunities within 90 days. Include content marketing demand, freelancer competition analysis, and premium pricing strategies. Rank by profit potential and client acquisition speed."

27. Digital Asset Creation
Prompt: "Transform [expertise area] into scalable digital products that generate [target income] monthly. Include [product formats], [distribution channels], and [pricing models]. Add content creation timeline and passive income projections."
Example: "Transform Excel expertise into scalable digital products generating $5,000 monthly. Include template/course formats, Etsy/Gumroad distribution, and tiered pricing models. Add 60-day creation timeline and 12-month passive income projections."

28. High-Value Consulting Launch
Prompt: "Package [professional experience] into consulting services commanding [hourly rate]. Include [target clients], [service packages], and [credibility building]. Add client acquisition strategy and pricing progression plan."
Example: "Package HR management experience into consulting services commanding $200/hour. Include small business target clients, compliance audit packages, and LinkedIn credibility building. Add referral acquisition strategy and premium pricing progression."

29. Rapid Business Validation
Prompt: "Test [business idea] based on [existing skills] for market viability within [timeframe]. Include [minimum viable product], [target customers], and [validation metrics]. Add launch strategy and scaling decisions."
Example: "Test meal planning app idea based on nutrition knowledge for market viability within 30 days. Include PDF guide MVP, busy parent customers, and pre-order validation metrics. Add social media launch strategy and app development scaling decisions."

30. Investment Income Acceleration
Prompt: "Use [current income/savings] and [knowledge areas] to generate investment returns of [target percentage] annually. Include [risk tolerance], [time commitment], and [learning requirements]. Add portfolio allocation and performance tracking."

Example: "Use $25,000 savings and tech industry knowledge to generate 15% annual returns. Include moderate risk tolerance, 5-hour weekly commitment, and options trading learning requirements. Add 70/30 stock/options allocation and monthly performance tracking."

🆘 Emergency Prompt SOS Guide

Scan this QR code to use the interactive artifact in Claude:

When AI Gives You Bad Results - Quick Decision Tree

START HERE: Is your result...

❌ **COMPLETELY OFF-TOPIC?**

→ **PROBLEM:** Unclear context or goal

→ **QUICK FIX:** Add "I need help with [specific task] for [specific purpose]"

→ **EMERGENCY BACKUP:** "Ignore previous response. Help me with [restate your goal clearly]"

📝 **TOO VAGUE OR GENERIC?**

→ **PROBLEM:** Missing specificity

→ **QUICK FIX:** Add exact details: numbers, names, constraints, examples

→ **EMERGENCY BACKUP:** "Make this more specific: [paste original request]. Include concrete examples and actionable steps."

🎭 **WRONG TONE OR STYLE?**

→ **PROBLEM:** Missing tone/audience specification

→ **QUICK FIX:** Add "Write this in a [professional/casual/friendly] tone for [specific audience]"

→ **EMERGENCY BACKUP:** "Rewrite the above in [desired tone] for [target audience]"

📏 **TOO LONG OR TOO SHORT?**

→ **PROBLEM:** No length specification

→ **QUICK FIX:** Add "in exactly [X] words/sentences/paragraphs"

→ **EMERGENCY BACKUP:** "Make this [shorter/longer]: [paste content]"

❓ **FACTUALLY WRONG?**

→ **PROBLEM:** AI hallucination or outdated info

→ **QUICK FIX:** Ask "Please verify this information and cite sources"

→ **EMERGENCY BACKUP:** "I need you to fact-check this and correct any errors: [paste content]"

🔄 **REPETITIVE OR CIRCULAR?**

→ **PROBLEM:** Unclear instructions or constraints

→ **QUICK FIX:** Add "without repeating information" and "focus only on [specific aspect]"

→ **EMERGENCY BACKUP:** "Give me 5 completely different approaches to [your goal]"

Emergency Prompt Formulas - Copy & Paste Ready

Universal Reset:

"Start over. I need [specific outcome] for [specific audience].

The most important thing is [key priority]. Please ask me

3 clarifying questions before responding."

Specificity Booster:

"Take this request and make it 10x more specific: [your request].

Include exact details, examples, and constraints."

Tone Corrector:

"Rewrite this content in a [professional/casual/enthusiastic] tone

for [specific audience]: [paste content]"

Quality Controller:

"Before answering, tell me: What additional information would help you give me the best possible response to: [your request]"

Format Fixer:
"Present this information as [bullet points/numbered list/paragraph/table]:

[paste content]"

📅 30-Day Prompt Challenge Calendar

Your Prompt Mastery Journey - Check Off Each Day!

WEEK 1: Foundation Building

- [ ] **Day 1:** Practice the C.A.L.M. framework on a work task
  Notes: ____
- [ ] **Day 2:** Create 3 different versions of the same prompt
  Best result: _______________________________________
- [ ] **Day 3:** Use a persona prompt ("Act as a [expert]...")
  Persona used: _____________________________________
- [ ] **Day 4:** Add specific constraints (time, budget, audience)
  Constraint added: _________________________________
- [ ] **Day 5:** Practice the "before giving your answer" technique
  Result quality (1-10): ____________________________
- [ ] **Day 6:** Create a prompt for a creative project
  Project: ____
- [ ] **Day 7:** Review and improve your worst prompt from this week
  🏆 *MILESTONE: Foundation Complete!*

WEEK 2: Intermediate Techniques

- [ ] **Day 8:** Use step-by-step breakdown prompting
  Task broken down: _________________________________
- [ ] **Day 9:** Practice example-based prompting
  Number of examples used: __________________________
- [ ] **Day 10:** Create a prompt with multiple output options
  Options requested: ________________________________
- [ ] **Day 11:** Use emotional/psychological context
  Context added: ____________________________________
- [ ] **Day 12:** Practice iterative prompting (build on responses)
  Number of iterations: _____________________________
- [ ] **Day 13:** Create a business-focused prompt
  Business goal: ____________________________________
- [ ] **Day 14:** Challenge: Combine 3 techniques in one prompt
  🏆 *MILESTONE: Technique Combiner!*

WEEK 3: Advanced Applications

- [ ] **Day 15**: Create a problem-solving prompt sequence
  Problem solved: _______________________________________
- [ ] **Day 16**: Use comparative analysis prompting
  Items compared: ______________________________________
- [ ] **Day 17**: Practice educational/training prompts
  Skill learned: _______________________________________
- [ ] **Day 18**: Create a planning or strategy prompt
  Plan created for: ____________________________________
- [ ] **Day 19**: Use research and analysis prompting
  Research topic: ______________________________________
- [ ] **Day 20**: Practice troubleshooting prompts
  Problem troubleshot: _________________________________
- [ ] **Day 21**: Create a creative/brainstorming prompt
  🏆 *MILESTONE: Advanced Practitioner!*

WEEK 4: Mastery & Innovation

- [ ] **Day 22**: Customize prompts for different AI personalities
  AI platforms used: ___________________________________
- [ ] **Day 23**: Create a complex multi-part prompt
  Parts included: ______________________________________
- [ ] **Day 24**: Practice rapid prompt iteration
  Versions created: ____________________________________
- [ ] **Day 25**: Use prompts for personal development
  Development area: ____________________________________
- [ ] **Day 26**: Create industry-specific prompts
  Industry: ____
- [ ] **Day 27**: Master the "assumption check" technique
  Assumptions challenged: ______________________________
- [ ] **Day 28**: Practice teaching others through prompts
  Person taught: _______________________________________
- [ ] **Day 29**: Create your signature prompt formula
  Your formula: ____
- [ ] **Day 30**: Design prompts for your biggest goal
  🏆 *MILESTONE: PROMPT MASTER ACHIEVED!*

Overall Challenge Stats:

- Days completed: _____ / 30
- Most useful technique discovered: _______________________
- Biggest improvement area: ______________________________
- Next month's focus: _________________________________

Fill-in-the-Blank Master Templates

Universal Prompt Framework

"I need help with ________________________ for ________________________.

Context: I am a ________________________ working on

________________________.

The outcome should be ________________________ and include

________________________.

Important constraints: ________________________

Most important priority: ________________________

Before responding, please ________________________"

Business Problem Solver

"Analyze this business challenge: ________________________

Background information: ________________________

Stakeholders involved: ________________________

Current resources: ________________________

Success looks like: ________________________

Biggest obstacle: ________________________

Timeline: ________________________

Please provide ________________________ options with ________________________ level of detail."

Creative Project Launcher

"Help me create a ________________________ for ________________________.

Target audience: ________________________

Mood/style should be: ________________________

Must include these elements: ________________________

Cannot include: ________________________

Inspiration sources: ________________________

Final format needed: ________________________

Please provide ________________________ and ask ________________________ clarifying questions."

Learning & Development

"I want to learn ________________________ for ________________________.

My current level: ________________________

Available time: ________________________

Learning style preference: ________________________

Practical application: ________________________

Success measurement: ________________________

Biggest challenge: ________________________

Create a ________________________ plan with ________________________ milestones."

Personal Productivity

"I need to ________________________ by ________________________.

Current situation: ________________________

Available resources: ________________________

Time constraints: ________________________

Energy levels: ________________________

Motivation factors: ________________________

Biggest obstacles: ________________________

Design a ________________________ system that includes ________________________."

Decision Making

"Help me decide between ________________________ and ________________________.

Context: _______________________

Important factors: _______________________

Success criteria: _______________________

Risk tolerance: _______________________

Stakeholders affected: _______________________

Timeline for decision: _______________________

Please provide _______________________ analysis and recommend _______________________."

📚 Personal Prompt Library Organizer

Category System - Check Your Focus Areas

📊 **BUSINESS & PROFESSIONAL**

- [ ] Strategy & Planning
- [ ] Communication & Emails
- [ ] Presentations & Reports
- [ ] Problem Solving
- [ ] Team Management
- [ ] Customer Relations

- [ ] Marketing & Sales
- [ ] Data Analysis

🎨 **CREATIVE & CONTENT**

- [ ] Writing & Editing
- [ ] Brainstorming Ideas
- [ ] Visual Concepts
- [ ] Social Media
- [ ] Storytelling
- [ ] Design Feedback
- [ ] Content Planning
- [ ] Creative Problem Solving

📚 **LEARNING & DEVELOPMENT**

- [ ] Skill Acquisition
- [ ] Research & Analysis
- [ ] Study Planning
- [ ] Knowledge Testing
- [ ] Concept Explanation
- [ ] Tutorial Creation
- [ ] Progress Tracking
- [ ] Goal Setting

🏠 **PERSONAL & LIFESTYLE**

- [ ] Life Organization
- [ ] Health & Wellness
- [ ] Financial Planning
- [ ] Relationships
- [ ] Hobbies & Interests
- [ ] Travel Planning
- [ ] Home Management
- [ ] Personal Growth

Your Top 10 Go-To Prompts

Rank by frequency of use (1 = most used)

Rank	Prompt Name	Category	Last Used	Success Rate
1	___________	________	_________	____________
2	___________	________	_________	____________
3	___________	________	_________	____________
4	___________	________	_________	____________
5	___________	________	_________	____________
6	___________	________	_________	____________
7	___________	________	_________	____________
8	___________	________	_________	____________
9	___________	________	_________	____________
10	___________	________	_________	____________

Alphabetical Quick Reference

A-E

- _______________________ (Category: ________)
- _______________________ (Category: ________)
- _______________________ (Category: ________)
- _______________________ (Category: ________)
- _______________________ (Category: ________)

F-J

- _______________________ (Category: ________)
- _______________________ (Category: ________)
- _______________________ (Category: ________)
- _______________________ (Category: ________)

- ________________________ (Category: ________)

K-O

- ________________________ (Category: ________)
- ________________________ (Category: ________)
- ________________________ (Category: ________)
- ________________________ (Category: ________)
- ________________________ (Category: ________)

P-T

- ________________________ (Category: ________)
- ________________________ (Category: ________)
- ________________________ (Category: ________)
- ________________________ (Category: ________)
- ________________________ (Category: ________)

U-Z

- ________________________ (Category: ________)
- ________________________ (Category: ________)
- ________________________ (Category: ________)
- ________________________ (Category: ________)
- ________________________ (Category: ________)

Prompt Performance Tracker

Prompt Name	Date Used	Context	Result Quality (1-10)	Notes for Improvement
___________ _	_________ _	_______ _	___________________ _	___________________ _
___________ _	_________ _	_______ _	___________________ _	___________________ _
___________ _	_________ _	_______ _	___________________ _	___________________ _
___________ _	_________ _	_______ _	___________________ _	___________________ _

Prompt Name	Date Used	Context	Result Quality (1-10)	Notes for Improvement
___________	_________	_______	___________________	___________________
___________	_________	_______	___________________	___________________
___________	_________	_______	___________________	___________________
___________	_________	_______	___________________	___________________

Custom Tags & Labels

Create your own organization system:

🔥 High Priority: _________________________________ ⭐ Favorites: ___________________________________ 🚀 Quick Wins: ___________________________________ 🔧 Needs Work: ___________________________________ 💡 Experimental: ________________________________ 📈 High Success Rate: ___________________________ 🎯 Specific Use Case: ____________________________ 🔄 Template Base: _______________________________

Monthly Review Checklist

☐ Review prompt performance scores ☐ Identify top 3 most successful prompts ☐ Note patterns in successful prompts ☐ Archive or delete unused prompts ☐ Create new prompts for emerging needs ☐ Update categories and tags ☐ Plan next month's prompt experiments

---

References

Deloitte. (2025). 2025 Global Human Capital Trends. https://www2.deloitte.com/global/en/pages/human-capital/articles/introduction-human-capital-trends.html

Schwartz, B. (2004). *The paradox of choice: Why more is less*. HarperCollins.

Singla, A., Sukharevsky, A., Yee, L., Chui, M., & Hall, B. (2025, March 12). *The state of AI: How organizations are rewiring to capture value*. QuantumBlack, AI by McKinsey. McKinsey & Company. mckinsey.com+4mckinsey.com+4mckinsey.com+4mckinsey.com+6mckinsey.com+6mckinsey.com+6

ABOUT THE AUTHOR

Dr. Elisa Janson Jones, MBA, EdD, CAIC™, is a leading authority on AI adoption, instructional design, and business transformation. With a Bachelor of Music, a Master of Business Administration, and a Doctorate in Education, she brings a uniquely interdisciplinary lens to the future of work and learning. As a Certified AI Consultant™, custom GPT developer, and creator of the C.A.L.M. AI Navigator™ framework, Elisa helps professionals and organizations integrate AI in practical, human-centered ways.

Her work bridges the gap between innovation and real-world application, empowering leaders to use AI not just efficiently, but ethically and intelligently. She is a sought-after keynote speaker, executive advisor, and workshop leader, as well as a trusted mentor to educators, entrepreneurs, and change-makers navigating digital transformation.

When she's not speaking or consulting, you'll find her adventuring in the high desert and alpine landscapes of western Colorado, where she lives with her family. An avid outdoor athlete and lifelong learner, Elisa believes in leading with curiosity, living with purpose, and helping others thrive in the age of intelligent tools.

www.ingramcontent.com/pod-product-compliance
Lightning Source LLC
LaVergne TN
LVHW020656110826
845149LV00012B/2018

* 9 7 9 8 9 9 9 6 3 8 1 0 6 *